The International Library of Sociology

THE INSTITUTIONS
OF P.RIVATE LAW
AND THEIR SOCIAL FUNCTIONS

Founded by KARL MANNHEIM

The International Library of Sociology

THE SOCIOLOGY OF LAW
AND CRIMINOLOGY
In 15 Volumes

THE INSTITUTIONS OF PRIVATE LAW

and Their Social Functions

by
KARL RENNER

Edited, with an Introduction and notes by
O. KAHN-FREUND

Translated by
AGNES SCHWARZSCHILD

Routledge
Taylor & Francis Group

LONDON AND NEW YORK

This translation first published in 1949
by Routledge

Reprinted 1998, 2001 by Routledge
2 Park Square, Milton Park, Abingdon, Oxon, OX14 4RN
711 Third Avenue, New York, NY 10017

Transferred to Digital Printing 2007

Routledge is an imprint of the Taylor & Francis Group

First issued in paperback 2013

British Library Cataloguing in Publication Data
A CIP catalogue record for this book
is available from the British Library

ISBN13: 978-0-415-17741-2 (hbk)

ISBN13: 978-0-415-86389-6 (pbk)

Publisher's Note

The publisher has gone to great lengths to ensure the quality of this reprint
but points out that some imperfections in the original may be apparent

CONTENTS

CHAPTER III
SOCIOLOGICAL ANALYSIS OF FUNCTIONAL CHANGE

INTRODUCTION

BY O. KAHN-FREUND, LL.M., DR. JUR.

Reader in Law in the University of London

KARL RENNER'S work on the Institutions of Private Law and their Social Function is an attempt to utilise the Marxist system of sociology for the construction of a theory of law. As a statement and formulation of an important aspect of Marxist doctrine and as a highly original contribution to jurisprudence the book has for many years been well known on the Continent. It is now, for the first time, made accessible to the English speaking world.

I

Renner's work is concerned with the sociology of law, and, more particularly, with the impact of economic forces and social changes upon the functioning of legal institutions. The legal institutions which he examines are those which are classified as belonging to the sphere of "private law": ownership in land and movable property, contracts of various types, mortgage and lease, marriage and succession. "Public law", which includes the organisation of the state and of local government bodies is outside the purview of his analysis.

It is one of the tasks of a sociology of law to explore the social forces which bring about the creation of legal norms and institutions and changes in the positive law. Renner's work does not deal with this aspect of the inter-relation between law and society. It does not investigate the problem how and why legal principles like that of the freedom of contract or of the owner's unfettered right of disposition come into being at a given stage of social development. He pre-supposes the stability and relative immutability of legal institutions such as property and contract, and he asks: how is it possible that, given unchanged norms, unchanged conceptions of ownership and sale, contract and debt, mortgage and inheritance, their social function can nevertheless undergo a profound transformation? How is it possible that—to take the most prominent example and the central theme of Renner's work—as a legal institution "property" can mean the same thing, say, in 1750 and in 1900, and yet in the latter year produce economic and social effects almost diametrically opposed to those it had in the former? How can one account for the functional transformation of a norm which remains stable? What, in particular, is the technique used by a developing capitalist society in order to adapt pre-capitalist and early capitalist legal conceptions to the needs of high capitalism without changing those conceptions themselves? How does society use the institutions of the law, what does it make of them, how does it group and re-group them? How does it put them to new services without transforming their normative content? How, in particular, has property been able to become the legal framework of a capitalist economy?

II

It will be seen that Renner postulates the normative "purity" of all legal institutions. It is impossible to understand his analysis without realising that he belongs to the positivist school of legal thought. In his view the legal norm is indifferent towards its social function, the economic effect extraneous to the definition of a legal concept. Institutions such as property, contract, succession by inheritance, are "neutral", "colourless", "empty frames", they are neither "feudal", nor "capitalist", nor "socialist". Their juridical analysis cannot teach us anything about their social or economic effect. Renner insists that the place which legal institutions occupy in society is a matter for the economist, for the political scientist, for the sociologist. A lawyer may be interested in it during his leisure hours, but he must not allow this interest to intrude upon his work, no more than the botanist as such may be concerned with the economic use to which others put the plants he studies under the microscope. Renner rejects the sociological or functional method of interpreting positive law itself. He is uninfluenced by and opposed to those trends of legal thought represented by jurists such as Ihering or the American realists who urge the judge and the lawyer to be aware of, and take into account, the social purposes of the legal norms which he applies, and to interpret them in their light.

No consistent positivist can ever admit that the normative content of legal institutions can be influenced by their function, by the factual results of their application. The "functional transformation" of legal institutions which Renner examines in his work is not—he emphasises it again and again—a transformation of these institutions themselves as part of the positive law.

It is not necessarily inherent in the positivist doctrine that the legal norm should be understood as a command or as an imperative. Kelsen, for example, holds that the logical structure of the legal norm is that of a hypothetical judgment. Renner, however, adheres to the view of the majority of continental positivists (which was also the view of Austin), that every norm is an imperative. Whatever the formulation in which it appears in codes, statutes, or decrees, it can, according to this doctrine, never be more than a command addressed by one individual to another. Renner insists that the law can neither control nature nor regulate man's relation to nature. The technical progress of mankind, the development of productivity is achieved "under the eye of the law, but not by means of the law". Nor does Renner admit that the law can ever fully control human associations and "groups", though he agrees that it may enhance their efficiency. Even where it purports to issue its commands to collective bodies, it can ultimately enforce them against individuals only. Similarly, the "collective" will which pretends to be embodied in legislation is, on ultimate analysis, the will of those individuals who enforce it.[1] Whether they are able to do so, and how, is not determined by the law, but by "the social conditions prevailing at that particular historical period".

Renner's conception of the law as a series of imperatives addressed by one individual to another is of profound significance for the whole of his theory. It goes without saying that these relations between individual "wills" which are alone capable of being moulded by the law exist in a social and in a natural environment. They derive their social meaning from the influence which this environment exercises upon them and which they in turn exercise upon society as a whole. It is, however, just this mutual impact which lies beyond the province of the law, as understood by positivism. "The lever which the law uses upon social facts is too short to control them. Legal ties are mere threads compared with the Herculean power of natural life. Yet this Hercules stretches his limbs so gradually and

---

[1] These views are not, of course, common to all positivists—Renner's positivism differs substantially from, e.g., Austin's.

imperceptibly, that the threads do not suddenly snap in all places."

Legislation is thus not seen as the prime mover of social change. It is, at best, a response of the law to a change which has already taken place in the womb of society. On this important point dialectical Marxism agrees with representatives of the historical school such as Savigny and Maine, albeit on very different grounds. Social and economic developments, transformations of the substratum which affect people's lives, are not, as a rule, brought about by the law, nor do they necessarily change the law itself. They do not occur by leaps and bounds. "The social substratum knows evolution only, not revolution." Revolutions, i.e. political revolutions, take place in the normative sphere. They may—and often do—lay the normative foundation for new evolutionary developments in society. They make room for social change, but they are not its *causa causans*. The belief that one can transform society by "decree" is stigmatised by Renner as a superstition, as "idolatry of legislation", "decretinism", and it is, in his view, a common characteristic of successful revolutions. He argues that it betrays a misapprehension of the social rôle of law as such and an over-estimation of its effectiveness.

It is inherent in Renner's approach—and he is at pains expressly to point out—that the crude formula which reduces the relation between economy and law to one of cause and effect does not meet the case. He refuses to describe the complex interdependence between the relations of production and consumption on the one side and the institutions of the law on the other by means of the simple architectural image of substructure and superstructure. In so far as the economic and legal systems of a given society can be understood in terms of cause and effect at all, changes in the economic relations are often the result of legal developments, though it is far more usual to find that a transformation of the economic system ultimately produces a change in the law. However—and this is one of Renner's cardinal arguments—not only does such a change never occur automatically (i.e. without a political development), it also invariably occurs after a time lag, which may have to be measured in centuries, During this time lag norms which, at an earlier period of history, may have been a true mirror of social relations, may cease to be an adequate expression of factual conditions. In extreme cases an institution may survive as part of the law, but lose all its social functions, a phenomenon—called *desuetudo*—of which English legal history offers examples (e.g. military tenure which had long ceased to be a living institution when it was formally abolished in the 17th century). As a rule, however, there is not a disappearance but a transformation of the social function. An institution may be put to the service of a variety of economic objectivés: to-day the ownership of land serves the provision of dwelling room no less than of agriculture or factory production. One economic effect may be produced by the alternative application of a variety of legal techniques: the provision of dwelling houses for the working and lower middle classes may be effectuated through the mechanism of the building society mortgage or through that of the lease.

Much more important, however, is the fact that under the conditions of modern capitalism economic results can only be achieved through the simultaneous operation of a multitude of legal institutions. Ownership taken by itself is incapable of serving the organisation of modern industry. It can do so only with the aid of a number of satellite or complementary institutions: company law and patent law, the contract of sale and the contract of employment. A simple economic process often corresponds to a whole group of legal categories. The subservience of many legal categories to one economic process is what Renner calls their economic function.

All economic processes, however, are themselves part and parcel of the social processes of "production" and "reproduction",[1] of the maintenance of the human species. Legal institutions can and must be understood as the tools used by society in achieving this ultimate aim. They are cogs in the mechanism of the production, consumption and distribution of the social product. This is what Renner calls their social function.

A simple photographic picture of a given society at a given stage of its development will fail to reveal the manner in which legal concepts and institutions are used and grouped for economic and social purposes. Society must always be viewed as a process, a dialectical process. Hence it is, as it were, a cinematographic picture which the sociologist has to envisage. Only thus will he discern the laws which determine the grouping and re-grouping of legal institutions, the sequence of uses to which they are put

---

[1]For the definition and explanation of re-production see Marx, *Capital*, Vol. I. pp. 577–8 (translation by Moore and Aveling).

and of arrangements into which they enter. Society handles the institutions of the law much in the same way as a child handles his bricks. It uses the same bricks all the time—or for a long time,—to-day to build a manor house, to-morrow to build a factory, and the day after to build a railway station. The number of bricks is limited: the manor house may have to be pulled down to make way for the factory. But—this is Renner's positivist axiom—the bricks remain the same. The law provides the bricks. What society makes of them, is none of the lawyer's business. The legal institution is a rigid abstract, a congeries of crystallised imperatives, and, owing to its very rigidity and abstract nature, a "fetish" in the Marxist sense, like the "commodity" concept of the economist. Renner builds the tenets of positivism into the structure of the Marxist system, and thus succeeds in extending the Marxist doctrine to the theory of law. The discrepancy between the normative content of the law (which is static) and its economic and social function (which is dynamic) is the key to its dialectical development.[1] This development can be summarised as the functional transformation of the untransformed norm.

The ultimate end of society, and hence the ultimate social function of the law, is the maintenance of the species. The maintenance of the species requires the organisation of society. Society organises itself in three different ways: it allocates to the individuals who are its members the work which is needed for production and reproduction, the power to command which is necessary to keep the organisation in being, and the factual "detention", the "having" of all things, movable and immovable. By its very nature every human society must have an "order of labour", an "order of power", an "order of goods". No matter whether it is a primitive tribe in Central Africa or a modern industrial community, whether it is feudal or capitalist or socialist, society must keep production and reproduction going, it must establish a hierarchy of subordination (and relations of co-ordination too), and it cannot dispense with a distribution of the handling and having of goods among its members. Lawyers may talk about corporate entities, public or private, but ultimately it is always an individual and an individual only who

---

[1] The parallel to Marx's analysis of the discrepancy between forces of production and relations of production in the Preface to the *Critique of Political Economy* is almost too obvious to be mentioned.

works, who commands, and who "possesses" (in the sense of the Roman detention) a thing.

All this would be commonplace, had it not been for the curious illusion created by capitalist society that it could live without an order of labour and of goods, and partly without an order of power. The legal order of feudalism deliberately allocated the control of land and goods, established the hierarchy of power, and imposed the duty to work in accordance with the social functions of possession, power, and labour. The function of the legal institutions corresponded to their normative structure. Capitalist society, however, pretended to be able to forego a functional organisation of possession and of labour. It covered the order of goods with a legal concept of property defined in the abstract, it avoided, in the name of personal freedom, a legal formulation of the duty to work. "*De jure* bourgeois society has no order of goods and no order of labour." Property was protected, whoever be the owner, and whatever be the purpose of ownership. Compulsion to work was—seemingly—abolished. Society pretended to abdicate in favour of the will of the individual. Yet, behind the smokescreen of abstract norms, behind the legal system of *a priori* categories, like "person", "property", "liberty", there was concealed an order of labour, of power, of goods, no less determined, no less purposeful than that of feudalism. But the laws which constituted the order of goods and of labour were not expressed, they appeared not as legal norms, for they were the economic "laws" governing capitalist production, distribution, and consumption. Society rules over production, distribution, and consumption whether it does so openly by express norms and through institutions such as feudal tenure and villeinage or under the guise of the law of property and free employment. The law of property is an order of detention which conceals its own objectives. It is—*sub specie historiae*—an ephemeral order, one of many such orders that have appeared in the course of the centuries. It is also part of an order of labour and of an order of power: the "imperatives" issued by the factory owner to his workers by virtue of his ownership of the plant take the place of the express norms which regulated the labour of the serf. The law of succession to property and those parts of company law which deal with the appointment of directors belong to the order of power no less than the law of feudal investiture which they replace.

The analysis of the social function of property and of its transformation in the course of the history of capitalism is the most important part of Renner's investigation.

III

Since the positivist assumption is one of the cornerstones of this analysis, it is useful to reflect on the question how far the structure of the Anglo-American common law precludes an application of the positivist doctrine. To what extent, in other words, is Renner's analysis without validity for a capitalist society whose legal system differs from any Continental system as fundamentally as does the English common law?

It would be quite fruitless—and it is not the purpose of this Introduction—to examine the validity of the positivist tenets. During the forty years which have elapsed since Renner wrote the first edition of his work the positivist theory of law has been subjected to the most searching criticism, both in Europe and in America. To repeat the arguments which have been advanced in favour of a functional approach to law itself would be equivalent to kicking at a door that is already open. Suffice it to remind the reader that, whatever be its logical merits, the positivist theory fails to yield a practical guidance to the judge, to the advocate, to the administrator. Positivism is a utopia. The law is neither consistent nor self-sufficient. Whatever theorists may say and whatever he himself may think and say, the judge constantly recurs to an analysis, articulate or inarticulate, of the moral, social, economic function and effect of the rules and principles he applies, and of his own decision. The task of the law-maker and that of the law-finder cannot be kept in water-tight compartments, and judges have always acted and will always act on the celebrated principle of the Swiss Civil Code of 1912 that, in the absence of a statutory or customary norm, the judge must decide "in accordance with the rule he would lay down if he were the legislator".

One cannot, however, dispose of positivism simply by stating that it is a utopia. Like other utopias it has its place in the history of human ideas, a place which is (at least partly) determined by the social and political environment in which it arose. Is it simply a response to the needs of capitalism? Is it the outcome of conditions peculiar to the European Continent?

Every legal system requires an element of ideological unity.

However much one may be aware that the application of the legal norm is, in many cases, a policy-making process, one cannot dispense with a principle which links one decision with another, which raises the judicial act beyond the level of the realm of sheer expediency. Without such a principle the practical lawyer cannot operate, without it the law cannot command the respect of the public. The fiction of logical consistency, however threadbare it may look to the critical eyes of our generation, did once provide this unifying principle. It does so still—up to a point—and it does so both on the Continent and in the common-law jurisdictions of the British Empire and of the United States. There is, however, an important difference between the place which this fiction occupies in continental legal thought and the rôle it plays in the common law world.

In a systematised legal structure such as the *Usus Modernus Pandectarum* and the modern Continental Codes legal institutions such as ownership, sale, marriage, appear as part and parcel of a self-contained logical entity, of an intricate network of major and minor premises. It is the task of the jurist, of the legal scholar, to analyse and re-analyse the normative content of the law, to make the logical network more and more refined and pliable. It is the function of the judge to find his decision with the help of the intellectual tools which the "science of the law" has put at his disposal. Every new factual situation must somehow be fitted into the existing system. That system is comprehensive and without "gaps". It stands firm like a rock, be it even in the midst of a turbulent sea of social change.

The conceptualist school of thought was, on the Continent, the dominant variety of positivism in the 19th century. It postulated the logical consistency of the legal system as a whole. The judicial process, it insisted, is of a strictly deductive nature. The norm which the judge applies is, in its view, incapable of being transformed by the process of application. Hence, the judicial decision itself can in no sense be considered as a source of law. It must justify itself exclusively by the process of deduction from abstract premises on which it is based.

Although this conceptualist doctrine has for many decades been discarded by the majority of continental scholars, it has left as its legacy the fiction of systematic consistency as the primary element of ideological unity in the law.

In this country and in the whole common-law world, the place of the systematic fiction is taken to a considerable extent by the fiction of historical continuity. Every decision appears in the cloak of a mere application or adaptation of pre-existing "principles" laid down in earlier judicial pronouncements. Where historical continuity and systematic consistency are in conflict, it is the former which prevails, and it prevails even where the question at stake is the interpretation of a statute. If law can be called a science, it is, in this country, an empirical not a speculative science. It is an answer—primarily—to the question: "what was done previously?", not a logical process untrammelled by previous attempts to grapple with a similar situation. The positivist utopia has its place in a systematic as well as in a casuistic legal structure, but, in the latter, the logical fiction will be pushed into the background by the historical fiction.

It is necessary to bear this in mind in reading Renner's analysis. But it is also necessary to remember what are the historical causes and events which account for this difference, and to avoid two all too frequent misapprehensions.

It is not, as is sometimes argued, the codification of the law which gives rise to the idea of systematic consistency. Germany before 1900 was the Mecca of "legal science". It paved the way for the Code which came into force that year, the Code was its fruit, not its root. On the other hand, large parts of Land Law, of Commercial Law, of Administrative Law, and of Criminal Law have been codified in England, but the "principle of precedent" continues to dominate these branches of law to such an extent that the highest Court had occasion to remind the lower instances that there was—after all—a codification.[1] Codification does not necessarily engender "scientific" legal thought (as Bentham erroneously assumed), a code can be survived by the fiction of historical continuity. While, therefore, the inherent connection between conceptual positivism and codification must not be overrated, it must be understood that in Renner's analysis the terms "law" and "written law" are largely synonymous. He does not draw a distinction between *"droit"* and *"loi"*, between *"Recht"* and *"Gesetz"*. The Austrian Civil Code had been in force for almost a century (since 1811), the German Civil Code had just seen the light of day when he wrote his book. In the background of his thought there was the *"ratio scripta"*, Justinian's Corpus Juris. What Renner says about the stability of the norm in the

[1]Lord Herschell in *Bank of England v. Vagliano*, [1891] AC 107, at p. 144.

face of a changing social substratum would not have been said, or not have been said that way, if customary and judge-made law had been within the scope of his analysis. Where the courts are openly recognised as law-making agencies, it is difficult, if not impossible to maintain the fiction that the norm is stable and unaffected by social change. Every case *"primæ impressionis"* is a living refutation of that fiction.[1]

Systematic positivism is, in this country, sometimes associated with the influence of Roman Law. To some extent this too is a misunderstanding. It is quite true that the systematic grouping of positive norms as "legal institutions" and the definition of these institutions (ownership, obligation, sale, hire, pledge, etc.) was one of the great contributions of the Roman mind to human civilisation. It is equally true that, as Ihering has formulated it,[2] it was the Romans who succeeded in "precipitating" legal conceptions out of the multitude of legal norms, and in building up an "alphabet" of legal concepts which is the pre-condition and indispensable tool of scientific legal thought. Nevertheless, no one who has endeavoured to compare the method of the common lawyer with that of the Roman jurist and of the 19th century continental legal scholar can fail to agree with Buckland and McNair[3] "that there is more affinity between the Roman jurist and the common lawyer than there is between the Roman jurist and his modern civilian successor". "Both the common lawyer and the Roman jurist avoid generalisations and, so far as possible, definitions. Their method is intensely casuistic. . . . That is not the method of the Pandectist. For him the law is a set of rules to be deduced from a group of primary principles, the statement of which constitutes the *'Allgemeiner Teil'* of his structure." The conceptual method which implies the "purity" of the norm and which claims to be capable of establishing and enforcing a *judicium finium regundorum* between "norm" and "substratum" is not inherent in Roman Law. It is the heritage of the *Usus Modernus Pandectarum*, of the "Roman common law" influenced by natural law concepts and by Germanic customs and developed on the Continent since the Middle Ages.

Neither codification nor the influence of Roman Law can account for the difference between the Continental and the Anglo-

[1]The only place where judge-made law is mentioned is at p. 199 where, characteristically, the norm appears as adaptable to the substratum.
[2]*Geist des römischen Rechts*, Vol. I, p. 42.
[3]*Roman Law and Common Law*, p. xi.

Saxon types of positivism. The axiom that the law is a logical system, self-sufficient, comprehensive, without "gaps", arose on the Continent as a response to the needs of the growing civil service state. Max Weber has demonstrated how the continental monarchies from the 16th to the 19th centuries availed themselves of the systematised structure of legal conceptions built up by the scholarly expositors of the Roman Law. The rigid frame-work of positive legal concepts made for unity of administration, it also facilitated the smooth operation and the supervision of the administration of the law by a judicial and administrative civil service, a civil service which was scattered over wide areas, but subject to a centralised control. It is not, of course, suggested that the growth of systematic positivism on the Continent can be entirely explained by a simple formula like this. Many factors, the influence of natural law not being the least of them, have contributed to the development of this particular type of what Weber calls the "formal rationality" of the law. It cannot, however, be denied that the social structure of the legal profession on the Continent and, above all, the political structure of the absolute monarchies were the "prime movers" in the creation of this unique phenomenon of a "logical utopia" in the law.

None of the sociological and political factors which, on the Continent, made for systematisation and for the restriction of judicial discretion to a minimum was present in this country, not, at any rate, since the middle of the 17th century.

In this country the unification of the law had been the work of the medieval monarchy operating largely through the common law courts. It is impossible to over-emphasise the historical importance of this fact. What was a problem still to be solved on the Continent at the inception of the capitalist era—the creation of a uniform law—was, in England, an accomplished achievement. Systematisation was very largely unnecessary, because it was not required in order to overcome the chaos of local laws and customs. Of all the important jurisdictions of Europe, England was the only one to emerge from the Middle Ages with a "*common law*". The heritage of feudalism in this country was a unified body of institutions and rules which, while lacking in logic, were nevertheless capable of being intellectually absorbed and—above all—capable of being applied throughout the country. The lawyer did not need the Ariadne thread of systematic thought to help him to grope his way through a labyrinth of "*Stadtrechte*", of "*coutumes*", etc.

Moreover—and Max Weber's sociological analysis has made this convincingly clear—the thought-processes of the common law can and should be understood as the outcome of the needs and habits of a legal profession organised in gilds and preserving the structure and the power of a medieval vocational body. The modern continental systems were developed in the universities by legal scholars for the use of officials. English law evolved as a series of gild rules for the use and guidance of the members and apprentices of the Inns of Court. It was due to political factors, to the failure of the absolute monarchy in England, to the aristocratic structure of the body politic in the 18th century, that the administration of the law remained in the hands of the lawyers' guilds. With some exaggeration one might say that it was the Revolution of 1688, not the refusal to "receive" Roman Law that, in this country, sealed the fate of systematic legal science in the continental sense.

The common law was developed by that branch of the legal profession whose main interest lies in litigation. It was, until well into the 19th century (and, to a degree, it still is), a series of rules of conduct for practising advocates, a comprehensive answer to the question: "how do I behave in court?" It was a body of practical and technical craft-rules, handed down from master to apprentice, and designed to instruct the advocate in the art of raising and defending claims. This largely accounts for its "empirical", for its casuistic as opposed to the continental logical and systematic method. The craftsman asks: "how has this—or a similar—case been handled before?" He is not very much concerned with the question, whether the answer is capable of being fitted into an abstract system. It is, of course, easy to over-emphasise the contrast between the two methods. Logical deduction was never absent from the thought-processes of English judges and advocates, and precedents have played and are playing an important and rapidly increasing rôle on the Continent.[1] We are merely concerned with a basic difference in outlook and with the historical factors which account for this difference.

The contrast between the methods of thought of university

---

[1] See for the various types of principles of precedent the analysis by Goodhart, *Essays in Jurisprudence and the Common Law*, pp. 49 sq.

trained and gild trained lawyers may also serve as an explanation
for the essentially "remedial" or "procedural" structure of
English legal ideas. English law does not pose and answer the
question: "what are the legal guarantees for the freedom of the
individual from arbitrary arrest?" It is content to ask: "in what
circumstances will you, the barrister, be able to obtain for your
client a writ of *habeas corpus* or a judgment for damages on the
ground of false imprisonment?" From a practical point of view
there is no difference between these two types of question. Nevertheless the contrast between the two formulations reveals the gulf
between thought processes influenced by natural law and
orientated towards a systematic structure of rights and duties,
and a method of argument whose primary pre-occupation is with
remedies, not with rights, with procedural form, not with juridical
substance. It will be seen that the difference in approach to the
law of property can and must be explained as a similar divergence
in method rather than in practical results. It is not so much in
the practical operation of legal institutions as in the intellectual
machinery which promotes that operation that systematic and
historical positivism, the continental and the Anglo-Saxon
methods, are divided.

The foregoing remarks are not intended to give a comprehensive account of the methodological difference between the two
types of legal thought, even less to give a full explanation of its
causes. What they are designed to demonstrate is that it is not
an inherent feature of capitalism as such to give rise to either
systematic or historical positivism. That the continental method
of approach was not adopted in England, that the principle of
precedent (in its English form) did not take root on the Continent,
has its social causes. But these causes must be found in the
structure of the body politic, not in the economic and social
function of legal institutions. The rising middle classes were
interested in what Max Weber calls the "calculability of chances".
They were inclined to press for a development of the law which
permitted their lawyers to predict the outcome of disputes. There
is no doubt that the needs of capitalism promoted the "formal
rationality" of the law, i.e. the decision of each individual case in
accordance with a rational thought process, not in accordance
with ethical imperatives, expediency or political maxims. This
formal rationality, however, is a common characteristic of
systematic and of historical positivism. As long as the judge

proceeds on lines which can be predicted, it is irrelevant to the lawyer's client whether the argument is empirical or speculative, based on precedent or on general principles. "Modern capitalism can equally flourish and show identical traits under legal orders which not only possess widely different norms and legal institutions, but whose ultimate formal principles of structure are as widely divergent from each other as possible."[1] "There is not inherent in capitalism as such any decisive motive for favouring that form of rationalisation of the law which, since the rise of Romanist University education, has remained a characteristic of the continental occident."[2]

The contrast between the continental legal systems and English law lies far more in "ultimate formal principles of structure" than in positive "norms and institutions". The practical results are very often identical, where the lines of reasoning which lead up to them are as divergent as possible. Renner's analysis is concerned with the function of legal institutions, and especially with the adaptation of the property concept to an almost infinite variety of social and economic uses. Whether and to what extent lawyers choose to clothe the practical operation of these institutions in general formulæ is largely irrelevant for an analysis of this kind. English law has never developed a fixed and rounded definition of property, but, from the point of view of a sociological investigation, it matters little whether the owner claims his property by virtue of a *rei vindicatio* arising from the institution of ownership as such or whether he avails himself of an action for conversion or of detinue arising from the right to possession and being in its origin and structure a species of a delictal claim. It is only a question of legal technique whether I ask: "what are the conditions for the acquisition of ownership?" or: "who is the proper plaintiff, who is the proper defendant in an action for conversion?" From the point of view of the function of the institution of property it is irrelevant whether I devise a systematic set of principles culminating in the monumental pronouncement: "*En fait de meubles, la possession vaut titre*,"[3] or whether I am content to say that, as against a defendant who has given value in good faith, the plaintiff is, in certain circumstances, estopped from pleading a title better than that of the defendant's

---

[1] Max Weber, *Wirtschaft und Gesellschaft*, p. 508.
[2] Ib. p. 509.
[3] Code Civil Art. 2279, there are, of course, in this case, formidable practical differences in detail, which do not affect the point made in the text.

alleged predecessor   The difference is very important for those who learn the law and those who teach it. It is equally important for those who apply it. It is of next to no account for those whose interests are involved.

A continental lawyer and an English lawyer engaged in a conversation upon the law of succession on death will find it very difficult to understand the "thought processes" of their partner. The Englishman will take it for granted that there must be a "personal representative", an administrator or executor, who as such has no beneficial interest in the deceased's estate at all, has merely powers and duties, but no rights of enjoyment. He will fail to appreciate what his colleague means when he speaks about an "heir" or "heirs" in whom the estate vests *ipso facto*, who is (or are) liable for the debts of the deceased, and entitled to keep the residue. Nevertheless, if they forget their legal techniques and look at the practical results with the eyes of their clients, they will soon be convinced, that English law—without saying so— embodies the principle of "heirship" no less than French law which defines an "*héritier*" and a "*légataire universel*" or German law which defines an "*Erbe*". Two bankruptcy specialists, one from the Continent and the other from England, will soon discover that it is not very relevant from a practical point of view whether the law gives an abstract definition of insolvency or enumerates a catalogue of types of conduct—known as "acts of bankruptcy"— which indicate an individual's inability to pay his debts.

The institutions of property, of heirship, of bankruptcy, and innumerable others exist—perhaps in a somewhat inarticulate fashion—on this side of the Channel as on the other. The normative content of the institutions varies in detail, not in fundamentals. Their social and economic functions are similar.

The language of Renner's analysis appears to envisage continental institutions only, its substance applies in this country as much or as little as it applies in its country of origin. The capitalist environment of the law favours the positivist approach. Whether positivism is more of the systematic or of the empirical variety may affect the degree to which legal institutions adapt their normative content to changes in their social environment. It does not affect the relevance and validity of Renner's question: given a set of legal institutions, how can they change their functions without changing their norms?

IV

In one respect the remedial and procedural method of thought opens up an access to Renner's work which is closed to the conceptual thinking of the continental systems: The legal notion of property which Renner uses throughout his book is in one way much more germane to Anglo-Saxon than to current continental ideas.

The continental Codes define property as the right to enjoy a thing and to dispose of it in the most absolute manner,[1] to deal with it as one pleases and exclude third persons from interference,[2] etc. Property or ownership appears as a relation between a person and a tangible thing—*plena in re potestas*—a relation which comprises both the legal title, i.e. the power to claim undisturbed possession as against third persons, and the right of beneficial enjoyment.

From the point of view of strict positivism the normal beneficial use of tangible things is legally irrelevant. If the law consists of a body of imperatives addressed to individuals (or even if it is understood as a series of hypothetical judgments on the application of criminal or civil sanctions), the property norm exhausts itself in the prohibition not to interfere with the thing except with the consent of the owner. What the owner does with the thing, whether he uses it for purposes of production or consumption, is, like all relations between man and nature, a matter outside the law. The law intervenes when another person withholds possession from the owner or disturbs his enjoyment. It is only concerned with pathological situations, and also, of course, with the acquisition and loss of the right of ownership, but the normal undisturbed enjoyment of the thing is of interest to the economist and sociologist only, not to the lawyer. The definitions in the Codes are, in this view, an intrusion of sociological upon legal thought. Renner adopts this positivist legal theory of ownership,

---

[1]French Civil Code Art. 544: "La propriété est le droit de jouir et de disposer des choses de la manière la plus absolue, pourvu qu'on n'en fasse pas un usage prohibé par a loi ou par les règlements."

[2]German Civil Code § 903: "Der Eigentümer einer Sache kann, soweit nicht das Gesetz oder Rechte dritter entgegenstehen, mit der Sache nach Belieben verfahren und andere von jeder Einwirkung ausschliessen."

Swiss Civil Code Art. 641: "Wer Eigentümer einer Sache ist, kann in den Schranken der Rechtsordnung über sie nach seinem Belieben verfügen.

Er hat das Recht, sie von jedem, der sie ihm vorenthält, herauszuverlangen und jede ungerechtfertigte Einwirkung abzuwehren."

§ 354 of the Austrian Civil Code is quoted in Renner's text.

and, within the framework of his investigation, this strict differentiation between the legal and the sociological property concepts
is of paramount importance.

Continental practical lawyers, having been brought up in the
system of one of the Codes, are accustomed to think and speak of
ownership as a relation between a *persona* and a *res*. The Codes
were written by university-trained draftsmen skilled in the
handling of highly abstract definitions. Claims which were to be
raised in the courts were understood as the outcome of substantive
rights fixed within the framework of a systematised structure.
The owner's right to obtain possession from a wrongful detentor,
to ward off a trespass or a nuisance were mere incidents of his
right of ownership. *Ubi jus ibi remedium.* The owner as such
claims "his own" by virtue of his right of property. The positivist
objection to the definition of this right as a relation between a
person and a thing appeared on a level of scientific and philosophical thought which was beyond the scope of the ordinary
lawyer's textbook learning. He was inclined to ignore, or to
dismiss as unpractical, the plea of the theoretical jurist that law is
only concerned with relations between persons.

In this country, however, and throughout the common law
world, the situation is the reverse. The definition of property
as the owner's power to deal with the thing as he wills lingers on in
some of the textbooks on "jurisprudence",[1] but this literature
plays no part in the consciousness of the practical lawyer or in his
working life. His attention is fixed on cases of conflicting interests,
he thinks in terms of "remedies" much more than in terms of
"rights". For reasons mentioned above English law grew up as a
number of rules giving a cause of action in certain situations, causes
of action for trespass, for nuisance, for conversion, etc. It is true
that the principle *ubi remedium ibi jus* has been defunct ever since the
Common Law Procedure Act, 1852, but Maitland's dictum:[2]
"The forms of action we have buried, but they still rule us from
their graves" has acquired, among lawyers, the fame of a proverb
and almost of a common place. The living law of this country
knows nothing of an abstract definition of property in terms of a
relation between *persona* and *res*. It offers no target to the conceptualist attack against the mixing of legal and sociological

[1]See Salmond, *Jurisprudence*, 9th ed. (1937), p. 339 (Ownership appears as ownership of a "right"), Paton, *Jurisprudence*, p. 393. Holland, *Jurisprudence*, p. 193, has the
positivist definition.
[2]*Lectures on the Forms of Action at Common Law*, No. 1, 1926 ed., p. 296.

methods. It is content to define those encroachments upon a man's right to possession which enable him to set in motion the machinery of the courts. It ignores the normal enjoyment of tangible things as long as it is not disturbed by others. The English law of property, both movable and immovable, is, in so far, much closer to the spirit of extreme continental positivist jurisprudence than the living doctrine of the law on the Continent itself. Renner's rigid distinction between property in the legal and in the economic sense, his insistence that, as a legal institution, property is no more than a bundle of powers to ward off interferences by others, should, in so far, strike a familiar chord in the minds of English lawyers.[1]

The absence in English law of a rigid definition of property could, however, in other respects, be a hindrance rather than a help to the understanding of Renner's argument. It is advisable to bear in mind the differences between the continental and the Anglo-Saxon approaches to the law of property. These differences arise partly from a certain equivocation inherent in the word "property". Partly—and in connection with this—they are due to a greater flexibility of the English property concept which sometimes enables it to come very near to what Renner calls "economic property". And some of the differences are inherent in the ability of English law to isolate from each other the various legal incidents of property which, owing to its conceptual structure, continental law is compelled to view as a whole.

The legal conception of ownership used by Renner could not be so unambiguous and so clear, if the term *Eigentum, dominium* (ownership) was the exact equivalent of the English concept of "property". Renner follows the terminology of all legal systems based on Roman law in confining the term "ownership" to tangible things. He protests against the "watering down" of this concept, its extension to what English law calls "choses in action", such as debts, patents, copyright, or shares in a company. The English lawyer does not find it incongruous to say that a claim for the repayment of a loan, a mortgage upon another man's land, or a share in a limited company belongs to a person's "property". Renner's sociological analysis, and, more particularly, his theory of complementary institutions must remain obscure, unless it is borne in mind that the comprehensive English

---

[1] The difference between the two conceptions of ownership is discussed in Buckland and McNair, *Roman Law and Common Law*, pp. 64 sq.

term "property" has no equivalent in the German language. A man may be the "owner" of the piece of paper (the share warrant) which embodies his right of membership in a company.[1] The membership right itself is not "property". "Property" which is not ownership of tangible objects plays a dominant part in modern economic life. Economic control has largely shifted from the "owner" as such to those who, in English terminology, "own" choses in action, not "choses in possession". This process does not affect a diminution in the role of "property" in the English sense, it does however vitally transform the social function of *dominium* or ownership in tangible objects.

It is necessary to insist upon another terminological point. The English word "property" is often used to connote the sum total of a man's assets, irrespective of their nature. For this the German language uses the word *Vermögen*. Sometimes—and particularly as used by Renner—this term comprises liabilities as well as assets, a man's "estate". In this sense the English term "property" signifies the totality of a person's economic and social power, it covers what Renner calls "ownership in the economic sense". In a system of "simple commodity production" there is a measure of coincidence between legal and economic property, between ownership in tangible objects (house, garden, tools, etc.) and the sum total of a man's worldly possessions. It is the essence of the functional transformation described by Renner that *"Vermögen"*, property understood as "assets", becomes a conglomeration of values without intrinsic functional unity. The English word "property" is ambiguous, but this linguistic ambiguity is the mirror of the change in the structure of society and of the function of the property concept which is the main topic of Renner's work.

The term "property", as used by Renner, then, should be understood as comprising a right in an individual tangible object only, an object which may be land or a movable thing. "Property" in a mere "fund", a unit of values, is inconceivable to Romanist legal thought. English law, on the other hand, is perfectly capable of giving effect to the idea of "floating" property,[2] of a "property" right which does not attach to any individualised asset, but to a "value" which may, at any given

---

[1] In other words: movable property is only that which, in this country, can be the object of an act of conversion. See Scrutton, L. J., in *Lloyds Bank v. Chartered Bank of India*, [1929] K.B. 40, at p. 35.

[2] or in Company Law, of the "floating charge" (which is unknown to Scottish Law).

moment, be represented either by land or by a bank account (i.e. a banker's debt) or by Government securities. It is very difficult indeed for a continental lawyer to understand the legislative technique which enabled English lawyers to adapt the institution of settled land to the needs of modern society. The rights of the members of the family other than the tenant in possession were originally "property" rights in the sense that they attached to the land itself. The land was "in fetters". The multitude of rights of "remainder men" whose concurrence was needed for any disposition over the land itself prevented its development for building purposes and even those improvements which could only be carried into effect with the help of mortgages. Legislation which culminated in the Settled Land Act, 1925, has, in effect, converted the "ownership" rights of the remaindermen in the land into beneficial "property" rights in the value of the land. The tenant in possession, now, significantly, called "estate owner" can (in certain limits) freely dispose, provided the proceeds of his transaction are paid into a fund vested in trustees to which the beneficial rights of the remaindermen continue to attach. Family "ownership" in the strict legal sense was out of tune with the requirements of modern society and had to be "softened" so as to become what Renner would call merely "economic property". Continental systems are not unfamiliar with rights in aggregates of values, funds, etc., but neither a husband's right in his wife's assets, nor an executor's power over the deceased's estate nor those of an administrator of a bankrupt's estate can, on the Continent, be classified as "property" rights.[1]

That English law has been able to develop a "property" concept which is so much closer to modern economic reality than the *dominium* of continental law, is largely due to the influence of Equity, and, more particularly, to the institution of the Trust. The strict separation between *jura in re* and *jura in personam*—the corner-stone of private law—is a necessary ingredient of a notion of property such as that used by Renner. The difference between the two types of rights is, of course, perfectly familiar to English law, but the line was blurred by the formulation of "beneficial" rights against a trustee of property—the "legal owner"—which, in certain circumstances, can be enforced by the beneficiary against third parties. These "equitable interests"—of which the rights of remainder men in a settled estate are now an example—stand on the border-line between *jura in re* and *jura in personam*.

[1] See also Notes 22 and 23 below.

To this day it has remained controversial whether an equitable interest should be classified as a right "in the thing", as "property" in the continental sense (as Lord Mansfield's logical mind would have had it[1]) or whether Maitland was right in arguing that they were extended *jura in personam*.[2] But—this is decisive—while the celebrated controversy may be of absorbing interest to scholars, it does not—and need not—usually cause any major anxiety to learned judges or to practising lawyers.[3] Nothing can show more clearly of how little account is the legal property concept within the framework of English law.

If a man is the sole beneficiary for life of a fund invested, say, in urban house property, and receives the rent every quarter day, he would hardly hesitate, in this country, to think of himself as "the owner" of the house. Yet the "legal estate" is vested in a trustee or trustees who hold the "title". The beneficiary's right is merely a right of enjoyment. This illustrates another fundamental difference between continental and English law: the *dominium* concept comprises both the legal title and the right to enjoy the benefits. If the subject-matter of the property right is a tangible object which is in the possession of the beneficiary, the right to be in possession is the only legally relevant aspect of the beneficiary's interest. But as soon as he enjoys his right with the help of "complementary institutions", e.g. contracts of lease, it becomes apparent that English law can do what continental law is incapable of doing: it can separate the power to protect the thing as against the outside world from the right to have its economic benefit. On the Continent title and enjoyment are welded together in the notion of ownership. The exigencies of practical life often require a separation, but, whenever that occurs, the law is forced to resort to complicated legal constructions, fictitious "agencies", and highly involved institutions *sui generis*. It cannot, as a rule, formulate the right to enjoy "economic property" as a legal institution. Continental systems must always ask and answer the question: "who is *the* owner?" They may divest "the owner" of his title and leave him with a mere beneficial right against an all powerful "agent" or they may leave him with a bare title without any economic interest. They cannot admit

---

[1]*Burgess v. Wheate* (1759),1 Eden 177.
[2]Equity, Lecture III.
[3]That even this most abstract jurisprudential problem can suddenly spring into practical eminence is shown by the two cases *Baker v. Archer-Shee*, [1927] AC 844, and *Archer-Shee v. Garland*, [1931] AC 212.

the possibility of a splitting of the ownership right as such.[1] This remains one and indivisible. English law has no objection to isolating the attributes of property from each other, largely through the machinery of the trust. Maitland has shown,[2] how the flexible trust concept was able to serve as a comprehensive substitute for the manifold complexities of legal thought in which continental systems are involved owing to the almost insoluble union between title and use. In developing the trust concept—in some ways its most original contribution to jurisprudence—the English legal mind has made it unnecessary and impossible for itself to search for a definition of property in the continental sense. Nor is this fundamental difference in approach exclusively due to the influence of Equity. The separation between legal title and beneficial use permeates many branches of English law. The relationship between the personal representative of a deceased's estate and the residuary legatee constitutes a major example, but it was moulded only partly by the Court of Chancery and partly by the ecclesiastical Courts.[3] Modern company law provides another instance: the English "nominee" shareholder is, in a parallel situation abroad, a mere agent. To such an extent is English law capable of isolating the functions of ownership from each other that a person who has neither title nor use can nevertheless be vested with the right to confer ownership, a "power of appointment". This may be a cloak for a variety of substantive rights ranging from something little short of economic ownership[4] to the mere office of selecting the owner of a thing with which the holder of the power has otherwise no concern at all.

Owing to its habit of looking at the powers and rights arising from ownership rather than at ownership in the abstract, English law has been able to introduce the time element into the property concept. The continental notion of property, like the *dominium* of Roman law, contains, as a matter of principle, the element of eternity. An "estate" which is limited to the life of a person or to a fixed period is not property. In this country property for a time (at least with regard to land) has been possible since the feudal age. English law sees as a species of ownership—tenancy

---

[1]This is subject to qualification. Thus the German *Reichs-gericht* has sometimes separated "economic" and "legal" ownership in cases in which property had been transferred merely for the purpose of securing a debt, a revival of the Roman *fiducia.*
[2]*Collected Papers*, Vol. I, pp. 353 sq.
[3]Holdsworth, *History of English Law*, Vol. V, p. 317, p. 321.
[4]This is implicitly recognised by Section 27 of the Wills Act, 1837.

for life, leasehold—what Roman law and modern continental thought can only define as a contractual right, or, at best, as a *jus in re aliena* such as a usufruct. The common law dissolves the idea of ownership in land into a multitude of estates distinguished by their relation to the time factor. The Law of Property Act, 1925, has curtailed the number of possible legal estates, but they still include the leasehold, and, by clothing the tenant for life of a settled estate with the dignity of an owner of the fee simple, the legislation of 1925 has emphasised the contrast between English and continental doctrine.

Very few of these differences between the two systems affect the practical working of the law. This is, however, irrelevant in the present context. Capitalist "property" was, of course, developed and protected on the Continent as it was in this country. But, owing to the greater flexibility of the English property concept, the changing function of the legal institution was more rapidly reflected in the normative sphere. It will be useful to revert to this point after having briefly surveyed the outline of Renner's theory.

v.

The analysis of the functional transformation of legal institutions takes as its starting point the "age of simple commodity production", i.e. a society in which the bulk of all producers of goods are independent peasants and artisans who own their means of production, employ little, if any, outside labour, and sell their products, in the majority of cases, directly to the consumer.

It was this social order of goods and of labour which prevailed in Europe when the Roman conception of ownership was "received" by the legal systems and became the central institution dominating practice and theory. The Roman *dominium*, the legal norm safeguarding to the individual the absolute unfettered control over a tangible thing, tallied precisely with the economic and social function of property. "There is always a moment in the history of human institutions when the legal system is the adequate expression of economic relations." The conception of ownership was the mirror of a society in which wealth mainly consisted of tangible things, things which formed a functional unit: the house containing workshop and tools, dwelling room and furniture, the self-contained entity of the farm. They were held together by their common dedication to one single economic objective: to safeguard a livelihood to the owner and to his family. The "own and patrimony" assisted the *dominus* in filling his place in the process of production and of distribution, and it served as the principal basis of consumption. Legal and economic property coincided: the notion of ownership applied to, and was the corollary of, a functional microcosm, an *universitas rerum*.

The owner, the "person", combined in himself many of those functions which were later separated: he purchased the raw materials, he converted them—with his own hands—into the finished product, he sold that product to the consumer. He was, in a sense, economically "free". When the institution of property was allied to its "twin brother", the law of personal freedom, the world of norms was at last fully adapted to the substratum, the world of facts. The French Revolution was only the last step in the break-up of antiquated feudal institutions. In the sphere of private law the legal concept of the abstract "*persona*" was the true image of a society in which economic functions were not as yet specialised.

The conceptions of the law of contract, such as sale, bailment, or loan for consumption (*mutuum*) operated mainly as auxiliary devices. Bailment and loan—as a rule gratuitous—did not as yet play a major part in the economic process, and this was accurately reflected in the rule of the Roman law that *mutuum* does not comprise interest, which is extraneous to the contract of loan. Money was still mainly used as a standard of measurement, as a means of circulation, or as unused treasure, not yet as capital. The law of commercial sales, in so far as it operated at all, was not a stimulus to, but a brake upon, production. It tended to petrify the productive system, to retard technical progress. The merchant stood between the producer and the consumer, he exploited the former by taking his profits away from him. The law of sale was not yet subservient to the law of property, it was antagonistic to it. Only one type of contract was of central importance: the contract of work and labour, *locatio conductio operis*, the form in which the craftsman realised the proceeds of his labour. It is noteworthy, that, in this country, the action of *assumpsit*, the main vehicle for the development of the law of contract, arose, in the 14th, 15th and 16th centuries, to a large extent out of cases of "work and labour."[1]

[1]Plucknett, *Concise History of the Common Law*, 3rd ed., p. 415, pp. 569–572.

The "unity" of husband and wife in the eyes of the law, whether expressed in a system of community of goods, in the husband's right to administer, use, and enjoy his wife's property, or in the "merger" of the wife's legal personality in that of the husband, was the adequate legal corollary of an economic system in which the family was a unit of production as well as of consumption. The principles of the English common law which governed the status and capacity of married women (and also those of infants), no less than the manifold continental systems of *régime matrimonial*, reflected a state of society in which the family was but one aspect of the "house", that *universitas* which, with its contents, was the property object κατ ' ἐξοχήν. Wife and children co-operated in the productive effort of the "house". This was the basis of their maintenance, and of the raising and training of the young. Why then should they have capacity to contract? Why should a married woman hold or administer property of her own?

Inheritance either in the family in accordance with some canons of intestacy, or, if need be, by will, was the adequate order of succession in this system of simple commodity production. No society can live without such an order. The production and reproduction of goods and of labour do not suffer an interruption. The individual dies, but, since the species continues to live, the order of goods and the order of power must be so organised that the vacancy is filled. The estate of a deceased artisan or farmer was a living entity, property still safeguarded the productive and reproductive process. No one, then, was better qualified to "succeed" than the children of the deceased who had been trained in the "house". And if they were not so qualified, the owner himself was the proper person to select a substitute. The law of inheritance *ab intestato* or by will fulfilled its social function. Legal and economic succession coincided, no matter whether it took the form of Roman heirship or of English personal representation.

Property, then, the central institution of private law, fulfilled, in the system of simple commodity production, the functions of providing an order of goods, and, in part, an order of power. It did so without any essential aid from other institutions. It was not, however, able, to guarantee for any length of time an order of labour. Outside labour was increasingly used by the independent artisans, and this was regulated not by the law of property itself, but by complementary norms, norms which were at first derived from public gild law, and subsequently from the law of free employment. It is at this point that the order of simple commodity production starts to break up, and the functional transformation of private law, and of the law of property in particular, begins.

VI

The law of property was substantially the same in 1900 as in 1600, but what had become of its social functions? Did it still provide an order of production? No: the producer now worked in another man's house, with another man's tools. The producer was still the *detentor* of the raw materials, the means of production, the finished products, but they were no longer "his". Ownership was no longer capable of expressing the order of goods.

Did it, then, fulfil its function to regulate consumption? No, the man still "occupied" the house in which he lived, but he occupied it as a tenant. The furniture which he "held" and used was, perhaps, hired under a hire-purchase contract. The house, the family, had long ceased to be a universal unit of consumption. The children were educated in schools, the sick cared for in hospitals, the old and invalid in homes.

The *universitas rerum* of the "house", that microcosm of tangible objects which had been the substratum of the property norm, had been torn asunder, but the norm survived the destruction of its substratum. The single pieces—things—which had been the constituting elements of a functional entity had been—in the Marxist sense—"expropriated". Each object—land, house, means of production, commodities for consumption—followed its own destiny.

The things which a man owns are no longer held together by a common function. Nothing except the fact of ownership itself links them together. If, and in so far as, they are consumers' goods—a dwelling house and garden, an allotment, furniture, etc.—they "belong" to their owner not only in the legal, but also in the functional sense. But the bulk of all the things which are privately owned have no intrinsic connection with the proprietor at all. They happen to belong to him—legally—, they would function just as well if they belonged to someone else. From his point of view their sole object is to be a title, a title to profits, a title to interest, a title to rent. It does not matter what the thing

is: it may be a block of flats, an agricultural estate, a factory, or
so many South African gold shares. The property object has
become "capital". But the law of property cannot by itself
endow its object with the nature of capital. It must be assisted
by complementary institutions most of which are to be found in
the law of contract.

Of these complementary institutions the contract of employment
was the first to appear on the scene, and it has remained the
principal actor in the drama. The contract itself is, like all legal
institutions, a blank without intrinsic social significance, and
adaptable to an infinite number of social objectives. In industrial
capitalism, however, it is also "blank" in a more poignant sense.
Whatever the law may say, from a sociological point of view this
is a "contract" without contractual content. It is a command
under the guise of an agreement. The employer, by exercising
his power to command, fills in the blank, and that power vests in
him by virtue of his *dominium*, his ownership in the means of
production. The legal institution of property, having ceased to
be part of the order of detention (in relation to means of production)—see above, p. 26—has become part of the order of labour.
Those who handle the tools, control the machines, "occupy"—
not in the legal sense—the factory space, use the raw materials,
and hold in their hands the finished products, are no longer
"owners". The law of property clashes with the social order of
goods, but, through its alliance with the contract of employment,
it organises the labour power of society. A brick has been taken out
of one edifice and been put into another. As simple commodity
production gave way to manufacture, and manufacture to factory
production, ownership became a *dominium* over persons. This
functional transformation was, of course, a long drawn out
process. It began with manual labour, but, as a consequence of
the industrial revolution, presently extended to intellectual work.

Property became part of the order of labour, but it also became
part of the order of power. It was almost a shock for a liberal
19th century lawyer to be told that anything outside the "State",
could participate in the organisation of a hierarchy. Was it not
one of the tenets of his creed that there gaped an unbridgeable
gulf between "public" and "private" law, between the subordination of "subjects" and the co-ordination of "free persons"?
Was it not the great achievement of the century that employment
had become a matter of private law? Renner maintains that

"the institution of property leads automatically to an organisation similar to the state. Power over matter begets personal power". If this is true, if, without any event or development capable of finding its way into the pages of a book on legal history, property gives rise to a hierarchy of subordination, to a subjugation of free persons, what has happened to the legal institution of personal freedom, to the *persona* itself?

The answer is that the abstract concept of the *persona*, so admirably fitted to respond to the needs of the craftsmanship age, had changed its function no less than the concept of property. The social corollary of the *persona* had disappeared. A man was no longer owner and worker, vendor and purchaser, all at the same time. In order to play a part in the social drama, it was no longer enough for a man to be a "person". That universal "mask" would no longer serve him, he had to wear a "character mask", the "mask" of a landowner or factory hand, rentier or agricultural labourer, merchant or industrialist. As industrial capitalism developed, the *persona* concept like that of the institution of ownership was prevented by its abstract nature from exercising any independent social function, because the universality of its normative content no longer mirrored the universality of its social purpose.

Property, as part of the order of power, subordinates the will of one person to that of another, but it also co-ordinates in a compulsory association those who work in the factory. Marx contrasted the planned production—the despotism—of the factory with the unplanned operation—the anarchy—of the market. Renner translated this contrast into terms of sociology of law. As a public law corporation receives its constitution from the superior "will", the State, so does the compulsory heteronomous association of factory workers. Its law and constitution is the command of the employer, his plan of production, the tempo of his machines. The law of the market, that voluntary autonomous association of capital owners, confronts the law of the factory as the law of free tenure confronted the custom of the manor. The worker is the unfree copyholder of the classical age of capitalism.

The analysis of the factory as a compulsory association, a *Herrschaftsverband*, is familiar to readers of Gierke. As early as 1868 he described the modern factory as "the domination of capital" which "in the relation of entrepreneur and worker" had created "a new form of economic *Herrschaftsverband*, to which contemporary law gives no more significance than that of a sum total of individual rights between the One and the Many, despite the fact that it is an independent organism interfering with public as well as private law".[1] The Conservative Gierke was the protagonist of the school of thought—in this country mainly represented by Maitland—which believed in the "real nature of corporate personality". This romantic theory of human associations was inclined to blur the line between legal and factual corporate entities. Renner arrives at the same point from the opposite direction. His strictly positivistic and, as it were, individualistic conception of the norm compels him to see human associations almost entirely as sociological, not as legal phenomena. The law has very little to do with the formation and operation of groups. There is no more "legal reality" in a corporate entity recognised by the state than in a factory, because there is no such thing as a legal reality of associations at all. There is little intrinsic difference between an association like a municipality and an organisation like that of the workers in a factory. Both are kept together by social forces beyond their control, and it is not very relevant that in one case, but not in the other, positive law recognises the association as a corporate body. Gierke was the antipode of the positivists. In his view all social phenomena are potentially "law", in Renner's view nothing is law except the control of individuals by individuals. Both regard legal incorporation as comparatively insignificant. *Les extrêmes se touchent.*

VII

The ownership of tangible things becomes property in industrial capital. This process transforms a host of other legal institutions.

It destroys the economic substratum of family law. The working class wife seeks work and earns wages outside the house, but she remains subject to those incapacities in the law of property and contract which have lost their meaning. In this country it was only by two Statutes of 1882 and 1935[2] that the law took account of the disappearance of the family as a unit of production. The transformation in the nature of wealth made the wife's incapacity

---

[1]Gierke, *Deutsches Genossenschaftsrecht*, Vol. I, p. 911.
[2]Married Women's Property Act, 1882. Law Reform (Married Women and Tortfeasors) Act, 1935.

to hold personal property a burden for the capital owning classes as well, but owing to the flexibility of Equity during its formative stages, the burden was largely removed by the development of the "separate estate" through the mechanism of the trust. The working class child had to be socially "of age" long before he reached the age of legal capacity. The Courts took, in this country, account of this fact, by gradually expanding his capacity to contract.[1]

The Poor Law, social insurance legislation, legislation on education and other social services were the—often belated—response of the law to the diminishing importance of the family as a unit of consumption. The care for the aged and for the sick, the training and education of the young had belonged to the sphere of the family when it was a living economic entity. The history of the social services is, to some extent, the story of the gradual socialisation of consumption. They should be understood as institutions complementary to family law.

When a man's estate had ceased to be a functional entity, the law of inheritance was no longer the guarantee of the uninterrupted working of the social mechanism. It is socially irrelevant whether the son of a share- or bond-holder or a stranger steps into the shoes of the deceased. What matters is who succeeds to managerial positions, civil service appointments, etc. This, however, is determined, to a large extent, by orders of succession outside the law of inheritance, except, perhaps, in relation to certain types of agricultural property. Renner suggests that the sale and purchase of business goodwills has taken the place of the law of heirship and of wills. To-day and in this country company law and manifold provisions and practices governing the appointment of public servants and others provide the true order of succession, while inheritance has been transformed to a mere transmission of "values".

When property becomes capital, the contract of sale, hitherto the enemy of the law of property, becomes its ally, or, better, its servant. The industrial producer appears himself in the market and appropriates the sales profit.

This enables him to accumulate capital and to improve production. Commercial law becomes an agent of technical progress when the "character-mask" of the owner is combined with that

---

[1] An infant's contract of employment is generally held valid. He can even sue upon it in a County Court. County Courts Act, 1934, Sect. 77.

of the seller. The independent artisan was reduced to bondage when the contract of sale was used against him by a middleman, the factory owner uses this type of contract to re-imburse himself for his outlay on permanent means of production and wages and to realise the "surplus value". The market itself becomes an institution complementary to property whether or not the law organises it as an "exchange", a *bourse*.

Presently a new actor appears on the scene and gives a new function to the law of sale. The capitalist merchant, unlike his predecessor of craftsmanship days, does not himself handle the goods: physical possession is "purified" into the handling of warehouse receipts, warrants, and other documents of title. The modern law of bailment begins to develop—and (one may add) also the modern law of carriage by sea and of insurance (which Renner does not mention). The merchant no longer deals with a worker directly. He leaves the economic function of exploitation to the owner of the means of production who has long since ceased to be a worker himself.

All this, however, is of minor significance, compared with the catalytic effect upon society of another type of commercial contract: the contract of loan. This legal institution re-organises the capitalist class itself. As an institution complementary to property it is second in importance only to the contract of employment. The latter had lifted the institution of ownership from the order of detention, made it part of the order of labour, and endowed it with the function of capital. It was the destiny of the contract of loan to separate again the property in goods and land, the power to command, from its capital function, and to crystallise that function into an institution of its own.

When money becomes a form of capital, *mutuum*, the contract of loan, is caught by the stream of evolution. Interest becomes an *essentiale negotii* in the functional, i.e. (from Renner's point of view) the non-legal sense. Capital owners are divided into managers and financiers, operating and non-operating capitalists. The entrepreneur who conducts his business with borrowed capital still exercises the domination over persons—that essential attribute of property in means of production—but it is the investor who disposes of the capital, and he does so without himself directly exploiting labour. He is divided by two removes from the labour which—according to Marxist doctrine—produces his interest. The mechanism of capital has become so refined that tangible property has ceased to be an essential ingredient of capital. Capital has ceased to function in the productive process, it has now, at last, assumed its proper rôle: to be a means of distribution.

The law of ownership at first subjugates other institutions and uses them so to speak as its satellites. But subsequently the "satellites" conspire against their "master". The contract of loan was not the only method by which legal *dominium* was deprived of its capital function, of its character of property in the economic sense. Company law was—especially in this country and in the United States—an even more powerful agent in this process. Renner does not pursue his analysis into this sphere. He merely mentions the fact that frequently the company is the *dominus* of the assets, and the controlling shareholder the owner in the economic sense. He does not show how the function of the limited company as an institution was itself transformed without any change in its normative content. An institution originally designed to "attract" morsels of shifting capital to one concentrated unit, has, to a large extent, been transmuted into an instrument enabling the owner to become a pure capitalist and to leave the entrepreneurial function to paid managers. Renner's attention is not attracted by those modern structures of holding (investing) and subsidiary (operating) companies which would have lent additional force to his argument. Nor has he anything to say about the growing ascendancy of the managerial over the purely financial power inside the mechanism of the business corporation which has been the most remarkable phenomenon in this field in our time. His analysis is still permeated by the dogma of the supremacy of finance over industry. The forty years which have passed since Renner published the first edition of his work have seen a re-union between control over physical substance and control over profits which 19th century thought would have refused to predict.

In relation to agricultural property the contract of lease separates the physical *dominium* from its entrepreneurial function. The position is very different from that obtaining in industry. There physical ownership and "command power" remained united, even where the former was deprived of its capital function through the operation of the contract of loan. In agriculture the owner in the legal sense is also the capitalist, but he divests himself of his rôle of entrepreneur, of his command-power, where he

2*

leases his property to a tenant farmer who employs agricultural labour. Much of what Renner says in this connection is less applicable to English conditions than many other parts of his investigation. Industrial developments in various countries have much more in common than the legal and economic forms in which agriculture is carried on. It is not usually true of this country that, as between land-owner and tenant-farmer, the capital to be invested is entirely supplied by the latter, and that it is he who appropriates for himself the interest on such capital. Renner insists that this type of agricultural property is of necessity inimical to technical progress. He argues that it deprives the tenant-entrepreneur of any stimulus to accumulate and to invest by threatening him with the forfeiture of his improvements on termination of the lease. This is much less true, if the capital is supplied by the landowner. In so far as in this country the situation is as described by Renner and the tenant finds the capital for investment, the Agricultural Holdings Acts have given him an expectation for compensation in the event of the termination of the tenancy. This legislation has gone some way towards eliminating the reactionary consequences of the separation between ownership and entrepreneurial control and of the principle *superficies solo cedit* which forms part of English no less than of Roman law. In spite of these differences there is a great deal in Renner's analysis which holds good for English conditions: where the landlord supplies the capital, physical ownership retains its character of title, it is—economically—a title for the appropriation not only of rent, but also of interest on invested capital. Legal and economic ownership are even more clearly combined than where interest accrues to the tenant, the entrepreneurial function of the latter is even more fully isolated, the owner of the *res* even more unequivocally the investor in every sense of the word.

Ownership in land and agricultural lease are legal cloaks which cover widely different economic situations. Thus an agricultural tenant who is a working small-holder—as he frequently is in many parts of the world outside this country—is economically in the position of a labourer. Here the lease is the equivalent of a contract of employment, and the physical owner retains his entrepreneurial rôle. His social function differs little from that of a farmer-owner who uses hired labour. Both take for themselves the ground-rent and, assuming the land is not mortgaged, the interest on capital. Their property, unlike that of the landlord who lets his land to tenant farmers, belongs to the order of labour, but not, of course, to the order of detention.

The institution of land ownership itself is no less ambivalent than that of the lease. The landowner, the owner-farmer, and the man with "three acres and a cow", are all "owners". How little this means one can see if one remembers that the small-holder's property is, amongst other things, a working tool, that it belongs to the order of detention as well as of labour. Far from being a simple phenomenon, it is in fact an economic hybrid, since the owner realises with the price of his produce three things at a time: wages for labour, rent of the land, and interest on capital. Renner postulates a society of peasant proprietors—smallholders—and he traces a functional development by which the titles to wages, rent, and interest become separated, with the transformation of peasant ownership to large scale landholding. This was not universally the development in this country, nevertheless the structural analysis is of general interest.

It goes without saying that the mortgage of land—both agricultural and urban—ranks high among those legal institutions which have deprived the *dominus* of the *res* of his capital function. A peasant proprietor is rarely in a position to find both the pur-chase price for the land and the capital required for the running of the farm. He has the option of retaining physical ownership and divesting himself of the economic enjoyment of the property—in this case he becomes a mortgagor—or of renouncing physical ownership itself by becoming a tenant. In his case mortgage and lease have similar functions. Where a landowner who has leased property to a managing farmer mortgages his estate, physical ownership continues as a mere title to rent, the title to interest lies elsewhere, and so does the entrepreneurial function: economic property is split in three, but it is itself separated from the "deten-tion" of the land which remains with the agricultural labourers who work it.

Urban as well as rural land offers examples for this transforma-tion of property by its ancillary institutions. Renner's indictment of the lease as an institution retarding economic progress may, in this country, be directed with greater force against the building lease than against agricultural tenancy. He envisages a world in which practically all town-dwellers live in rented flats or tene-ments. But the social function of the building society mortgage is very closely akin to that of the urban lease. The "ownership" of a house bought with a building society mortgage (and collateral security) has the economic function of a tenancy combined with the ideological function of property. The building society mortgage supplies perhaps the most powerful evidence for the truth of Renner's thesis that ancillary institutions may reduce legal ownership to an empty form, or, as one might say, to a mere ideology.

It also serves as an example of the seemingly paradoxical phenomenon that ownership which had so often used the contract of employment as its complementary institution, can, in turn, become socially ancillary to the latter. The wage-earner also dons the "character mask" of an "owner", an owner of an allotment, of furniture, etc., and, if he is in a position to "accumulate" savings, even of a "creditor". He does not, however, accumulate capital, but a consumer's reserve fund, designed to supplement his wage income, which may, nevertheless, be capital in the true sense in the hands of the borrower. Owing to their ubiquity and adaptability legal institutions like ownership and loan may serve opposite social purposes at the same time. This is not without political significance. The transfer of invested capital to public ownership can be misunderstood or misrepresented as an attack upon the consumers' reserve fund of those who are "owners" and "investors". The property concept can ultimately serve the political function of creating the illusion that factual situations are identical because they happen to be reflected in the same legal institution. The higher the standard of living, the wider the spread of savings, the greater is the ideological function of property and—correspondingly—the need for insisting upon the contrast between the comprehensiveness and unity of the property norm and the multifariousness of its social substrata.

Loan, joint stock company, lease, mortgage—all these and others together—bring about that "mobility" of the capital function which enables it to attach to itself a multitude of different norms whose legal structures have little or nothing in common. They were originally destined to serve the institution of ownership but eventually they force it to abdicate from that dominant social position which still casts its shadow in the world of norms.

VIII

It is impossible to read Renner's work without being constantly reminded of the distance which separates our own time from the time when the book was written. Legal positivism, the belief in the relative stability of the normative system, flourished during a long spell of uninterrupted peace. It was, in a way, a juris-prudential reflection of the age of liberal capitalism.[1] The absence of major legislative regulations which affected the economic system engendered an atmosphere in which the norma-tive framework of society appeared to be stable and its conceptions fixed. The First World War administered a mortal blow to the conceptual utopia. The events which followed, inflation and catastrophic unemployment, gave it the *coup de grâce*. The con-cepts of property and of contract were thrown into the melting pot, when the institutions of private law, like their counterpart, the laissez-faire economy, proved unable to safeguard the life and expansion of society. Renner's positivist doctrine is "dated", it is to-day no more and no less than an important and interesting phenomenon in the history of human ideas.

But it is not only the jurisprudential foundation of Renner's investigation, it is his picture of society itself which is manifestly conditioned by the circumstances of an age which is no more. The social facts which he presupposes are those of 1900, not those of 1946. The social substratum of the norms of private law has changed more rapidly in this half-century than at any previous period of history. Trade unionism has reduced the factual com-mand power of property, the association of the workers in the factory is no longer as compulsive and as heteronomous as it was 50 years ago, the hold of the investor over industrial property no longer as firm as in the days when "finance capitalism" seemed to be the ultimate outcome of the capitalist age. Renner mentions cartels occasionally, but the world which forms the background of his analysis is not that of industrial monopolies, of price-fixing trade associations, of international cartels in which we live, it is still the world of competitive capitalism.

The additions to his text which Renner inserted in the 1929 edition of his book show how well aware he was of the profound transformation in the world of norms which had occurred since 1904. That transformation has been even more rapid since the

[1]This point is further developed by Friedmann, *Legal Theory*, pp. 148–149.

beginning of the "great depression" and during the Second World War. It is unnecessary to elaborate the point that, wherever we look, whether at agriculture or urban house property, at the distribution of the social product between wages and the "accumulation fund", at minimum wage legislation or at price control, the sovereignty of "economic property" has been broken. It is to-day impossible and misleading to study the functioning of the "property norm" in isolation from public law. It is public law which to-day determines to an ever increasing extent the economic and social function of property. No lawyer and no jurist can to-day afford to ignore the influence which revenue law exercises on the operation of such institutions as the law of wills or company law. Indeed a second volume would be needed to describe even in outline the revolution which has overtaken the social functions of the institutions of private law.

All this is obvious. Yet those who urge it as an objection to the theoretical importance and practical usefulness of Renner's work can be met by a plea of "confession and avoidance". The material which Renner uses, the examples which he gives to demonstrate the working of his method and his theory may be out of date, the jurisprudential foundation of his structure may have been shaken by the course of history. Nevertheless the method itself remains fruitful, and can and should be used for a better understanding of many legal developments of our own time. It is as true to-day as it was fifty years ago that legal institutions may thoroughly change their social function as a consequence of a transformation in their environment. It is also true that the legal profession is apt to ignore this process. Definitions and precedents linger on, social phenomena and processes are "construed" in terms of concepts designed to cover situations intrinsically antithetic to those to which the norm is now made to apply. A feeling of uneasiness, some vague sense of the "unreality" of the atmophere,[1] of the clash between "law" and "truth and substance",[2] sometimes finds expression in judgments and indicates that a transformation of its substratum has condemned the law to produce paradoxical results.

It would be easy to give many examples, but it should be sufficient to remind the reader of a few instances which are familiar to every lawyer:

[1]See, e.g., *Sugar v. L.M. and S. Ry. Co.*, [1941] 1 All E.R. 172.
[2]See, e.g., *Kerr v. John Mottram, Ltd.*, [1940] Ch. 657.

It is the theory of English law that a contract is a freely concluded agreement. The norm postulates an exchange of offer and acceptance. The party who accepts does not express his willingness to be bound by an agreement in the abstract, he gives his legally relevant assent to the precise terms proposed by the offeror. It is an admirable formulation for a process of bargaining between two equal partners, engaged upon an exchange in a market. Precisely this legal institution, however, has been put to the service of monopoly. The monopolist and his client are parties to a "contract". A passenger who takes a railway ticket "accepts" the terms "offered" by the company. A householder "contracts" with the local authority or public utility company which supplies him with gas, water, or electricity. The law cannot admit that these acts are acts of submission, that these relations are power relations, it must "construe" them as agreements, it must press into the form of a contract what has no contractual substance whatsoever. Conditions by which a monopolist excludes or limits his legal liabilities are "deemed" to have been freely accepted, if "reasonable notice" was given to the other party, e.g. by the magic formula "for conditions see back" on a ticket. The customer has "assented" even if he is blind or illiterate.[1] It would be difficult to find more cogent evidence for the relevance of Renner's thesis that the function of a legal norm can undergo a process of dialectical transformation when its social substratum is transmuted. To-day a large part, if not the majority, of commercial contracts derive their substance from terms and conditions laid down by trade associations or similar bodies. They are "standard contracts", the parties—or at least one of them—merely "adhere" to these *contrats d' adhésion*, but the law does not—and cannot—make a distinction between an offer which results in free bargaining and the process of private legislation which enforces obedience upon those who approach its orbit. The legal forms of the competitive era have survived into the age of monopoly. The change in society has transformed their function. As long as private monopolies exist, relations of sub-ordination must be hidden behind the veil of a legal norm which signifies co-ordination.

That the assets and liabilities of a corporate person are not those of its members, that a limited company cannot be regarded as the agent of its shareholders, is a norm designed to enable a

[1] *Thompson v. L.M.S.*, [1930] 1 K.B. 41.

number of capitalists to carry on business without incurring its full risk. The limited company was intended to be a "joint stock" enterprise. That was the economic substance of which the institution of commercial corporate entity was the form. That form, however, has survived into an age when the concentration of a larger or smaller number of business concerns in the hands of one entrepreneur or group of entrepreneurs has become a dominant feature of the economic system. In the form of "parent" and "subsidiary" companies corporate entities with limited liability have become convenient accounting devices, but it is still the law that a shareholder—be it even a parent company—is not liable for the debts of the company. The law does not admit that a "change in quantity" may become a "change in quality". If it did, there would be no one-man company, the "joint stock" principle could not have been used to enable a business man to "convert" his enterprise into a "company", and thus to escape personal liability.

Some of the most remarkable functional transformations of legal norms have, in this country, resulted from the changes which have occurred in the production of consumers' goods and in the buying habits of the public. To a certain extent these changes illustrate Renner's thesis. They are, however, even more significant as evidence that its application is limited in a system of judge-made law. In other words: these changes show not only how the function of the norm was transformed by developments of the substratum, but also how subsequently the Courts adapted the content of the norm to its new function.

According to English law[1] a seller who in the course of his business supplies a certain description of goods is liable to the buyer if they are not fit for the purpose for which they were bought. He is, however, thus responsible only if the buyer "expressly or by implication, makes known to the seller the particular purpose for which the goods are required, so as to show that the buyer relies on the seller's skill or judgment". There is a proviso "that in the case of a contract for the sale of a specified article under its patent or other trade name, there is no implied condition as to its fitness for any particular purpose". In 1893, when this rule was enacted—it was a codification of existing common law principles—the law was still able to deal with the sale of goods under a trade name in a mere proviso. It was still possible

[1]Sale of Goods Act, 1893, Sect. 14 (subs. 1).

to envisage as the normal form of transaction, say, between a grocer and a housewife, the personal recommendation of an article by the seller, a recommendation based on experience and on the reputation of its intrinsic merits. It was fair to assume that the purchase of a branded article involved a reliance on the buyer's own, rather than on the seller's judgment. In this case the transformation of the economic substratum has been little short of revolutionary. The standardisation of consumers' goods, the growth of the production of proprietary articles has reduced the rôle of the retail distributor's "judgment" to a mere selection among competing brands. But for the peculiar characteristics of a judge-made law, this economic change would have enabled the proviso to "swallow" the rule, to exclude the seller's liability and to impose upon the buyer the full risk of the seller's reliance upon the advertised merits of proprietary articles. This reversal in the economic effect of a rule of law was, however, prevented by the Courts. They interpreted the Section in a way which it is not easy to reconcile with its wording and which, in substance, amounted to the making of a new rule and to the adaptation of the norm to its new substratum. What they said was that, if a branded article is bought for a particular purpose upon the recommendation of the seller, this is not a case "of a contract of sale of a specified article under its . . . trade name" at all.[1] Thus, it is only where the buyer relies on the manufacturer's "recommendation", the advertisement, where the now customary method of distribution operates upon the mind of the ultimate consumer himself, that the retailer is free from this liability.

This example illustrates the ability of a casuistic and empirical system of law-making to reduce the time lag between social and legal change. A much more notable and famous instance is provided by the way in which the law of negligence was adopted to the changes in the production and distribution of consumers' goods. The English law of tort, no less than the law of contract, is ill equipped to meet the needs of an age of standardised mass consumption. The law of negligence, in particular, insists upon the presence of a personal "duty to take care", of some kind of "proximity" to enable a man to recover damages from another. How could such a system cope with the requirements of a society in which human beings were brought into contact through channels that did not seem to involve any "proximity" at all?

[1] *Baldrey v. Marshall*, [1925] 1 K.B. 260.

Was not the law of negligence deprived of some of its essential functions, was it not, in some ways, set at nought, when every man's health depended on the organisation of factories hundreds of miles away? When the compliance with certain involved standards of industrial technique was the "duty" on the fulfilment of which the physical integrity of ultimate consumers depended? And how far could the failure to comply with these standards be called "negligence" if no one was able to prove that the producer, the entrepreneur, or any of his servants was himself to blame? How, in other words, could the law of negligence function in a society in which injuries might arise from some flaw in a technical network far too complicated to be unravelled by any outside observer? Here is a case of economic developments which seemed completely to frustrate the operation of a norm. The British Courts[1] did consider the negligence concept to be sufficiently flexible to help the consumer of injurious goods to recover damages from the producer. Was this alleged "application" of the law of negligence an act of legislation? Or was it merely an interpretation of the existing law? Where, in such a case, is the borderline between a reaction of the substratum upon the working of the norm and a change in the norm itself?

Every student of English law is familiar with the survival of the names of former feudal realities as symbols for capitalist institutions. To borrow Bagehot's terminology, the term "fee simple" is merely a "dignified" and, therefore, deceptive nomenclature for ownership. This use of feudal symbolism for capitalist reality, this imperceptible and gradual transformation of institutions without a change of name is, in fact, a process in which it is difficult to disentangle the substratum and the norm. What produced the conversion of copy-hold into a species of ownership? Was it the depreciation of the currency in the 16th century or the action of the law which gave the copy-holder a remedy in the King's Courts?[2]

It is not—this must again be emphasised—as if the norm was, in this country, immune from the impact of the change in its substratum. Nor is it the case that it adapts itself immediately and automatically. Rigidities exist, here as everywhere, and often they have been and are still more obdurate in this country than on the Continent. But the social and political position of the

[1]*Donoghue v. Stevenson*, [1932] A.C. 562.
[2]Holdsworth, *An Historical Introduction to the Land Law*, 1927, p. 44.

judiciary has enabled them to translate into norms many changes which, on the Continent, had to await the intervention of the legislature. Owing to the fiction of continuity these transformations have often been inarticulate, sometimes unconscious. This is what O. W. Holmes called "the paradox of form and substance in the development of law". In a classical passage[1] he points out that "in form" the growth of the law is logical. "The official theory is that each new decision follows syllogistically from existing precedents. . . . On the other hand, in substance the growth of the law is legislative. And this in a deeper sense than that what the courts declare to have always been the law is in fact new. It is legislative in its grounds. The very considerations which judges most rarely mention, and always with an apology, are the secret roots from which the law draws all its juices of life. I mean, of course, considerations of what is expedient for the community concerned. Every important principle which is developed by litigation is in fact and at bottom the result of more or less definitely understood views of public policy; most generally, to be sure, under our practice and traditions, the unconscious result of instinctive preferences and inarticulate convictions, but none the less traceable to views of public policy in the last analysis. And as the law is administered by able and experienced men, who know too much to sacrifice good sense to a syllogism, it will be found that, when ancient rules maintain themselves . . . , new reasons more fitted to the time have been found for them, and that they gradually receive a new content, and at last a new form, from the grounds to which they have been transplanted."

Such is the prestige of the law that its fictions and its conventions are apt to become habits of thought among its own disciples and among the public. The ever-changing forces of society incessantly mould and transform the law, and yet it pretends to stand aloof and prides itself of its immutability in a tumultuous world. While it seems to be a spectator of the great social drama, serene and imperturbable, it suffers all the agonies and fights all the struggles of an actor in the play. Holmes as well as Renner, each in his own way, point to the reality which lies behind the fiction. It is as a guide to essential realities that Renner's book needs to be read, and that it teaches a permanent lesson.

[1] *The Common Law*, pp. 35–36.

TRANSLATOR'S NOTE

IN Dr. Renner's treatment of his subject one meets with a novel approach; and he makes use of many concepts unfamiliar to the English reader. It has therefore not always been possible to give a translation which makes easy reading and at the same time does justice to Dr. Renner's arguments. As a lawyer, I have regarded it as my paramount duty to be faithful to the original. I am sure that the intelligent reader will readily overcome the difficulties in style which I have been unable to avoid.

It is my happy duty to express my profound gratitude to Mr. Leonard Lyons, B.A., A.C.A., for his invaluable help and unfailing patience. He has been at great pains to leaven the dough of Continental scholarship with the spirit of the English language.

I am also greatly indebted to Dr. Kahn-Freund for his friendly guidance, especially in the choice of legal terminology.

For Renner's quotations from Marx's *Capital*, I have adopted the translation by Moore-Aveling (London 1920) for volume i, and that of E. Untermann (Chicago 1907, 1909) for vols. ii and iii. I have, however, not been able to trace the quotation on p. 59 and have translated it myself; I have dealt similarly with the quotations on pp. 127 and 205 of passages from *Capital*, vol. i, which appear in the German text but are omitted in the above translation.

AGNES SCHWARZSCHILD.

CHAPTER I

LEGAL INSTITUTIONS AND ECONOMIC STRUCTURE

Section i. THE PROBLEM

I. NORMS

OUR modern law is crystallized in a countless multitude of codes, statutes and orders, rulings of authorities and judgments of courts; and of contracts and other acts of private individuals. What is to be the law is set forth in writing and in print: so what had a merely subjective, nebulous existence in the mind of man is rendered objective. In this way the notions of the individual are removed from the control of his fluctuating psychology and are made permanent. The law appears thus to be established, stable and fixed; it becomes statute. (*I*)

Consider first the language in which law is embodied. The terminology of codes of law varies widely. Nowadays it is most usual to find the indicative mood: assertions, definitions and conditional statements. For example: "The family relationship is established by the contract of marriage"[1] (*2*) (assertion)—"The right of ownership is the legal power to dispose at will of the substance and fruits of an object, and to exclude all others from interfering with it"[2] (*2a*) (definition)—"Whosoever intentionally kills a man is guilty of murder and is liable to capital punishment"[3] (*3*) (conditional statement). This kind of legal norm is very similar (*4*) in form to the law of physics that when the temperature drops, the mercury in a thermometer falls to a lower level. There is a formal analogy between the laws of nature and the rules of law: the former control the relations among natural objects, the latter regulate the relations among men; moreover, both appear to operate as superior and superhuman powers. The world would seem to be divided into a realm of reason and a realm of nature, the first governed by the rules of law (side by side with the rules of morality), and the second by laws of science. According to

---

[1] § 44 Austrian Civil Code. (*5*)
[2] § 54 ibid.
[3] § 211 German Criminal Code.

tradition both laws are of superhuman or divine origin.[1]

On closer investigation of the legal norm, however, we observe that the indicative changes into the imperative. In relation to murder, for example, the individual is told: "Thou shalt not kill", and further: "If you have killed intentionally, you shall yourself suffer death." The biblical imperatives "Stone him!"—"Crucify him!" are thus moulded into legal rules. And in relation to property the owner is told: "You may dispose of the substance and fruits of your own property as you please", and at the same time a command is given to all other members of the community: "None of you is to limit or to interfere with the owner's pleasure". Every norm in its indicative form assumes a fetish-like character, akin to a law of nature, transcending the individual, superhuman, even divine. If the norm is resolved into imperatives directed to the individual and telling him "you ought", "you ought not", "you may", "you can", it appears immediately less unnatural, though still not acceptable as self-evident. The analogy with the law of nature is now meaningless, for nature knows no controlling common will, nor an individual will that is controlled.

The ancients usually spoke in direct imperatives when they recorded their norms in stone and metal, on papyrus and parchment, e.g. the code of Hamurabi, the Mosaic decalogue and the Twelve Tables of Rome.[2]

Such imperatives are the elements of the legal order. They are

[1] ". . . a realm of rational beings (*mundus intelligibilis*) as a realm of ends . . ." (Immanuel Kant: *The Fundamental Principles of the Metaphysics of Ethics*, transl. by Otto Mantney Zorn, p. 56). "Thus a realm of ends is possible only by analogy with a realm of nature, but the former according to maxims only, that is self-imposed, the latter only according to laws resulting from causes acting under external compulsion" (ibid. p. 57). The world of reason and the world of nature confront each other. Man as a natural and at the same time reasonable being has a part in both of them, '. . . first, in so far as he belongs to the world of the senses, he is subject to laws of nature (heteronomy); secondly, belonging to the intelligible world, he is subject to laws which are independent of nature and have their basis not in experience but in reason alone" (ibid. p. 73). This entire conception of the legal world "as a lawful order of actions which in general resembles the natural order" (as it is held to be by Kant), is based on a very narrow historical abstraction derived from a society of private owners connected solely by competition and contract. Hence also Kant's definition of the law: "The law is the sum-total of conditions, under which the personal wishes of one man can be reconciled with the personal wishes of another man, in accordance with a general law of freedom."

Once society is split up into atoms, the social law, analogous to the natural law, re-establishes a relation between these atoms. It is clear that this kind of philosophical dogma is the ideological superstructure upon a system of simple commodity production.

[2] Characteristically, in the language of the ancients the imperative mood is much more highly inflected than in modern languages; in fact it has, in the passive as well as in the active voice, nearly as many forms as the indicative mood. This is especially true of Greek. Peoples whose economic life rested on the ancient patriarchal family, i.e. a small community of slaves under the jurisdiction of the master or "*despotes*", hence

addressed to the individual and claim his obedience. Aiming at the will, they limit or enlarge, break or enhance the individual will (autonomy) and hence confront it as an extraneous will (heteronomy). This relation of wills is fundamental to the law, there is no mystery about it, nothing metaphysical, supernatural or divine. From the psychological and physical aspect, the highway robber who attacks the wayfarer in the wood with the alternative command of "Your money or your life" attempts to impose his own will upon that of another person in the same way as the law seeks to impose its authority, with its instant readiness to apply civil sanctions or with the threat of punishment and criminal sanctions. How the authority of another person (the "heteronomous will") is imposed on the wishes of an individual (his "autonomous will") is a matter of common experience. He is coaxed or threatened, talked round or browbeaten; fraud and coercion, either physical or mental (hypnosis), play their part.

There is however, this mysterious difference: that in modern times all law is laid down, in the name of all citizens, by the state, conceived as an entity. Instead of one man's will prevailing over the will of another, the common will is regarded as imposed upon that of the individual. How this common will arises—for it is clearly not the *volonté générale*—is one of the fundamental problems of jurisprudence; but we need not concern ourselves with this question.

For the purpose of the present investigation we will take it for granted that the state lays down the law which confronts the subject as the common will and claims his obedience; we will not examine whether the state in this aspect is real, an actual entity, a person; nor will we enquire whether this unity of the state corresponds in any way with a real unity of the society within its borders. [1] (5) Let it suffice that the legal order is in fact imposed

upon personal command and obedience, used the imperative very much more than we do, since we replace it by impersonal rules. "The factory door is opened daily from 5.45 to 6 a.m." This assertion, which does not refer to a subjective agent, can only be justified as a prophecy. As such it would make no more sense than the statement of the criminal code "the murderer is punished by death", since in actual fact only a proportion of murderers meet with their punishment. Just as this rule of the criminal law is based upon an imperative, so is the rule of the factory door; it tells the porter to open the door daily at 5.45 and to close it at 6 o'clock. Where a norm takes the form of an assertive rule, the commanding and obeying individuals disappear from sight; where it takes the form of an imperative order, the relation between these individuals is emphasized. Ancient laws which employ the imperative are thus fascinating in their powerful expression. Modern laws prefer an obscure diction which makes it necessary to go through a process of interpretation to find out who are the persons concerned and what are their duties.

[1] "To regard society as a single subject is to regard it in the wrong way, i.e. in a speculative manner" (Karl Marx: *Neue Zeit*, No. XXI, vol. I, p. 718).

upon the individual will of the citizens as a unified common will, and that in actual fact it operates as a unified whole. It is one of the most important functions of legal science to analyse the process by which a unified common will arises from a chaos of conflicting individual wills. But this analysis does not form part of our present task.

Of greater interest to us is another part of legal theory which I will call the analysis of positive law; distinguishing it as a separate branch from general legal theory, for it has its own functions and methodology. It is not the object of positive legal analysis to investigate the origin of the common will, its essence, its growth or decay. Its object is to analyse the legal norms contained in the sum total of positive legal provisions, arranging them in accordance with their inherent nature, and to reduce them to a system. For the chaotic multitude of norms can neither be understood nor expounded, neither taught nor applied, without previous co-ordination. We have to classify the norms according to their constituent elements, (6) which we will call "legal characteristics". Positive legal analysis distinguishes rules of private law and rules of public law, (7) and divides the former, in accordance with the particular relations of individual wills with which they are concerned, (8) into rules of the law of property, of obligations, of family relationships, and of succession. Such analysis treats a loan, for example, invariably as a relationship between the wills of two persons, creditor and debtor, concerning the giving and returning of an object; it pays no regard to whether the creditor exploits the debtor—as is usually the case—or whether the debtor exploits the creditor—which may also happen—or to whether the loan concerns a debt of honour or a commercial credit. Positive legal analysis has no other task than to ascertain all the legal norms relevant to the facts and to apply them to the case in hand. This exhausts the function of positive legal analysis. The question how loan transactions collectively react upon the economic system, upon particular classes or upon society as a whole, in short the social effect of the norm, transcends its legal structure. (9) However interesting these social repercussions may be to the lawyer as a side-line, they are the province of the economist and sociologist. They lie outside the province of systematic legal analysis, just as the economic use of the tobacco leaf lies outside the province of botany. (10)

2. LEGAL INSTITUTIONS AND THEIR COMPONENT NORMS

There is a radical difference of approach when we consider norms from the standpoints of law and of economics. Systematic legal exposition enquires whether the norms establish rights; it distinguishes absolute and relative rights, (*11*) rights *in personam* and rights *in rem;* (*12*) it is the juridical aspect of the rights which decides their classification. Rights are conceived as having a life-cycle: a right is acquired; it is enforced against interfering third parties; it is lost. (*13*) If the right is exercised in a normal way without disturbance, it remains outside the scope of legal analysis. (*14*) Yet it is just this day-to-day exercise that reveals the value of the law in the life of the community.

In the eyes of the law a landowner exercises his right whether he plants corn or tobacco on his soil, or leaves it untilled; but in this continuing exercise of his right the landowner is not the concern of the law; he is of no interest to the lawyers and judges who are agents of the law. No contract is involved, no lawsuit, no judgment; but the normal and undisturbed exercise of a right is none the less of paramount economic and social importance. To the lawyer the acquisition and extinction of a right, and interference with it, are normal incidents. The economist regards these events differently: for him they are at the most symptoms of a disease, abnormalities which he mentions in an appendix. (*15*) A right of real property is to legal analysis a homogeneous concept where no further differentiation is possible. Yet if this right is exercised in different ways, there will be different economic and social consequences. The economist is therefore bound to establish different categories of land-holding: small-holders' property, peasants' property and landed estate. (*16*) He will examine how these affect the density of population, conditions of labour, imports and exports, and so forth. He will treat the small-holding, the farm and the large estate as distinct economic institutions. As an example, the rentcharge of the parents (*17*) is normally part of the economic institution "farm" but it is a totally different institution in the eyes of the law. Between legal and economic institutions there is no point-to-point correspondence.

Positive legal analysis builds up legal institutions from their (*18*) constituent norms, in accordance with formal legal characteristics. The legal theorist disregards the economic and social significance of an institution, as is only right; for he is applying a method which is peculiar and necessary to positive legal analysis. Contrast the methods of the economist who looks for unity of economic purpose when he classifies the works of mankind which make up an economic institution. Thus he speaks of the institution of peasant-holding, although now and then (*19*) the owner does not farm the land himself but leases it to a tenant. The holding is then partly in a different legal category. In practice it often happens that the same term is used indifferently for a legal and an economic institution; and this may lead to confusion.

Quite a number of economists—some of them of considerable repute—demand that the lawyer should fuse the economic and legal methods. These theorists themselves apply a combination of these two methods in their own field. (*20*) They regard with deep disfavour [1] the civil lawyer's concept of the right of property—the rigid individualistic concept of Roman Law which emphasizes the absolute character of property: connoting unlimited power. Just as the bourgeois economist sees everything in terms of value—a glass of water in the desert, the baritone in the opera, and the favours of a prostitute—so do these economists regard everything as property—debts, copyrights and patent rights. Their definition of property would even include ownership in "legal relationships" and "rights" [2] (*21*) And when they are able to refer in this connection to medieval Germanic Law, they claim to have strikingly exposed the alleged one-sidedness of the contemporary theory of civil law, a theory that is foolish enough to aim at an interpretation of civil law as legislation has made it. (*22*)

In our legal system there are more such seeming inconsistencies. As we all know, the law relating to property is split up into three parts: civil law, criminal law and law of administration; legal analysis follows the legislator in making these divisions of one legal institution. Moreover, the civil law of property is a mere illusion without the law of civil procedure, its most important complement in the sphere of public law. For this subdivision legal theory has good methodological reasons and good practical reasons. Surely the concept of property, a concept of civil law, should not be made to include restrictions and obligations imposed on the owner by

---

[1] Cf. Adolf Wagner: *Grundlegung*, 3rd ed., II. 1–3, p. 185 and § 126 ff.
[2] Cf. Adolf Wagner, l.c. p. 268. This definition of property comprises the total of an individual's rights capable of pecuniary assessment. Julius Ofner in his *Sachenrecht* has happily coined the term "*suum*" of an individual for this total of his rights; he distinguishes it from the narrower concept of property. Cf. also Kant: *Allgemeine Rechtslehre*, Part I. "*Das rechtlich Meine.*"

the law of administration, such as liability to land tax. Adolf Wagner actually demands that the civil lawyer's definition should embrace "the possibility to restrict by law the owner's power of disposal, and even to impose on him obligations to perform certain acts". This suggestion will appear monstrous to all lawyers. They well know that every right is conferred by the law, that it has no existence but for the law; that this same law may in any particular case impose personal liabilities upon the owner and encumbrances upon the *res* or subject-matter of the ownership; just as it can compel all citizens to act in a certain way, and can encumber all things within the territory of the state. Should the teacher of law have to recite the principles of constitutional and legal theory every time he wishes to define a legal institution? (*23*)

And what would be the position if the constitution itself were to lay down the rule that "property obliges and should be made to serve the common good"—as does the Weimar Constitution in Art. 153? A programmatic pronouncement of this kind is a command addressed not to the citizen but only to the legislator, enjoining him to translate these obligations into legal norms, while to the citizen it merely gives an exhortation. But, be that as it may, is the right *in rem* called "property" affected by the duties of the owner as a citizen? (*24*)

Or does this formulation mean that our private property as we know it thereby becomes social property? Can all this prove anything more than that the owner is not sovereign but remains a subject of the state? Property is absolute in the sphere of private law; in the sphere of private economics it is equally absolute; this is of paramount importance to the economist. Tamper with this, and you reduce the economic system of private capitalism to the confused medley of qualified statements which serves the champions of private economy when they compile their principles, guides and text-books for business men and students.

There is no greater stumbling block in the path of knowledge than the mingling of various methods. The unity of a legal institution derives from the unitary character of the norms from which it is built up. How such an institution affects social life, is quite another matter. We shall in due course meet many illustrations of this point; for the moment a few examples will suffice. Contract (*25*) remains one and the same legal institution, though it may serve an infinite variety of purposes—economic or otherwise—marriage as well as prostitution. In particular, the contract of loan does service for charity and usury alike. Conversely, the same economic purpose may be achieved by a variety of legal institutions. For instance "share-cropping" can be carried out either by an agreement of partnership or by a contract of service, providing for a partial payment in kind. The settlement of an estate *inter vivos* for a limited period is a substitute for testamentary succession and has a similar economic effect. The discrepancy between a legal institution and its extra-legal effects gives us a clue to the reason why so many laws are superfluous or ineffective. (*26*) Thus, even where the law permits the unrestricted partition of real property, the transmission of rural property by strict entail is maintained, wherever practicable, by will, although there is no compulsion by law. (*27*)   As we shall see later, this discrepancy, this constant divergence between legal norm and social efficacy provides the only explanation for the evolution of the law.

It will be our task to show that the historical development of the law, and the growth of individual laws and their decay, flow from the disparate development of legal and economic institutions; also that the change in the social functions of legal institutions takes place in a sphere beyond the reach of the law and eventually necessitates a transformation of the norms of the law.

We can never hope clearly to understand this process of origin and decay of the legal order, if we cloud over the difference between legal and economic institutions with psychological and ethical jargon.   Stammler's investigations [1] suggest another approach against which we have to be on our guard. This would be to conceive of the legal institution as a mere form and a product of conceptual doctrine, with the economic function as the real material content.   But the real content of a legal institution is given by its constituent norms; and there is no other.   The legal definition of an economic institution, for instance the usual lease of the small-holder, is by no means a mere "form" to the economist.   The legal postulation of the concept "exercise of a right" also reflects its material content.   It is meaningless, if not misleading, to use the abstract categories of form and substance whereas the real distinction is between the material content and the exercise of a right. (*28*)

It is true, however, that like practically everything in this

---

[1] Rudolf Stammler: *Wirtschaft und Recht nach der materialistischen Geschichtsauffassung,* 2nd ed., 1906. *Theorie der Rechtswissenschaft,* 1911.

bourgeois world, legal institutions have a two-fold nature, according to their constituent norms on the one hand and their social significance on the other. Both can and must be taken into consideration.[1] From the lawyer's point of view legal institutions are norms or imperatives moulded into assertions, printed or written on paper, more or less adequately expressed. Their existence compared with that of men of flesh and blood is as insubstantial as that of railway shares compared with the permanent way or rolling stock of a real railway, or that of treasury notes compared with real bars of gold. The same society which economically transforms the wage labour of the miner into stocks and bonds, transforms it legally into the clauses of a statute or deed. This comparison is not based upon a mystical falsification of facts. Just as the fetish "commodity" reflects the actuality of use-value, so the fetish "law" reflects the actual relations of human beings. (*29*)

Every legal institution is to a conceptual approach a composite of norms, a total of imperatives. In the case of property, the most important imperatives convey that no-one shall withdraw from A.'s factual power of disposition a thing which belongs to A, and no-one shall disturb his quiet possession of the thing, etc. (*30*) The lawyer sees the same institution of property wherever the same composite of norms applies. It does not matter to him whether the object is land, a retriever, a loaf of bread or a family portrait without intrinsic value. (*31*) Legal analysis confines itself to collating the totality of norms, the systematic understanding, logical exposition and practical application thereof. Legal analysis is of necessity determined by history like its arsenal of concepts, its terminology. It is of necessity empirical; by the same token the *corpus juris civilis*, the "*Sachsenspiegel*" and the German Civil Code are all empirical. (*32*)

A legal institution regulates the factual relationships of living beings and successive generations, it regulates facts which are in a constant state of flux and it is—like law in general—nothing but one aspect of the subject-matter which it governs.

Can the legal institution remain rigid and unchanged if man and matter undergo continual change? At first the answer seems

---

[1] The purely legalistic approach which does not consider the social function may be described, following popular usage, as legal formalism, if it is kept in mind that the term is not used with reference to Stammler's distinctions. As we use the term, every real and genuine legal analysis is formal; the whole of legal doctrine, however, must be more than that.

to be in the affirmative, for "right must remain right". For centuries the law was considered divine, immutable and constant like
the deity itself. The mere idea that man should engage in an
attempt to change the law, was blasphemous. Even One who
came into this world to change the whole order of humanity
believed himself in duty bound to say that he had come not to
destroy the law but to fulfil it. For thousands of years all change
in the law was carried out in the belief that men had at last arrived
at the right interpretation of the old law. (33) The general conviction that men can make the law, that human society makes its
own laws, is an achievement of the last few centuries. The thesis
that man can create the law has gradually been accepted, at first
in the form of state parliamentarism within the narrow confines
of the various countries. To-day every child knows that parliament
exists in order to make laws. But we can still not explain satis-
factorily how it is possible that parliaments can obtain a right to
legislate; if it is accepted that parliament makes all laws by virtue
of the constitution, the question remains, who gives them the right
to legislate.   Indeed, these are most controversial questions.
Parliament exercises its right to make laws in the name of the
community. It is a mere organ, it is argued, through which
society expresses itself. But it is still obscure exactly how society
makes its new laws. At this point the legal norm is no longer—as
in the case of positive analysis—the beginning, content and end
of the study. Here it appears as the result of a process which
belongs to another province, that of "law in the making". This
province is the counterpart of that with which we are concerned
and which deals with the social functions of the legal institutions.
For our study the norm and the legal institution are no more than
the starting point. Thus we see that the legal institution is the
end of one process, that of the evolution of law, and the beginning
of another, that of the social effects of the law. We can only
develop a complete theory of the law if we supplement positive
legal analysis by an investigation of the two adjoining provinces,
the origin and the social function of the law. The three together
form the whole of legal science.

This legal science, consisting of three parts, again is an empirical, not a speculative science. The subject of this empirical
research, however, is not a *corpus juris*, a charter, a given statute or
other document. If it were conceived as positive legal analysis
only, Kant's motto, taken from a different context, would justly

apply to it: "a merely empirical theory of law is like the wooden head in Phaedra's fable—it may be beautiful, a pity only that it has no brains". [1] Both at the beginning and at the end of legal analysis there is a social theory of the law which correlates it to all non-legal elements of our life, co-ordinating it like a cog to the whole machinery of social events.

3. THE ECONOMIC AND SOCIAL FUNCTIONS OF THE LEGAL INSTITUTIONS

Our enquiry, then, is not concerned with positive legal analysis, the systematic exposition of legal institutions, a field which has been amply covered by others.   Nor are we investigating the problems of the creation of law.   We shall refrain from analysing the questions as to how the norms originate which make up the legal institutions, how a legal norm grows from its economic background, and what are the economic causes of the creation of legal norms.   This field, it is true, has not been cultivated, but we shall keep away from it.   We propose to examine only the economic and social effect of the valid norm as it exists, so long as the norm does not change.

Those acquainted with socialist literature will at once perceive that we have taken as our subject the mutual relations between law and economics.   The traditional Marxist school conceives the economic relations as the substructure and the legal institutions as the superstructure.   "Substructure" and "superstructure" are metaphors, borrowed from architecture; it is obvious that they serve only to illustrate the connection, not to define it in exact terms.   This superstructure, according to Marx's well-known formula, [2] comprises not only law but also ethics and culture, in fact every ideology.   This terminology must therefore apply to many facts other than those relevant to the law, whose structures

---

[1] *Metaphysische Anfangsgründe der Rechtslehre, Einleitung in die Rechtslehre.* B.
[2] Preface to Marx's *Critique of Political Economics*, transl. by N. I. Stone, N.Y. London, 1904.   "The sum total of these relations of production constitutes the economic structure of society—the real foundations on which rise legal and political superstructures."

Friedrich Engels, Preface to Marx's *Der achtzehnte Brumaire*, 3rd edition, Hamburg, 1885: "The law according to which all struggle, whether in the political, religious, philosophical or any other ideological field, is in fact only the more or less clear expression of struggles among social classes whose existence and hence collisions are again conditioned by the degree of development of their economic position, their methods of production and their manner of exchange dependent thereon."   And many other passages.   Cf. also note 1, p. 227.

are completely different and must be separately defined. The relation between the philosophy of an age and the economic substructure of that age is obviously determined by key concepts quite different from those of legal norm, exercise of a right, and the like. We must desist, therefore, from attempting to give a general exposition of the Marxist concept of superstructure. We must recognise that each of these social phenomena, which in their general aspects are quite aptly illustrated by Marx's metaphor, requires a specific investigation. We attempt this investigation in regard to law.

Our previous explanations have made it clear that the relation is not merely one of cause and effect. It would be no solution of our problem to say that the economic structure generates the norm. Such an assumption could apply only to one of the fields of learning, that concerned with the creation of laws. Yet the mechanism by which economy as the causal factor brings about the effect of law, is obscure and unexplored. It probably would not become intelligible by any ultimate abstraction, such as the application of the primitive categories of cause and effect, nor does Stammler's formula of the regulating form and the regulated substance make it any clearer. In the second province, that of positive legal analysis, the concepts of cause and effect generally mean little; the main concern here is obviously that of motive, means and ends, and the appropriate method of explanation is teleological, not causal. If we were to describe the superstructure of the law in the third field (that of the economic and social efficacy of the norms) as exclusively the effect of the social and economic substructure, our conclusions would be proved to be absurd by the very facts to which they refer.

It is mere platitude to say that laws can influence economy sufficiently to change it and can therefore be considered as causes of economic results. Marx, of course, was the last person to deny this. "The influence of laws upon the conservation of the relations of distribution and consequently their influence upon production must be specifically determined" (*Neue Zeit*, p. 744). Laws are made with the intention of producing economic results, and as a rule they achieve this effect. Social life is not so simple that we can grasp it, open it and reveal its kernel like a nut, by placing it between the two arms of a nutcracker called cause and effect. Although he was much occupied with legal problems, Marx never found time to "determine the influence of the laws" (as above);

yet he saw the problem clearly as is proved in particular by the following methodological hint: "The really difficult point to be discussed here, however, is how the relations of production as relations of the law enter into a disparate development. An instance is Roman civil law in its relations to modern production" (ibid. p. 779). (*34*) We make use of this hint in the formulation of our problem: (1) Law which continues unchanged in relation to changing economic conditions; (2) Changed economic conditions in relation to the new norms and the new law. Our study, however, will be concerned with the first part of the problem only.

We start with a definite legal system based upon a definite economic foundation as it appears at a given moment of history. All economic institutions are at the same time institutions of the law. All economic activities are either, like sale and purchase, acts-in-the-law, or, like farming one's own land, the mere exercise of a right; or if neither, like the work of a mill-hand at his loom, even though they are extra-legal activities, they are nevertheless performed within definite legal conditions. We see that the act-in-the-law and the economic action are not identical.

The process of eating has a physiological, an economic and a volitional aspect but it is not an act of will with the qualities of an act-in-the-law. Yet the conditions under which it takes place are determined to some extent by the law.

The circulation of goods in a capitalist society (*35*) is mediated by sale and purchase and by ancillary contracts: these are transactions for which the law of obligations provides various forms. (*36*) Production, however, is not in itself an act-in-the-law. It can be the mere exercise of the right of ownership, as in the case of the peasant. In the capitalist factory, however, the legal aspect of production is more complicated. For the capitalist, production is the exercise of his right of ownership, since factory and machines are his property. For the worker it is the fulfilment of a legal obligation which has been established by the contract of employment. In so far as it is the latter, it is an act-in-the-law; in so far as it is the former, it is the mere exercise of a right. Thus a simple economic category is equivalent to a combination of various legal categories, there is no point-to-point correspondence. A number of distinct legal institutions serves a single economic process. (*37, 38*) They play a part which I will call their economic function.

Yet every economic process which in theory is an isolated unit

3

is only part of the whole process of social production and reproduction. If the economic function is related to this whole, it becomes the social function of the legal institution.

A comprehensive exposition of the functions fulfilled by the legal institutions at every stage of the economic process has been given in *Das Kapital*, Marx's principal work. No other investigator, either before or after him, was more aware of their importance for even the most minute details of this process. We shall see that no other economic theory gives so much insight into the connections between law and economics. Marx's predecessors and successors either refused to recognise the problem or could not do it full justice.

If we regard a social order as static and confine our attention to a certain moment of history, then the legal norms and the economic process merely appear as mutually conditioned and subservient to one another. Within the economic structure economic process and legal norm appear as the same thing: the former seen as an external, technico-natural event, the latter as an inherent relation of wills, seen from the point of view of individual will-formation. We call the external, technico-natural process the substratum of the norm.[1] This sounds very plausible. But we can no more study the laws of gravity from a stone in a state of rest than we can learn the art of cooking from the cook who was pricked by the Sleeping Beauty's spindle. All that we can observe is that in a state of rest legal and economic institutions, though not identical, are but two aspects of the same thing, inextricably interwoven. We must define and describe this co-existence.

This observation, however, only stresses the fact that they are mutually determined. We must study the process in its historical sequence, the gradual transition of a social order from a given stage to the next. The inherent laws of development can only be revealed if the events are seen in motion, in the historic sequence of economic and legal systems. If we examine two consecutive periods, chosen at random, we may obtain results which, though they apply to these particular periods of transition, cannot claim to be generally valid. To decide the function of the law in general, we have to study inductively all social orders as they appear in the course of history, from the most primitive to the most highly developed. By this method we obtain the general categories of

[1] The concept of the substratum will be dealt with in detail on pp. 84, note 3, 86 f., 252 ff.

the social order and at the same time the general functions of the law.

This procedure is legitimate in spite of the fact that every individual stage of development has its specific nature and is subject to its peculiar laws. Marx frequently refers to general principles of this kind, declaring them to be justified. "All periods of production have certain characteristics in common . . . production in general is an abstract concept, but a reasonable one in that it really establishes and emphasizes what is common, and thus saves us repetition." ". . . a unity brought about by the fact that the subject, mankind, and the object, nature, are always the same" (*Neue Zeit*, vol. 21, p. 712). Yet Marx disparages these general abstractions in economics often enough to fortify our objections against them. One of his reasons was the tendency of economists, which still exists, to regard the categories of the capitalist order as eternal and sacrosanct. Another reason lies in the limitations of his own task, viz. to explore and describe one individual period only. "Yet it is the very difference from what is general and common which is the essential element of a particular development." If Marx had concentrated upon the definition of peculiar characteristics of one epoch as he found them, he might have given a description in the manner of a research student, but the laws of social development would have remained hidden from him. Marx, however, seeks to explain the specific historical phenomenon alongside with previous individual forms as being merely an individual manifestation of the general principle. In this way he discovers inherent connections within the development.

The following may serve as an example: "Surplus labour is a general social phenomenon as soon as the productivity of human labour power exceeds the immediate needs of life, but its appearance in the feudal epoch differs from that in the capitalist epoch—in the former it is villeinage, in the latter surplus value."

We cannot dispense in our enquiry with a general survey of the functions performed by the legal institutions. Every individual function which is historically determined is correlated to the whole and can only be clearly understood within its context. A diagrammatic exposition of the functions at least clears the field. A concrete detail cannot be demonstrated otherwise than by relating it to the general whole. "A phenomenon is concrete because it integrates various determining factors, because it is a

unity of multiplicity. If it is thought out, it appears as the product
and result of an integrating process."

NOTES, CHAPTER I, SECTION I

(*1*) Renner envisages only that portion of the law which is crystallised in statutes. What he says about enacted law applies with
almost equal force to judge-made law, especially in a system
dominated by the principle *stare decisis*. The jurisprudential distinction between "written" (statute) and "unwritten" (judge-
made) law, has nothing to do with the point made by Renner.
The "fixation" of the law discussed in the text may be brought
about through the medium of legislation or through that of
precedent. In this country the history of mercantile law shows
the transition from (fluctuating) custom to (crystallised) judge-
made law. This occurred in the 17th and 18th centuries. The
legislative codification of some parts of mercantile law in the 19th
and 20th centuries merely changed the form in which the law was
crystallised. A reader who is familiar with Ehrlich's *Fundamental
Principles of the Sociology of Law* (English translation: Harvard
University Press, 1936), will perceive that Renner's conception of
law is the antithesis of Ehrlich's. All that Ehrlich calls "the living
law" (see in particular chp. xxi of his work), is from Renner's
point of view no law at all. It is the extra-legal functioning of
the legal norm.

(*2*) This form of legislative "statement" is sometimes to be
found in English codifying statutes. E.g. Marine Insurance Act,
1906, sect. 17: "A contract of marine insurance is a contract based
upon the utmost good faith, . . ." Administration of Estates Act,
1925, sect. 7 (1): "An executor of a sole or last surviving executor
of a testator is the executor of that testator." Larceny Act, 1916,
sect. 1 (1): "A person steals who, without the consent of the owner,
fraudulently and without a claim of right made in good faith,
takes and carries away anything capable of being stolen, with
intent, at the time of such taking, permanently to deprive the
owner thereof."

(*2a*) This form is far more frequently used in this country than
the "statement". E.g. the definition of a bill of exchange in sect. 3
of the Bills of Exchange Act, 1882, as that of a partnership in
sect. 1 of the Partnership Act, 1890: "Partnership is the relation
which subsists between persons carrying on a business in common
with a view to profit."

(*3*) The usual form of criminal legislation. See, e.g. Offences against the Person Act, 1861, sect. 1. For a general discussion of legislative style with many examples drawn from Roman, English, American, French and German law: Freund, *Legislative Regulation*, 1932, pp. 190–230.

(*4*) The continental method of legislative formulation is more apt to create the deceptive impression of a similarity between legal norms and natural laws than the form of statutory enactment traditional in this country. In many cases in which the Continental legislator uses the assertive form, English statutes say that something "shall" be, or shall be "deemed" to be the case. Compare, e.g., Art. 215 Code Civil, in the form of the Law of 18th February, 1938 ("La femme mariée *a* le plein exercice de sa capacité civile. Les restrictions à cet exercice *ne peuvent* résulter que de limitations légales ou du régime matrimonial qu'elle a adopté") with sect. 1 of the Law Reform (Married Women and Tortfeasors) Act, 1935 (. . . a married woman *shall* (*a*) be capable of acquiring, holding, and disposing of, any property . . .)

(*5*) It is a fact that, from the point of view of the individual, the norm *appears* as something imposed by a superior will. This simple psychological fact cannot be denied, whatever "theory" of the state one may choose to adopt. The superior will *appears* to the individual as emanating from "the state", an entity. Renner states this psychological fact which is perfectly compatible with the statement made in subsequent passages of the book that what *appears* as the will of a super-personal entity is *in reality* only the will of individuals. The statement in the text is not intended as an endorsement of the Austinian theory of sovereignty. The difference between the "collective will" as a psychological phenomenon and as a "reality" is discussed by Kelsen, *Hauptprobleme der Staatsrechtslehre*, p. 163 (quoting Wundt, *Grundriss der Psychologie*, pp. 384, 385).

(6) This classification is the proper province of "academic" law. In this country the pioneer work done by Anson for the law of contract stands out as the classical example. For an analysis of this process see the passage from Ihering, *Geist des römischen Rechts*, quoted in the Introduction.

(*7*) The rigid division between "public law" and "private law" was still widely insisted upon when Renner published the First Edition of his book. It was never adopted in this country. Although it was clear that certain branches of the law—constitutional, administrative, criminal law—had to be classified as "public", and others—law of contracts and torts, law of property—as "private", the borderline remained indistinct, and numerous theories were advanced in order to arrive at a clear differentiation. Ulpian's criterion ("Publicum jus est quod at statum rei Romanae spectat, privatum quod ad singulorum utilitatem," D. I. 1, 1, 2), i.e. the distinction between "public" and "private" interest, was rejected by many as deceptive and spurious. They contended that the "true" criterion was the difference between relations of sub-ordination and relations of co-ordination. All this is to-day only of historical interest. The reasons why the Anglo-Saxon world refused to adopt the differentiation are set out by Kelsen, *Allgemeine Staatslehre*, pp. 89–90. He shows that it owed its origin not only to the Reception, but also to the political exigencies of the absolutist state and to the influence of the theory of the *"ragione di stato"*. Sovjet legal theory and practice has adopted the distinction between Public and Private Law without, however, arriving at a definite criterion (Schlesinger, *Sovjet Legal Theory*, *passim*, especially pp. 252, sq.).

(*8*) The division of private law into law of property, law of obligation, family law, and law of succession is generally adopted on the Continent and the student is often in danger of seeing it as something necessarily inherent in the structure of law. This impression is largely created by the scheme of the principal Continental Codes, which is undoubtedly a useful legislative device. The syllabuses of the Continental Universities usually adopt the subdivisions embodied in the Codes.

(*9*) The sentence: "the social effect of the norm transcends its legal structure" may be regarded as the watchword of positivism. Friedmann, *Legal Theory*, p. 251, quotes a dictum of Lord Finlay in *Crown Milling Co. v. R.* [1927], AC 394, at p. 402: "It is not for any tribunal to adjudicate between conflicting theories of political economy." The spirit of legal positivism which has informed Renner's thought is still very prevalent in this country. It often prevents judges from realising that, though they may not be called upon to adjudicate between conflicting theories of political economy, their decisions may yet be influenced by them. Contrast with Lord Finlay's dictum the words of Cardozo (*The Judicial Process*, p. 102): "The teleological conception of his function must be ever in the judge's mind," and, again (p. 172), his call for a "spirit of self-search and self-reproach" among the judges. Here, indeed, are two conceptions of the judicial process which are well-nigh irreconcilable. They correspond to the antithesis of the conception of the nature of law used by Renner and by Ehrlich (see above, note 1).

(*10*) Would the botanist have taken the trouble of investigating the structure of the tobacco plant if the plant was of no importance to human society? Does the lawyer trouble to ask questions which are devoid of social relevance? That "the social effect" of the norm does not always transcend its legal structure can be seen from the history of the doctrine against "clogging" the equity of redemption of a mortgage in this country. This doctrine invalidates any agreement between the mortgagor and mortgagee by which the former's right to redeem the mortgage is fettered by any condition imposing duties additional to that of paying capital and interest. It also makes it impossible to render a mortgage irredeemable. The doctrine was formulated in the early 18th century expressly with a view to protecting necessitous borrowers. In a famous decision—*Kreglinger v. New Patagonia Meat Co.* [1914] A.C. 25, the House of Lords re-formulated the doctrine in the light of the modern function of money (see *Fifoot*, English Law and its background, p. 266). It has now been held that a mortgage may be made irredeemable where the borrower is a company (*Knightsbridge Estates Trust Ltd. v. Byrne and Others*, [1940] A.C. 618). Though this decision was based on the Companies Act, 1929, it was partly justified by the consideration that "there is no likelihood of oppression being exerted against the company" (*per* Viscount Maugham). This is but one example showing that—contrary to Renner's opinion—the social character of a loan may have something to do with the judicial formulation of the rules which apply to it. The "botanist" is, after all, concerned with the economic function of the plant. That, on the other hand, the law is perfectly able to disregard the economic functions of a legal institution, if it chooses to do so, is shown by the example of the "ticket" contracts mentioned in the Introduction.

(*11*) Rights of a "relative" nature are those existing strictly as against one particular person: rights arising from a contract, out of a tort, or the rights of husband and wife against each other. "Absolute" rights are rights against all the world: e.g. rights arising from property, or a parent's right to the custody of his child.

(*12*) "Personal" rights are "relative" rights which refer to money or money's worth, rights *in rem* are "absolute" rights which refer to money or money's worth. The line between *jura in personam* and *jura in rem* is, in this country, blurred by Equity. See the Introduction.

(*13*) The metaphorical personification of "rights" which are said to have a "life-cycle" is germane to Continental legal thought. Owing to the existence of a highly integrated system of legal abstractions, it is capable of conceiving of legal institutions— which are, in fact, merely groupings of legal norms—with the help of a symbolic imagery taken from organic nature. Such language is alien to the "remedial" method of Anglo-Saxon legal thought.

(*14*) See the Introduction. This idea goes back to Kant, *Metaphysik der Sitten, Rechtslehre*, Teil I, § 11 (Cassirer ed., vol. 7, p. 63).

(*15*) The "normal undisturbed" exercise of rights is of no interest to the law as long as the latter is exclusively concerned with the protection of private interests. The modern transition from the "negative" to the "positive" state forces the law to regulate normal and not merely marginal situations. To-day the law enforces the observance of a proper course of estate management and husbandry in agriculture (see Part II of the Agriculture Act, 1947), it regulates the exercise of a house owner's property right through housing and rent legislation, it controls investment through exchange regulations. Town planning law assumes the functions previously exercised by private "restrictive covenants". The view that the law is only concerned with situations of conflict has become untenable.

(*16*) Modern legislation in America, on the Continent, and in this country adopts categories previously alien to legal thought. It speaks of "homesteads" (in America and in Germany), it distinguishes between working class houses and other houses (Housing Act, 1936, Part V), between "small dwellings" and other dwellings (Small Dwellings Acquisition Act, 1899). It is interesting to note that, "throughout the long history of housing legislation", Parliament has always refused to define the term "working classes" (Hill, *Complete Law of Housing*, 3rd ed., p. 183, Note (e)).

(*17*) The parents' rent-charge is the right to maintenance of the retired peasant and his wife against the son who has taken over the farm. This right is often crystallised into fixed money payments or regular deliveries in kind, and secured by a registered mortgage or rent-charge.

(*18*) See the reference to Ihering's *Geist des römischen Rechts* in the Introduction.

(*19*) In view of the prevailing system of agricultural tenure in Austria, Renner treats peasant proprietorship as the rule and tenant farming as the exception. Modern legislation designed to enforce a proper and planned utilisation of the soil in the interest of food production applies to farmer-owners as well as tenant farmers. The law is compelled to disregard distinctions which do not affect the economic essence of the exercise of the right.

(*20*) Economists and sociologists have always been constrained to use the term "property" in the wider sense in which it is also used by English law. The narrow concept of property which is confined to ownership in tangible objects and which derives from Roman law is useless to the social sciences. The conflict between various terminologies which Renner describes does not exist in this country (see the Introduction).

(*21*) See the Introduction. "Ownership" in "rights" is a legal absurdity from the point of view of Pandectology. "Rights" belong to a person's "property" in the sense of *Vermögen* (see von Tuhr, *Der Allgemeine Teil des Deutschen Bürgerlichen Rechts*, Vol. I, pp. 313 *sq.*)

(*22*) The rigid conception of ownership was alien to medieval German law. See *Gierke, Deutsches Privatrecht*, Vol. II, p. 349. Renner's polemic is directed not only against conservative economists like Adolf Wagner, but also against jurists belonging to the "Germanistic" school (see, e.g., *Gierke*, l.c., p. 348, note 2). In all relevant respects the Germanistic school was unfavourably disposed towards the property concept used by Renner. It was inclined towards an extension of the "ownership" concept to incorporeal property (choses in action) (see, e.g. *Gierke*, l.c., p. 367), and towards the recognition of "ownership" in a fund, an estate (ibid. p. 64, note 71). Above all, it denied the "absolute" character of property and held that restrictions imposed upon it by public law, by the law of "natural easements", etc., were inherent in the very concept of the right (ibid. § 120 *passim*). There is, to say the least, a community of ideas between the socially minded conservatives (*Katheder sozialisten*) of the concluding decades of the 19th century and the Germanistic school of legal thought. Greek law was very much more akin to medieval Germanic than to Roman law. See Vinogradoff, *Historical Jurisprudence*, Vol. II, chp. x.

(*23*) One answer to Renner's question might be that legal concepts such as ownership and contract are necessary tools of the lawyer's trade, but that they become dangerously misleading simplifications, especially in the minds of students, unless their purely conceptual nature is emphasized by the teacher. He cannot be expected to detail *expressis verbis* the whole of administrative law when mentioning the word "property", but he can be expected to remind his students that "property" and "contract" are abstractions, and that neither the absolute dominium of a person over a thing nor the "free" meeting of the minds which these conceptions postulate has any relation to practical experience. Another answer is that, throughout his work, Renner uses a strictly Romanistic conception of property which is not by any means universally accepted even on the Continent. It is true that this concept was embodied in the French, Austrian, German, and other Codes, and it is also true that its use brings into sharp relief the contrast between property in the legal and property in the economic sense, between the absolute unfettered power over a thing granted to the owner by the law and the economic emasculation of that right which occurs when the capital function attaches to rights other than physical ownership. Yet, this conception of ownership has, for more than half a century, been the target of sharp attacks, not only, as mentioned in the previous note, by the "Germanistic" school, but also by those who held that the limitations of the right of property by public law were inherent in the nature of the right, not, as it were, accidental additions to its definition. In order to appreciate this controversy (which—in spite of its seemingly verbal character—symbolises a profound cleavage in legal and sociological thought), one must realize that the definition of property embodied in the Code Civil represented a triumph of one trend of 18th century natural law philosophy over another, equally important, trend (see for an analysis of its political background, Laski, *The Rise of European Liberalism*, p. 228). The idea of the "absolute" character of the domination over a thing was—in the history of human ideas—closely connected with that of its "inviolability" and "sanctity" which derived its polemical pathos from the fight against feudal burdens and restrictions. From the *Déclaration des Droits de l'Homme et du Citoyen* it found its way into numerous constitutional texts. It had, of course, been fully developed by 17th and 18th century political thought, and it would be hard to find a more radical statement of its meaning than that copied by Blackstone from Burlamaqui (*Commentaries*, 1821 ed., I, p. 147). There was, however, another line of legal and philosophical reasoning, articulate in the 18th century, submerged from the French Revolution until about 1875, but re-asserting itself with renewed vigour since that time. From Locke to Fichte we find numerous political thinkers reflecting upon the limitations of the right of property, limitations derived from the conditions of its (supposed) origin which also provided its justification. We find, moreover, in 18th century philosophical thought, indications (e.g. in Montesquieu) or clear expressions (e.g. Rousseau, *Contract Social* I, chp. ix) of the idea that, by its very essence, the right of property was limited by the needs of the community, needs which are crystallized in the laws of the state, e.g. by its *jus eminens*, its right of expropriation. Throughout the first three quarters of the 19th century, however, legislation and legal doctrine denied that these limitations were more than accidental phenomena, that they were part of the essence of the institution. Restrictions of the owner's right in the public interest were thus made to appear as something transient, fortuitous, anomalous, at variance with the permanent "sacred and inviolable" character of the institution. The "neat" separation between public and private law was maintained and served a very definite ideological purpose. A strong counter-movement set in by 1875. Ihering's *Zweck im Recht* (see especially 4th ed., Vol. I, pp. 404 ff.), published in 1877, contains a vigorous attack against the "individualistic" theory of property and asserts that "it is not true that the 'idea' of property comprises the absolute power to dispose" (p. 408). Restrictions on this power, and the right of expropriation appear, from the point of view of Ihering's social theory of property (p. 411), not as something abnormal or as an encroachment upon the idea of property. Duguit's idea of the "droit social" was, in many ways, a development of Ihering's ideas, and these two great jurists are only the protagonists of a movement of legal thought which, under the impact of new tendencies in the field of social reform, refused to view the idea of property in the light of that "absolutism" which corresponded to the traditional learning of the Pandectists and to that tendency of natural law which had found expression in the great documents of the French Revolution (see for a clear analysis of these developments: Hedemann, *Fortschritte des Zivilrechts im 19. Jahrhundert*, Vol. II). It must therefore be understood that Renner's treatment of the relation between property and public law is not in line with a *communis opinio* of legal thought on the Continent, even as it was at the time when the book was written.

(*24*) This provision of the Weimar Constitution (like others of its kind) was interpreted as a "legislative programme" which did not bind the legislator.

(*25*) "*Vertrag*" is a wider conception than "contract". It includes not only an agreement which gives rise to obligations, but any agreement of legal consequence, e.g. marriage, marriage settlements, and conveyances.

(*26*) Examples in English law are: Section 4 of the Marine Insurance Act, 1906 (invalidating marine insurance contracts made in the absence of insurable interest), Section 18 of the Gaming Act, 1845, and the Banking Companies (Shares) Act, 1857 (Leeman's Act). All this legislation has remained ineffective in the face of social facts.

(*27*) The Nazi Government found it necessary to make descent by strict entail compulsory by its Hereditary Farm Legislation, now repealed by the Allied Control Council.

(*28*) Stammler summarized his Neo-Kantian philosophy of law in 1922 in a *Lehrbuch der Rechtsphilosophie*. The theory of "form" and "matter" is summarized on pp. 111–115. For a description and criticism of Stammler's theory see Friedmann, *Legal Theory*, pp. 87–95.

(*29*) The "fetishistic" character of commodities and of money in a capitalist economy is explained by Marx in *Critique of Political Economy* (Popular Edition of the Marx-Engels-Lenin Institute, p. 36). "A social relation of production appears as an object existing independently from the individuals." "The specific relations into which individuals enter in the course of the productive processes of their social lives appear as specific qualities of a thing."

(*30*) Compare the quotations from the French, Swiss, and German Codes in the Introduction.

(*31*) On the political significance of this legal ideology see the Introduction.

(*32*) In the sense in which Renner uses the term in the text legal terminology is "empirical": the lawyer is constrained to take his norms from the statutory material which is given to him. The grouping of the norms, however, the crystallisation of concepts from these norms, and the building up of a system are speculative processes. In a legal order in which systematic thought prevails over the principle of precedent, the empirical process is subservient to non-empirical speculation. This is not the case where *stare decisis* has been adopted.

(*33*) Renner's theory of ancient legislation is that associated in this country with the name of Sir Henry Maine (*Ancient Law*, Pollock ed., pp. 12 *sq.*). Other legal historians call this theory a "myth" (see, e.g., Seagle, *The Quest for Law*, pp. 106-107). According to them even the Archaic Codes were written with the object of changing the law, not merely of fixing pre-existing law.

(*34*) Another instance is the relation between the common law and modern production. The painful and laborious process of adapting English company law to the exigencies of modern production and commerce is an example (see about this Formoy, *Historical Foundations of Modern Company Law*, and the recent article by Horrwitz, "Historical Development of Company Law", 62 *Law Quarterly Review*, 375).

(*35*) Not only in a capitalist society. See Schlesinger, *Sovjet Legal Theory*, p. 215, as to transactions between state enterprises in contractual form, and, in general, Gordon, *Système du Droit Commercial des Sovjets*, Paris, 1933.

(*36*) The law of obligation comprises contract, quasi-contract, and tort. What is meant is chiefly the law of contract.

(*37*) See the Introduction. From the point of view of modern developments the most important "legal categories" which enter into this combination are those of company law and patent law.

(*38*) It may be doubted whether the lack of correspondence between legal institution and economic function is inherent only in capitalism. It seems that in the Sovjet Union a very complex structure of legal institutions is needed in order to safeguard the productive process. The discrepancy between legal institution and economic function would seem to arise from the division of labour in modern industrial society.

Section ii. THE ORGANISATION;
AND THE CORRELATION OF THE FUNCTIONS

EVERY social system presupposes socialised man. He must have arrived at the stage where language and tools (Franklin's "tool-making animal") have already been developed in the tribe. Furthermore, the tribe must have developed into a community that is conscious of its own existence. We will refer to this type of community as an organisation. This term clearly expresses the consciousness of co-operation, differentiating it from the concept of organism.

Animal society is held together by physiological and biological laws, the laws of nature. They become rules of collective human activity as soon as man realises that it is these laws which hold the tribe together, that is to say, as soon as the tribe begins deliberately to act in the way in which the law of nature compels it to act. Thus the most ancient form of family constitution is an application of the natural laws of selection and heredity. [1] The description of this process of application is the concern of that branch of legal learning which deals with the creation of law. It is there that it must be demonstrated how, once recognized, the natural laws of preservation of the species are gradually transformed into social conventions and eventually into a code of conduct; how, in form and in effect, the laws of society progressively diverge from the laws of nature; and how these laws of society finally evolve in a way peculiar to themselves and, as division of labour proceeds and social differentiation increases, develop inherently conflicting tendencies. In short, this code of conduct re-formulates and con-sciously remoulds what had been the process of natural cause and effect into teleological imperatives addressed to the individuals in the name of the community. It now determines their actions with the same precision as previously instinct and inherited disposition had determined them. This code of conduct is the foundation of social life and brings about the order of society.

If the preservation of the species is the natural law for every social order, then every economic and consequently every legal institution must fulfil a function therein. Marx and Engels have called this preservation of the species the production and repro-

[1] Engels proves this by various instances in his *Origin of the Family, Private Property and the State.*

duction of the material conditions of life on an expanding scale. It is the production and reproduction of human individuals as well as of their conditions of existence. [2] Thus all legal institutions taken as a whole fulfil one function which comprises all others, that of the preservation of the species.

I. THE ORGANISING FUNCTIONS

The most important and precisely defined stages of this process of reproduction of the species are clearly perceptible in the economic system of our time. "The bourgeois order of society is the most highly developed and differentiated organisation of production known to history" (*Neue Zeit*, ibid. p. 776).

If we begin by applying a static method of analysis to the reproduction of the species, that is to say, if we consider it as mere production during the life-span of one generation, we see that it has a two-fold aspect: on the one hand, it is a physiological and technical life-process as it might take place in a bee-hive. On the other hand, it appears in the form of changing relations of wills, [3] since it also takes place in the consciousness of individuals and the community.

Whatever the stage of evolution, where men establish relations with one another, society as the common will must always subjugate the individual will. Society must be able, in one way or another, to dispose of the working power of the individual. [4] Every society is a community of labour and has its peculiar

[1] "Whatever the form of the process of production in a society, it must be a continuous process, must continue to go periodically through the same phases. A society can no more cease to produce than it can cease to consume. When viewed, therefore, as a connected whole, and as flowing on with incessant renewal, every social process of production is, at the same time, a process of reproduction" (*Capital* i, pp. 577–8). "In economic forms of society of the most different kinds, there occurs, not only simple reproduction, but, in varying degrees, reproduction on a progressively increasing scale" (ibid. p. 609). "According to the materialistic conception, the determining factor in history is, in the final instance, the production and reproduction of the immediate essentials of life" (Engels, *Origin*, p. 1).

[2] "On the one side, the production of the means of existence, . . . on the other side the production of human beings themselves, the propagation of the species" (ibid. p. 2).

[3] Cf. among others the following quotation: "This juridical relation, which thus expresses itself in a contract, whether such contract be part of a developed legal system or not, is a relation between two wills, and is but the reflex of the real economical relation between the two. It is this economical relation that determines the subject matter comprised in each such juridical act" (*Capital* i, p. 56). We would say that the economic relationship is the substratum of the legal relationship.

[4] This can be achieved by direct or indirect means, by direct legal compulsion or by indirect inducement brought about by other institutions—in capitalist society, for instance, by the wage-labourer's lack of property.

regulations of labour. In terms of the law this means that the individual will is subject to the common will. [1]

There is nothing metaphysical, however, about this common will. In spite of man's belief for three thousand years, it does not command from above like a voice beyond the clouds. It comes into being as an individual will endowed with power, just as the social exchange value is materialised in the form of money. Wherever the community has the power of command, as it has in every society, it exercises this power by means of individuals acting as its organs. (40) There is no society without regulation of power. [2]

If society does not superordinate or subordinate the individuals, it co-ordinates them and makes them equal before the law. Yet there can be no co-ordination without regulation.

There is no equality outside society in a fictitious pre-social state. [3] Equality is a creation of law and society.

Legal institutions designed to regulate the order of labour and of power and the co-ordination of individuals have an organising function in that they integrate the individual into the whole.

In all the older legal systems, the direct subordination of the individual to the common will, that is to say the direct regulation of power and labour, is manifest. [4] Master and slave, lord of the

---

[1] The capitalist order of economy alone creates the sophistic illusion that it has no regulation of labour, that labour is the result of free and autonomous will. The factory-owner knows better. He puts up the rules of labour on the factory walls for all to see. Yet the bourgeois lawyer would not notice this for a long time. Only within a quarter of a century after the first publication of this thesis has legal analysis endeavoured to understand the legal nature of factory rules. (39)

[2] An anarchist cannot conceive of freedom without the absence of all order, especially the regulation of power. This anarchist conception of freedom which must be distinguished from the political conception, is a negation of society itself. "Man's right to freedom is not based upon a union between man and man, but upon the isolation of man from man. It is the right to isolation, the right of the individual to be self-contained." Marx, *Nachlass* i, p. 418.

[3] Teachers of natural law have called this state a *status naturalis*, although it is against nature.

[4] The actual distribution of power among the individuals who apply it (the regulation of power), the actual distribution of the socially necessary labour among those individuals who have to perform it (the regulation of labour) and the personal selection and appointment of individuals for both tasks (the order of devolution) are in most of the known social systems a matter of public law. Organised society as the common will achieves these things by direct measures. As Marx has put it, subordination, superordination and co-ordination of individuals and their succession obviously appear as their own personal relations, and they are therefore not disguised as social relations between objects. Feudal tenure and succession, for instance, were at the height of the feudal period entirely *publici juris*. At this time, indeed, nearly every institution was one of public law, and there was practically no contrast between public and private law. (The Canon Law shows this even more clearly.) At the initial stage of the capitalist system, however, only the most indispensable provisions of public law are added to the private law by way of complementary institutions of public law. (43)

manor and serf are characters of a bygone order of labour. Their relations of subordination and superordination are direct and personal. "No matter, then, what we may think of the parts played by the different classes of people themselves in this society, the social relations between individuals in the performance of their labour, appear at all events as their own mutual personal relations, and are not disguised under the shape of social relations between the products of labour" (*Capital* i, p. 49). Bourgeois society has successfully developed the illusion that labour is not a social duty but a private affair for which no regulation of labour is required. (*41*) One of Marx's merits is to have proved that with freedom of property and contract, general co-ordination of individual wills becomes in fact a subjection of the will and the compulsion to work inside the factory, though what happens here was or could at least be imagined to be no concern of the law. (*42*) The legal structure of this sphere into which the civil law has failed for a long time to penetrate, has only during the last twenty-five years been made the object of legal analysis. It has only now been recognised that the "imperatives" which the factory foreman shouts to the worker at the noisy machine, imply a daily creation and administration of new law. How simple were, in comparison, the "direct relations of subjection" (*Capital* i, p. 51) in the pre-capitalist era!

The process by which any given society preserves its own species through history, that is, the process of reproduction in the course of generations, must be continuous. It follows from this postulate of continuity that each member of society, whether ruling or working, should be replaced by another, when he is no longer capable of wielding his sceptre or tool. That new member of society is substituted for the old, the old member is "succeeded" by him. Hence every legal system has its order of succession or devolution, it has legal institutions whose function is to regulate succession. Within the bourgeois system these institutions make up the law of inheritance. (*44*)

The preservation of the species, however, demands not only legal continuity, but also physical procreation, the raising, education and training of the growing generation. This, indeed, was the first common interest of society, it was here that the creative spirit first expressed itself in effective norms. The order according to *gentes* is the oldest complete legal system. It is these institutions whose function is to safeguard the existence and continuity of the family, which enabled mankind to rise from the tribal stage to that of organised society.

2. THE ECONOMIC FUNCTIONS IN PARTICULAR

Society thus organised as an aggregate of integrated individual wills now directs the thousands of its tentacles towards nature. "Labour is, in the first place, a process in which both man and Nature participate, and in which man of his own accord starts, regulates, and controls the material reactions between himself and Nature. He opposes himself to Nature as one of her own forces" (*Capital* i, p. 156). The relations between man as a social being and nature are not simply those of a natural individual, they are intrinsically social. This means that society as a whole always retains disposal over the territory and material objects which it has occupied and assimilated. An organised society can never give up the power to dispose of the goods which are indispensable for its preservation, yet it cannot itself seize and keep these goods except by entrusting them to its constituent members as its "trustees", as it were, to be used in its name. Whatever the social system, disposal of all goods that have been seized and assimilated must be regulated by the social order as the rights of persons over material objects. Only thus can the continuous and undisturbed process of production be ensured. Every stage of the economic development has its regulation of goods as it has its order of labour. The legal institutions which effect this regulation, subject the world of matter bit by bit to the will of singled-out individuals, since the community exists only through its individual members. (*45*) These legal institutions endow the individuals with detention so that they may dispose of the objects and possess them. Even communal property is always in individual hands, just as the regimental colours are in the hands of the standard-bearer. (*46*) Legal terminology offers no better word for this than "detention", for the term *gewere*, which was used in medieval Germanic law, has unfortunately become obsolete. (*47*) *Habere* and *detinere* is a general and necessary legal institution for every social system, and the bourgeoisie is inclined to regard it as a justification of "property". But we shall see that it is only in transitional stages of world history, that this state of detaining appears as private property. We say that the function of those legal institutions which effect the allocation, the social regulation of goods, is to regulate detention. [1] It may as well be termed the function of assignation: for what, from the point of view of the subject, appears as detention, is allocation or assignation from the point of view of the law.

The regulation of labour and goods determines the legal form of the process of preservation of the species, since it regulates the power of disposal over labour and means of production.

Three stages are generally distinguished in this process: production, distribution, and consumption. Accordingly, the legal institutions concerned with it fulfil three different kinds of function, those of production, distribution, and consumption.

Every member of society must have a share, however humble, of the annual product, regardless of whether he has taken an active part in production or not. He can obtain this share, his fund of consumption, only by means of legal institutions. To-day this function of consumption is fulfilled by property; also, in other ways, such as by life-tenure (usufruct) or by rural rent-charge; (49) recently by social insurance, and when all these fail, by the Poor Law. (50)

Nowadays distribution takes the form of circulation of commodities in the legal forms of sale and purchase. In the Middle Ages it was quite different, it occurred in forms like corvée (unfree labour) and tithe.

In modern times the function of production is mainly fulfilled by property and contract of service, though numerous other legal institutions play their part. (51) In the Middle Ages this rôle was taken by serfdom and villeinage; in antiquity by slavery.

The element of detention is common to these three functions. All three are integral portions of the regulation of goods, considered separately. In the course of our enquiry we shall find that from these general functions special and partial functions can become differentiated. For the time being this survey must suffice.

3. THE CONCEPT OF THE SOCIAL FUNCTION

Our survey has listed the functions of the legal institutions in the most general way. It comprises general abstractions which

---

[1] It should be borne in mind that detention in legal terminology means mere possession and disregards every legal qualification. We use the term as denoting possession on behalf of society, but again without regard to other legal qualification. (48)

are as valid as the abstractions of production, consumption, and social order in general. It is evident that production, consumption and distribution take specific forms at every stage in the development of a concrete society. This form is made specific by special economic institutions, viz. special technical procedures and legal institutions peculiar to them. By means of these general common characteristics we are now able without constant repetition to give shorter descriptions of these specific forms and of the process of change.

These functions, of course, merge into one another. The assignation of a piece of land in a Roman colony to an ex-legionary is also universal succession into the position of the native owner (who was either killed or taken prisoner and sold as a slave). The transfer of a farm from father to son either *inter vivos* or by inheritance serves the appointment of a successor to the departing farmer and at the same time the continuity of the family. As the successor also becomes the master of the farm hands, the transfer has an organising function as well. (*52*) If we correlate all specific effects of a legal institution upon society as a whole, the individual partial functions become fused into a single social function.

A legal institution is a composite of norms. If in the change of economic systems it has remained constant but its functions have either increased or diminished, changed or disappeared, then we speak of a change in the functions. By way of example let us consider the vestals who had to keep the fire ever burning on all the hearths of the community. We may well imagine that as long as they existed, the sum total of the laws relating to them remained unchanged and the relevant norms remained constant. With the discovery of flint and steel, however, all economic functions of the vestals were taken over by a substitute. Here we should be entitled to say that the economic revolution—for the discovery took place in a sphere outside the law—deprived the legal institution of its social function, made it redundant and led to its final abolition. (*53*)

Conversely, we may imagine that a legal institution retains its function and economic significance, though the norms which make it up have been transformed. Imperatives may have been added, taken away or altered, yet the essence will have remained of what was commanded. This, too, is neither unthinkable nor unhistorical. The bill of exchange, for instance, has retained all its economic functions, but the law relating to it no longer includes the personal liability of the debtor to imprisonment for debt. Similarly, the institution of capital punishment has retained its function although the norms have disappeared which provided for its various modifications such as quartering and mutilation. (54)

Thus we find two possibilities of legal development, the change of norms and the change of functions. Legal doctrine must examine both, in order to find out their mutual relations and the laws of their evolution.

However much the functions of the legal institutions may change, no function can remain unfulfilled permanently without involving the destruction of society itself. If a function is no longer served by one legal institution, another must be substituted for it; there is no vacuum in the legal system. We shall see that legal institutions can within certain limits take each other's place. [1] (55) As a rule, however, new institutions are required. Whence do they come? How do they compensate for the old?

In our terminology the organic character of the legal order is the fact that the totality of legal institutions existing at a given time must fulfil all general functions. This means that the law is an organised whole determined by the needs of society. Every legal institution as part of it, therefore, is more or less closely related to all others; and it is its function, not the content of its norms, which make for this connection.

The organic nature of the legal order implies further that all institutions of the civil law and their complementary institutions are also connected with the public law. Without it they can be neither effective nor intelligible. Property, for instance, is inoperative without the law of civil procedure, and this is inoperative without the law relating to the organisation of the courts. Property itself can never be fully effective, since public law imposes restrictions and encumbrances on it, such as taxes. Every institution of private law has its counterpart in public law; we shall have to refer to this correspondence in due course. The general opinion of the capitalist era, however, would have it that the complementary institutions of the state should do no more than guarantee the full efficacy of the private institutions; they should not in any way abolish or deflect them. (56) Therefore, as long as we confine ourselves to describing the capitalist system of economy, we must

---

[1] The right in rem of the servitus aquaehaustus can in case of need be replaced by the obligation of the owner to allow the drawing of water.

leave the institutions of the state out of consideration. (*57*) They only come to the fore where the development of the law points beyond the capitalist system. (*58*)

In spite of this organic character of the whole legal order, in spite of the interconnection of all individual institutions of private law, history exhibits an unceasing change in the norms and functions of the legal institutions. Above all we must strive to obtain a clear picture of the magnitude and significance of these transformations which may occur entirely outside the realm of the law and its commands, and wholly or partly below the level of society's collective consciousness. We must start on a journey through economics in order to obtain a clear understanding of the efficacy of the law. We must become acquainted with the limits of its powers and train our eye to perceive the problems involved in the change of norms.

Moreover, we shall thus gain insight into the legal system of our time. Property is still the fundamental institution, therefore we must concentrate mainly on property. As we consider principally the efficacy of present-day property, learning to understand the changes it has undergone, we prepare the ground for the understanding of its future development.

Notes, Chapter I, Section II

(*39*) This remark refers to the voluminous literature and case law which developed in connection with enactments such as the German Works Councils Act of 1920, under which the works rule had to be agreed between the employer and the workers' representatives. In this country legal writers have not yet taken sufficient notice of the fundamental principles involved in enactments such as the Coal Mines Regulation Act, 1887, the Coal Mines (Check-Weigher) Act, 1894, and the Check Weighing in Various Industries Act, 1919, or of the production committees established under various collective agreements (see "Joint Production Committees in Great Britain", ILO *Studies and Reports*, Series A, No. 42, Montreal 1944, and see Richardson, *Industrial Relations in Great Britain*, 2nd ed., pp. 155 *sq.*). For a description of the "Factory Committees" in the Soviet Union, see Webb, *Soviet Communism, A New Civilisation*, 2nd ed., Vol. I, p. 182.

(*40*) The principle of organic representation, by which the representative of a corporate entity acts as its organ, not as its agent, is only gradually adopted in this country. It was Lord Haldane who formulated it, probably for the first time, in an English case (*Lennard's Carrying Co., Ltd.*, v. *Asiatic Petroleum Co., Ltd.* [1915] AC 705). The practical importance of the difference between agency and organic representation was recently demonstrated by Welsh (*The Criminal Liability of Corporations*, 62 LQR 345). Renner assumes the validity of the doctrine as a matter of course,—another instance of the influence of Continental legal thought on Marxist legal theory.

(*41*) Apart from the Essential Work Orders an enactment such as Section 13 subs. 2 (b), (c), and (d) of the National Insurance Act, 1946, makes it difficult to say that present English law fails to recognise a "legal duty" to work. Refusal to work involves disqualification for receiving unemployment benefit. "Direction of labour" by incentives varying from persuasion to compulsion has become an essential institution of society.

(*42*) Renner puts this in the past tense. The whole body of labour law can be understood as the conversion of a relation of extra-legal subordination into a legal relationship.

(*43*) The development of a large number of legal institutions regulating the "order of power" (labour law) and the "order of devolution" (e.g. regulations governing the civil service) have made it impossible to maintain the rigid distinction between public and private law on the Continent.

(*44*) Among the many legal norms, which supplement or supplant the law of succession as the order of devolution, company law, the legal rules governing the appointment of trustees, the principles of local government law, and, most important, the law regulating parliamentary elections, may be mentioned.

(*45*) *Detinere* in Roman Law signifies the actual having of a thing which may or may not be coupled with "possession" in the legal sense. The Roman concept of *detinere* broadly corresponds to the English concept of possession, except that a servant entrusted with the goods of his master has detention according to Roman, but not possession according to English law. Renner's choice of the word "detention" for the actual "having" of a thing is thus a very fortunate one.

(*46*) "Property" means here the thing, not the right. See also below, note 289.

(*47*) Renner's reference to *Gewere* (seisin) is somewhat misleading. Though, as Maitland points out, seisin may originally have meant possession in the physical sense, it acquired a "technical meaning" in the course of the medieval development.

Neither the copyholder nor the leaseholder had seisin. *Gewere* or seisin was by no means identical with physical "having" (see Pollock and Maitland, *History of English Law*, Vol. II, pp. 29 *sq.*, and *Gierke Deutsches Privatrecht*, Vol. II, pp. 187 *sq.*).

(*48*) All private "having" of things appears here as "detention" on behalf of society, no matter whether the quality of ownership is given to this *detinere*.

(*49*) See above, note 17.

(*50*) This enumeration is incomplete. Public Health Legislation, Education Legislation, and Housing Legislation might have been mentioned. The legal principles governing Industrial and Provident Societies, Friendly Societies, and, in certain respects, Trade Unions, also come to mind.

(*51*) Together with many other institutions, such as company law, patent law, etc.

(*52*) Renner suggests a dual process of sociological investigation: an analysis of the role which each legal institution plays in the organisation of labour, of devolution, of detention, etc., and a subsequent synthesis showing how the various functions of one institution are brought into harmony. Modern institutions which might lend themselves well to this type of inquiry would be: the contract of life assurance (which is a mode of investment and an instrument promoting the concentration of financial power as well as a method of devolution), the restrictive covenant, the hire-purchase contract, etc. The more judges and lawyers abandon positivism and turn towards a functional approach to the law, the greater the practical importance of the methods suggested by Renner.

(*53*) A more modern example is the implied authority of the master of a ship to hypothecate the ship, freight, and cargo by a contract of bottomry or respondentia. This authority exists only if the master is unable to communicate with the owner. It is an ancient institution of great historical interest, and, as the number of decided cases shows, it was of considerable importance until late in the 19th century. To-day it has lost most of its practical significance, owing to the invention of wireless telegraphy, and also, as Gutteridge points out (Smith, *Mercantile Law*, 13th ed., p. 538, note (a)), owing "to the development of banking facilities in modern times". See further below, note 278.

(*54*) In this country land settlements provide an example for a change of norms which has left the social function intact. This change of norms by which the rights of the members of the family (other than the tenant for life) have been made to attach to a floating asset instead of the land itself has been mentioned in the Introduction.

(*55*) Public town planning supplants private building schemes under restrictive covenants, the private company takes over the social functions of the partnership, etc.

(*56*) See note 7 above. What Renner says, is still unfortunately true of much of our law *teaching*. It is no longer true of the practitioner's work. No conveyancer can afford to ignore town planning legislation, no company lawyer can look upon company law in isolation from income tax legislation. The conception that "private" law institutions can be understood as self-contained entities isolated from their "public" law environment is rapidly becoming an academic prejudice.

(*57*) This was possible, perhaps necessary, forty years ago. To-day, owing to the development of state activities, it has become impossible.

(*58*) Even within a capitalist system the law may "point" beyond it. It is submitted that this is the case to-day in this country.

CHAPTER II

THE FUNCTIONAL TRANSFORMATION OF PROPERTY

Section i. PRINCIPLES AND METHODS OF ANALYSIS

I. PATRIMONIAL PROPERTY

THE right of ownership, *dominium*, is a person's all-embracing legal power over a tangible object. (*59*) It is a right, i.e. a power conferred upon a subject (person) by the law. (*60*) This right is absolute, the imperatives upon which it is based are addressed to all persons without exception and claim their respect. (*61*) Its content is the power to dispose of the object, and this power is all-embracing. The owner in his capacity as owner may dispose in any manner:[1] he may, for instance, use the object, consume it, destroy it or abandon it. Ownership is not, therefore, an aggregate of individual rights, it implies unlimited possibilities of disposal. Whatever the manner of disposal, it is an exercise of the right. Any restriction of this power of disposal, whether imposed from outside by legislation or self-imposed by contract, only affects the exercise, not the right itself; it affects the owner, not his ownership. As far as the object is concerned, ownership is a universal institution: all corporeal things, even land, (*62*) can be objects of ownership if they are recognised as such by the law and are not by special provision put *extra commercium*.

Ownership is equally universal with regard to the subject. Everybody has an equal capacity for ownership, and he may own property of every description. (*63*) These are the norms which are characteristic of this institution.

This legal concept is the most simple and self-contained concept imaginable. No wonder that at the time when it was first developed, its logical, abstract and convincing simplicity should have made it appear as an eternal category of all law, immutable in the past and in the future. And yet—medieval law did not know this form of assignation of a thing to a person, except in the case of movable property. (*64*) Several persons were capable of

---

[1] Restrictions of the personal capacity for ownership (infant, prodigal, bankrupt) or public liabilities (taxes, etc.) imposed upon the owner affect the right of ownership neither legally nor with respect to its general economic function.

having simultaneously rights *in rem* of equal rank in the same piece
of land, a *res* was capable of being in the *"gewere"* (seizin) of
several persons, (*65*) and an enactment as late as the Austrian
Civil Code knows *dominium directum* and *dominium utile*[1] (superior
and inferior ownership), i.e. two kinds of ownership in the same
res. (*66*) It is indeed possible to carve out of the universal right of
disposition selected powers of disposal or beneficial enjoyment and
to constitute them as separate *jura in rem.* We shall see that this
is what is happening again in modern times, though the conceptual process is entirely different. (*67*)   It was not until the
Reception that, owing to the powerful, even violent, invasion of
the Roman Law, (*68*) the concept of ownership forced itself upon a
totally different system of law, so that commodity production
might take the place of feudal economy. (*69*)

This concept has its twin-brother—the right of personal liberty.
Each individual can, in relation to all others who are subject to
the norm, do as he pleases.   And it would be as meaningless to
dissolve the right of personal liberty into the freedom to sleep, to
take a walk, to make the sign of the cross, as it would now be to
dissect ownership into individualised powers. (*70*)

This right of personal liberty has removed the feudal order of
labour: the guild in the town and serfdom in the country. For the
Continent its birthday is the French Revolution. In the sequence
of events it comes later than civil property. English law did not
experience the violent Reception which occurred on the Continent;
and, to this day, it has preserved a large variety of rights of
possession. (*71*)   It did, however, go through a similar transformation in a long process of adaptation. (*72*)

By means of these two institutions, human society is now
dissolved into isolated individuals, and the world of goods is split
up into discrete items of nature. There is no regulation of labour
and goods directly controlling production, circulation and consumption, linking man to man, or man to nature, or correlating
the objects. The individual and his property work freely according
to his autonomous will.   This will is autonomous vis-à-vis the
community and the common will; the social rule abdicates after
having married *persona* and *res* through the property-norm. The
structure of society is now dominated by the relationship between
person and property just as it used to be dominated by that
between master and slave.   The social atoms bustle about in a

[1] § 357.

free interplay of forces, and from the point of view of society as a whole there is no rule or law to regulate their movements. But since the system of human economy as a whole is, and must always be, subject to a regulating order, these elements henceforward move about in accordance with a new law, a third law which is neither a law made by the state nor a law of nature. The elements repel and attract each other, they associate and dissociate, a process which we can observe in every-day economic life. In their own imagination they are autonomous, but in reality they are dominated by a social power. This power, not having been consciously established like a public authority, operates just like a law of nature vis-à-vis natural forces, and therefore appears like a law of nature. Yet it is a law of society, a superhuman force which remains below the level of consciousness, because otherwise it would be a social regulation. This self-contradictory law is nothing but the law of value of the capitalist mode of production. We need not prove this fact here, but we have to bear it in mind.

We take these norms which make up the institution of property as a given fact and now raise the question of its social function. We start with the historical beginnings of the institution, with the period of simple commodity production,[1] the initial stage of bourgeois society. For there is always a moment in the history of human institutions when the legal system is the adequate expression of the economic relations, when superstructure and substructure are in conformity. This, of course, is true only for what is typical, not for every individual case, as the law as a general norm has regard to the typical only.[2] We will now endeavour to piece together a picture of this period.

When production by individual craftsmen was at its zenith, the town as a rule consisted of houses for one family only. A whole poetry of the house was built round this type, Schiller's "*Lied von der Glocke*" made it immortal. House connotes family, witness the

---

[1] Like all other great stages of economic development, the system of simple commodity production never existed in absolute purity but was always combined with other forms of economy, natural economy, feudal economy, the economy of guild monopolies (Kautsky, *Agrarfrage*, p. 60). Our task to examine the specific essentials of every form of economy is not affected by the consideration that none of them was ever in history developed in undiluted purity.

[2] I have not overlooked the fact that nearly all institutions which, as we shall see, develop the functions of property, characteristic of the capitalist system, already existed in previous periods. They were, however, unimportant exceptions to a rule, abnormal forms of the exercise of ownership, whereas to-day they are the usual forms. Similarly, nearly all the legal forms which would be applicable in a socialist commonwealth, are already now in existence, though their functions have not been fully developed. (73)

House of Schroeder, [1] (74) and the names of peasants' houses in a farming community used side by side with the family names. House means occupation (commercial and business houses) and wealth. It connotes not only the building but *pars pro toto* the whole undertaking as well as the people engaged in it. A person's property, his patrimonial property, his house and home and everything around it, is at this period not merely a logical form of the law, but it is a quite distinct material entity, *a universitas rerum*, though the lawyer of to-day would see in it only a jumble of disjointed property-objects. (75)

This patrimony of a person provides the locus of production for the master and the members of his household, it contains workshop and storeroom, rooms for spinning and sewing, a kitchen garden and other land for cultivation and usually a share in the communal wood. (76) It provides, in the form of the small street shop, the premises for the turnover of goods. As the craftsman produces directly for a customer, one transaction covers sale, purchase, in short, the whole of distribution, the realisation of value and surplus value. At the same time the patrimony also serves as the place and as the framework of consumption as home and hearth, cellar and larder. [2] Thus all material conditions of production and reproduction, nearly all their material components are physically combined into a universal, self-contained and organic world of objects which derives its individuality from the person of the owner. So, for example, the house of Schroeder.

House here connotes an actual entirety composed of things as well as of persons. An economic purpose, not the law, gives unity to this real cosmos. It is the substratum or fundament to which the legal norm or rule refers. [3] At the stage of simple commodity production, then, the "house" was capable of being conceived in terms of law. It is evident that only a legal institution fit to embrace a comprehensive complex of objects could be adequate to this substratum. (77)

As the owner is surrounded mainly by other owners of the same

---

[1] Schroeder is the name of a commercial firm which is the central figure in a novel describing this period: *Soll und Haben*, by Gustav Freytag, *A.S.*

[2] As we can read with some nostalgia in *Soll und Haben*.

[3] Thus a village is made up of persons settled in the same place and their dwellings. The law takes this composite of facts—territory and persons—and transforms it into the parish. The parish is a creation of the law, but the law does not create it out of a void, it builds upon an actual foundation. In our terminology, the village is the substratum, the parish the normative structure. The problem of substratum and normative structure is part of the problem of the legal superstructure and must be examined separately for every legal institution.

status, and as the legal institution can and must be comprehensive also with regard to the powers it confers upon the person, since moreover his material microcosm scarcely affects that of his neighbour, he has full jurisdiction over his world of objects, *rei suae legem dicit.* His dominion is absolutely unlimited, as no neighbour is interested in interfering or would stand interference. [1]

This absolute character of the legal institution, its comprehensiveness with regard to the powers it confers and the objects it comprises, adequately expresses the actual independence of the goods. These goods are concentrated in organic microcosms, but the owners are situated next to one another without any organic correlation. Such was the typical substratum of the law at a time when the person was declared free and property sacrosanct.

This fact, the microcosm of goods, [2] alone enables property to serve the function of production without friction. (78) Within the large world of goods there are always inherent connections which cannot be dissolved but must be severed. The flow of water, the general lay-out of the land, the necessity for roads, the mere fact of contiguity of homes in the town and the fact that if everything is partitioned, the boundary line still remains common, all these circumstances prove that nature, like society, forms a collective whole. The legal institutions which take account of these circumstances, such as easements—both natural and acquired—do not in the least disintegrate property. On the contrary, they are necessary conditions of its exercise, they are complementary institutions which enable property to serve its function of production. (79)

Distribution, the other function of property, works even more smoothly. If we leave society out of consideration, as it is expedient to do at this stage, for many reasons, we see that immediate production for customers brings the commodity at once to the consumer, so that its whole value is realised for the producer. He is remunerated for his labour—surplus labour as well as necessary labour—the whole of the surplus value finds its way into the workers' pocket, no surplus product is extracted from society

---

[1] Interference only occurs outside the sphere of the house. It is impersonal and objective in form. The microcosm sends out spores, the commodities which have been produced within. In the beginning tradition and guild rules provide a certain regulation.

[2] The legal institution does not effect a co-ordination of goods. It is, on the contrary, indifferent towards them, one corporeal object is as good as another. This indifference was possible, however, only because there existed a pre-legal cosmos which provided a factual order of goods.

so as to maintain a "public authority" as was done in feudal
times in the form of the natural rent yielded by the fees. Hence
the necessity to tax owners or to increase the prices of commodities. Duties, whether direct or indirect, which were of no
consequence in feudal times, thus became necessary complementary institutions. Feudal society provided its public organs with
surplus labour and surplus produce by an open and conscious
regulation of labour and goods. (*80*)

As regards also the maintenance and continuity of the population, property fulfils its function in an adequate manner.
Procreation is automatically regulated according to the supply of
goods, and the reproduction of the species in accordance with the
reproduction of goods, i.e. the subsistence provided by the
"house". Moreover, the patrimony comprises the nursery and the
kindergarten and provides vocational training for the growing
generation. (*81*) Finally, it also regulates unproductive consumption by offering a retreat for the old and the sick. (*82*)

Property provided for everything but the regulation of labour.
At first it was public law which regulated the employment of
journeymen and apprentices and the organisation of the workshop,
and, at least at the initial stage of "personal freedom", exercised a
certain control. Journeymen and apprentices were still members
of the master's household and personal freedom took them only
gradually out of the house community. (*83*)

The description of patrimonial property applies to an even
greater extent to the peasant farm which was still mainly run as a
closed domestic economy, not yet engaging in regular production
for the market and offering only its surplus for sale. Here the house
community of the workers was even more rigorous; where labour
was performed for wages by people who lived outside it, this was in
the nature of mutual help between neighbours. Economic and
social relations of this kind were most purely developed in districts
in which isolated farmsteads predominated over self-contained
villages.

House and farm provide the type to which the legal institution
was consciously or unconsciously adapted. At the time when the
property norm was established, this was its substratum. The
decisive moment of adaptation is different from country to
country, but always historically ascertainable. (*84*) We take note
of this adaptation but we do not investigate its origin, we do not
ask whether it was the law which determined the economic system

or vice versa, we do not examine cause and effect. We simply take norm and substratum, as they exist side by side, as the actual starting point of our investigation.

2. TRANSFORMATIONS IN THE SUBSTRATUM OF PROPERTY

Within a few generations this substratum has been completely revolutionised. As the culminating point of this development in Western Europe we may provisionally take the time when Marx's *Capital* was published (1867).

Let us begin with this cardinal fact: the law of property has not changed. (*85*) The *Code Civil*, (*86*) the Prussian Land Law, (*87*) the Austrian Civil Code (*88*) and so forth (*89*)—all these codifications which record the victory of the property norm, contain norms which are still valid to-day. (*90*) The property norms of the new German code (*91*) are even somewhat more strict than those of the earlier codifications. There has been no change of norms.

In the world of facts, however, the changes have been so numerous that the mere thought of them is startling. The house for one family (*92*) and the whole microcosm which permeates it, are veritably smashed into pieces. We have no longer a house, only an address. (*93*) The idea of the home has been reduced to a mere number in a street or block of flats. As occupiers of lodgings, we have managed to get ourselves expropriated; we no longer live in our own castle. (*94*)

The question arises, what has taken the place of the family house? One part of it, the workshop, has been turned adrift. In the most favourable case it may be in the basement if the people live in a tenement. (*95*) But as a rule the many small workshops have become merged into large factories. The same applies to the storeroom and to the spinning and sewing room which have been welded together into mammoth textile works. The small kitchen gardens have given way to the establishments of the market gardeners in the outskirts of the city; (*96*) the patrimonial fields and shares in the woodlands to the vast latifundia of the exporting countries; the small corner shops have been detached or concentrated in huge department stores; living accommodation is concentrated in tenement buildings, the larder in delikatessen shops, the cellars and to some extent the kitchens in restaurants. The microcosm has been broken up into atoms, and these atoms have formed new groupings. (*97*)

More than that: the nurseries are concentrated in public establishments, kindergartens, children's homes, schools and finishing schools. The rooms reserved for aged relatives have been replaced by homes for the aged, the sickrooms by hospitals. Journeymen and apprentices live outside the house community, and even mothers-in-law are mercilessly boarded out.

What we see before our eyes is a revolutionary change of the substratum of property and of its component objects. The material microcosm is broken up and its *membra disjecta* grouped again according to a new law. This law no longer attaches to the individuality of the legal *persona*, the person who holds these parts together and is their master. Yet the material world still remains an organic and coherent whole, and this finds expression in a new law of grouping which we will discuss later. There could, however, have been no shifting of the *res*, unless there had been in fact a change in the dominant *personae* as well. The "patrimony" of simple commodity production was bound to become separated piece by piece from the previous owners in the process of its actual disintegration. In the eyes of the law this exchange of dominant *personae* is alienation from the point of view of the owner and appropriation from that of the new *dominus*. It is not enforced by the law, it is factual expropriation and appropriation. It is only in these terms of a factual shifting of the dominant *personae* of property and other kindred legal institutions, not in terms of a change of ownership imposed by a Court or authority, that Marx uses the conception of "expropriation". No other meaning must be attached to it.

A constantly increasing number of people is affected by this process, as we all know from our own experience. There has been a long series of undeniable expropriations which, once they have occurred, have become facts with which we have to reckon. Their importance cannot be diminished by the obvious reflection that these fragments of the old microcosm of which the former owners have been deprived, had to be appropriated again by somebody else. Their importance could not be denied even if every expropriated person at the end of the process possessed the same amount of value as before. This series of expropriations is evidence, at the very least, of an enormous revolution in our whole lives.

Like the naïve person quoted by Marx, we are made to wonder: "By what law, or series of laws, was it effected?" (*Capital* i, p. 775).

The answer is that no Act of Parliament with its hundred-and-one sections has pulverised the microcosm. Fundamentally, the norms which make up the law have remained absolutely constant, and yet an enormous revolution has occurred without any change of norms.

Let us consider what remains in the owner's hands at the end of the process, assuming that the value of the newly appropriated objects is equal to that of which he has been deprived. We know that in the majority of cases what remains is as good as worthless; but we will not enlarge on this point here.

The expropriated appropriator possesses perhaps a tenement house, a factory, a store of merchandise, but always a corporeal thing, a single or collective object which fulfils a strictly limited and separate function, and besides this he may own money, an object whose function, it is true, is universal. Moreover, he will have a few consumer goods. We see that nowadays the property of a person, modern possessions, are totally different from the former "patrimony". No longer do we find a microcosm of objects which derives its unity from the purposive connection with the owner. Instead of the House of Schroeder we have an engineering factory, a department store, a spinning mill and so on. The modern possessions of an individual are as a rule an inorganic jumble of objects; a personal relation to the owner exists only for consumer goods. (98) Other goods are grouped and individualised by their technical and economic functions, such as tenement houses, factories, warehouses and so forth.

Karl Marx shows in detail which natural and social laws (not law in the technical sense) were responsible for this "evolution". He begins as we shall do with the period of simple commodity production. He first proves that within its framework, all commodities are exchanged in accordance with their value, to wit, the average socially necessary labour-time required for their production. He further proves that value and price are as a rule equivalent; for during this economic phase the soil, the raw material and the labour of the owner, as well as that of other persons, are absorbed by the product in about equal proportions, so that the conditions of production remain undifferentiated. Value and surplus value, ground rent, profit, in short all the economic categories can be reduced to labour and the results of labour. At this stage of simple commodity production the fact becomes apparent that labour alone creates value. (99)

Marx's monumental achievement begins where he demonstrates the necessity of the transition from simple commodity production to capitalist production, and subjects the latter to analysis. This analysis is also invaluable for legal history. It revealed to him the truth that the transformation of its social functions will in the end result in a transformation of the norm itself, that the evolution of the law is determined by economic relations.

We must bear in mind that the development of the legal institution first took place at its two opposite poles, the *persona* and the *res*. Yet the content of the right, the total and absolute legal power of a person over a *res*, was not affected by the process of transformation. Only a change in the right or norm would have been a transformation of the norm itself. [1]

Every change is on the one hand expropriation of the *persona*, i.e. the owner, and appropriation by a new *persona*. On the other hand it means a splitting up of the *res*, i.e. the patrimony, into its component elements which are grouped again into modern units of possession. Marx has given a scientific analysis of this process of world history, and in the second section of our treatise we shall only have to follow his thoughts.

3. THE RIGHT OF PERSONAL FREEDOM

Property as a legal institution is indifferent towards subject (*persona*) and object (*res*). *De jure* it only regulates detention without being concerned with the identity of the persons or the type of the goods. The law protects possession, the power to dispose of the *res*. A system of private law is content to know that material wealth is firmly held by the individuals, it does not care what use they make of it or who they are. (*101*) Everybody, even the child, even the *nasciturus*, is capable of ownership, (*102*) and every owner has unlimited authority to act. Finally, private law is not interested in the destiny of social man-power, it ignores any conscious regulation of labour, it does not recognise an obligation to work. (*103*) As far as the legal appearance is concerned, our law might just as well govern the life of the gods on Olympus, or life in the Elysian fields, knowing neither toil nor sweat. No wonder that this appearance of the law evoked enthusiasm in

---

[1] A genuine transformation of norms might have occurred at the two opposite poles: by limiting the capacity to own property and by declaring a larger number of *res* as *res extra commercium*. Neither of these things has in fact taken place. The transfer of private property to state ownership, the organisation of material goods as state monopolies do not involve a change in the institution of property, as far as its legal content is concerned. It is well known that public property is governed by the rules of private law. (*100*)

its creators, the men of the bourgeois revolution, no wonder that it nearly led them to consider it as the essence of super-human wisdom. (*104*)

There is no legal regulation, then, of goods or of labour within bourgeois society, whereas the whole of the medieval world was obviously built on such conscious regulation. Society, the conscious organisation of mankind, in the eyes of the law an entity, here denies its own consciousness. It prefers blindness to recognition of the distribution of the goods, it pretends to be deaf so that it need not listen to the complaints of the dispossessed, it abdicates as a legal entity, as the common will, in favour of the individual will. [1] But though it feigns death, it is alive, and inanimate stones cry out where it remains silent. Production and reproduction of the species still remain part of a social process. They acquire this social character below the threshold of consciousness; and this social character finds expression in a regulation of labour and goods which is not embodied in a legal norm but in a law of nature which is also a law of society. It is an order full of contradictions, fetish-like in character, understood by nobody before Marx. The so-called bourgeois society, distinct from the political society of the organised state, is not conscious of itself. It confronts the individuals as a dark power of nature, a ghostly, inhuman force which does not talk in imperatives to the members of the community, which does not utter commands or threats, which does not punish afterwards in forms of law, which requires to be divined by speculation and destroys him who does not grasp it, which achieves its object by the force of blind matter and allows this matter to rule over man.

Yet we have seen that simple commodity production constituted an organic system of law and economics—what was it that brought about the change? That period had its traditional public regulation of labour which worked adequately, it had various complementary institutions which provided especially for the dispossessed (church property, etc.). There were whole legions of paupers, beggars, vagrants, and monks, who lived on alms, parts of the surplus product of working owners. The existence of these people was itself the result of the disintegration of older social functions. To-day we cannot even imagine the innumerable

---

[1] We are not yet concerned with the question, how far contemporary law engages in a direct regulation of labour and distribution of goods. In the beginning this legal intervention was of practically no consequence, and if we leave it out of consideration, our picture of rising capitalism is only imperceptibly falsified. (*105*)

masses of the poor at that time. (*106*)   Without working themselves, they absorbed a large part of the social surplus product.
The social question of those times was not the fate of the worker
but the incorporation of the vagrant into the social process of
production, the transformation of the beggar into a worker.   In
his chapter on primitive accumulation Karl Marx describes the
solution of this problem.   Here, however, we will not discuss it
further.   An institution of private law now becomes predominant,
an institution which heretofore was only occasionally used as a
subsidiary measure, now takes the place of the regulation of
labour by public law.   This is the private contract of employment
and service, *locatio conductio operarum*, and in practice it soon
became the normal institution, though the law did not establish
or extend it by special provisions. (*107*)   In order to make room
for this new institution, to remove all obstacles to its expansion,
the commodity producers smashed up the old traditional regulation of labour [1] by revolutionary methods, replacing it by the right
of personal freedom, the negation of every conscious control of
labour.   We may describe this right as the ownership of a person
in his labour-power.   Though not in any sense a legal definition,
this description would illustrate clearly the effects of this personal
freedom.   We shall see that for the propertied classes this right
means much more than, and something quite different from, mere
autonomy of the working individual.   However, in the beginning,
personal freedom was achieved for the whole of society, it was
universal, and it was this freedom which inspired in its enthusiastic advocates the hope that it would make all workers
owners.   But the absolute, abstract principle of freedom is, like
every abstract principle, merely an empty legal frame.   What was
to be its social content was not determined by the beautiful dreams
of those who fought for it and codified it, but by hard facts below
the plane of the law.   The social function fulfilled by this complementary institution of property, its economic significance for
the dispossessed part of society, is described by Marx as follows:

"On this assumption, labour-power can appear upon the
market as a commodity, only if, and so far as, its possessor, the
individual whose labour-power it is, offers it for sale, or sells it,
as a commodity.   In order that he may be able to do this, he must

---

[1] "The rules of the guilds . . . by limiting most strictly the number of apprentices
and journeymen that a single master could employ, prevented him from becoming a
capitalist" (*Capital* i, p. 352).

have it at his disposal, must be the untrammelled owner of his capacity for labour, i.e. of his person" (*Capital* i, p. 146). "The second essential condition . . . is this—that the labourer instead of being in the position to sell commodities in which his labour is incorporated, must be obliged to offer for sale as a commodity that very labour-power, which exists only in his living self. For the conversion of his money into capital, therefore, the owner of money must meet in the market with the free labourer, free in the double sense, that as a free man he can dispose of his labour-power as his own commodity, and that on the other hand he has no other commodity for sale, is short of everything necessary for the realisation of his labour-power" (ibid. p. 147).

By means of this complementary institution, simple commodity production had reached the climax of its development. From now onwards it was bound rapidly to pass over into the capitalist method of production. This reversal took place without any change in the law, it was not reflected in the active consciousness of society. Once the system of commodity production was fully developed, no external impetus accounted for its transformation; this was brought about entirely by inherent forces. If at one stage of development economy and law were adequate to one another, if the law was adapted to this particular economic system which it sought to conserve, every further development was bound to lead to discrepancies. It is at this point where we begin to get interested in the development.

4. THE SOCIAL CHARACTER MASK OF THE PERSONA AND THE ECONOMIC FORM OF THE RES

Now no other link exists between man and matter than that of *do ut des:* I give—I take, and of *do ut facias:* I pay—you work. No central will is responsible for the assignation of goods and labour to the various purposes of society, they move as if on their own, in independent circulation.

Just as water constantly changes its physical and geological form (the states of ice, water, and steam, and the geological forms of source, brook, river, sea, and cloud) so does every item wrested from nature and occupied assume specific technical and social forms and functions at every stage of the process of circulation.

And so with man. Like actors appearing to-day in one part, to-morrow in another, the individuals play specific parts in the

total drama of the life of the species.   Each actor wears the
economic character mask suited to the scene in which he appears. [1]
This economic character mask indicates the social function of the
individual in the complete process of social life.

Thus Marxist economics goes right to the core of the actual
process and embraces in its entirety the whole of its immense and
powerful meaning: the life process of the human species.   The
theory of marginal utility and other such theories regard phenomena with the mentality of the isolated individual, from the
economic frog's-eye view; but Marx contemplates the whole of
society and its total wealth, its immense accumulation of goods
and its legions of people in their mutual relations; he regards these
first as static, in a given period, say one year of production, then as
dynamic, in a succession of years of production, during the course
of generations.   The masses of goods appear now as continually
fluctuating, and men as in constant motion.   The feeding of individuals with goods ripe for consumption, for instance, is only a
transitional stage in this process, the goods are not eliminated from
it, they re-appear in the cycle of the species reproduced in labour-
power.   Individual consumption is reproduction of mankind.   If it
be true that mankind exists as a social entity, it is certain that this
process of production and reproduction in its entirety is nothing
but the economic problem itself.   Any so-called individualistic
economic theory, approaching the problem from the point of view
of the individual mentality, may be able to solve problems of
psychology and philosophy, but the economic problem is beyond
the comprehension of such theories. [2]

---

[1] It is evident that the economic part is but one aspect of the individual. A man
who in economic life plays the part of a usurer, for instance, may out of business hours
befriend the arts or even be a philanthropist or a member of an ethical society. Every
psychologist who deserves to be taken seriously comes up against the problem: what
part do economic opportunity and the necessity of usury play in fitting the human
soul to its rôle? and he must detail the characteristics of this "soul of the usurer".
Marx on many occasions gives shrewd analyses of economic character-types, often
with reference to poets such as Balzac and others. There is no doubt that general
human psychology is a presupposition of economics—Marx is not concerned with
this kind of platitude—but quite specific economic systems are presuppositions of
blood feud and feudal fidelity, and give rise to the psychology of usurer, capitalist and
worker.

[2] In regard to subjectivist theories we opine that a comparison of subjectivist and
objectivist methods is misleading. No economist has described the psychology of the
agents of production as subtly as Marx, none has analysed the economic motivations
of individual wills at every stage of production so carefully and shrewdly. Marx takes
the commonplaces of a so-called general theory of individual motivation for granted
and develops a specific theory of individual motivation based upon the specific functions of the individuals which leads to the recognition of definite economic character-
types. His approach is a combination of the subjectivist and objectivist method, a

Within the whole of this process every stage (production, circulation and consumption), and in every stage every element (commodity, natural object and labour) must play a quite specific part which is determined by its relation to the whole of society. In Marx's terminology the form (value-form, capital-form, equivalent-form) [1] is nothing but a given element of the process crystallised as a concept at a certain stage, and the part played by this element in this process is its function. [2]

Thus the money form: "Its specific social function and therefore its social monopoly is to play the part of general equivalent in the world of commodities". And similarly one can cite innumerable dicta regarding other elements of production. [3]

We consider it characteristic of Marx's theses that they show the significance of every element of production (labour-power and power of nature, man and matter, *persona* and *res* of property, in its most derivative forms and combinations in all stages of the process of preserving the species) and describe their function in the social life of mankind. [4]

NOTES, CHAPTER II, SECTION I

(*59*) See the terminological remarks in the Introduction.

(*60*) Renner adopts Savigny's view of the nature of a right as

most lucid correlation of internal and external happenings. But it is more than that, for he proves that every single event, subjective and objective at the same time, is determined by the existence of society, by the social conditioning of man and matter. Marx's method differs from Menger's in that it is not one of individual psychology but of social psychology, though by no means a purely psychological method.

[1] Stammler's distinction of form (law) and matter (economy) transfers the formal element completely into the realm of the law. Yet the purely economic thing (capital) has in fact its definite form before the law becomes concerned with it. A definite amount of money, for instance, the legal character of which is beyond dispute, assumes the economic form of equivalent in an act of exchange, the economic form of capital in a loan transaction, the economic form of means of circulation in the circulating process, and the economic form of hoard in the owner's stocking.

[2] It would be a profitable piece of research to analyse the concepts "form" and "function" to which Marx adheres in his *Capital*, and to demonstrate Marx's theory of form and function, in a separate treatise.

[3] "The different kinds of labour . . . are in themselves, and such as they are, direct social functions, because functions of the family which . . . possesses a spontaneously developed system of division of labour" (*Capital* i, p. 49). Subsequent quotations will show that Marx generally adheres to this terminology.

[4] Recently, there has been much talk about Othmar Spann's universalist theory. This is a play with concepts, while disregarding the substratum, and is therefore neither of philosophical nor of economic value. If special emphasis must be given to universality of approach, Marx's method is *the* universalist method *par excellence*. Our previous expositions have made it crystal clear that he alone conceives of man and matter in their universal relation to the totality of human life.

a power conferred by law (Savigny, *System des heutigen römischen Rechts*, Vol. I, p. 7). This formulation is more in line with the positivist foundation of Renner's thought than Ihering's definition of a right as an interest protected by law (Ihering, *geist des römischen Rechts*, Vol. III, p. 338).

(*61*) For "absolute" right see above, Note 11.

(*62*) It is one of the peculiarities of English land law that it has continued to use a feudal nomenclature for capitalist institutions. That the law recognises ownership in land need hardly be said, but the layman and the beginner are surprised and puzzled by the fact that it should still be called "fee simple".

(*63*) This is not entirely true of English land law. "A legal estate is not capable of . . . being held by an infant" (Law of Property Act, 1925, sect. 1 (6)). The practical importance of this principle is smaller than may appear at first sight. The infant can not be the holder of the legal estate, i.e. the holder of the power to represent the *res* as against outsiders, but he can, of course, be beneficial "owner", holder of an equitable interest. The legal estate is vested in trustees. Corporations are, in this country, incapable of owning land, unless they are enabled to do so by statute (as are all registered companies formed for the acquisition of gain—Companies Act, 1929, sect. 14) or by a special licence in mortmain under the Mortmain and Charitable Uses Act, 1888.

(*64*) Feudal tenure and seisin occupied the place of what is in modern law ownership. The "real actions" were available not to "the owner", but to the person having a better right to the seisin (Pollock and Maitland, l.c. Vol. II, pp. 46 *sq.*; Holdsworth, *Historical Introduction to the Land Law*, pp. 124, 128.) Renner's statement would seem to apply with greater force to English than to German medieval land law (see Gierke, l.c., Vol. II, p. 189).

(*65*) Pollock and Maitland, l.c., Vol. II, p. 75, speak of "a great rule of substantive law" which established "a graduated hierarchy of seisins and of proprietary rights". "Seisin generates a proprietary right—an ownership we may even say—which is good against all who have no better, because they have no older, right. . . . The man who obtains seisin obtains thereby a proprietary right that is good against all who have no older seisin to rely upon. . . . At one and the same moment there may be many persons each of whom is in some sort entitled in fee simple to this piece of land. . . ."

(*66*) For the theory of "divided ownership" and its complex and interesting history see Gierke, l.c., Vol. II, p. 368, and *Genossenschaftsrecht*, Vol. II, p. 163; Vangerow, *Pandeken*, Vol. I, § 302 (pp. 637–638); Dernburg, *Preussisches Privatrecht*, Vol. I,

§ 182 (pp. 446–448); Hedemann, *Die Fortschritte des Zivilrechts im 19. Jahrhundert*, 1930, p. 3. This theory was the result of an attempt to press the feudal institutions of medieval and post-medieval law into the conceptual framework of Roman law and of a misunderstanding of the latter, with the disastrous results of such a process familiar to students of Bracton's theory of possession. The medieval jurist did not find any difficulty in understanding the co-existence of "ownership" rights vested in the lord and his tenants. The Glossators and Post-Glossators misused the Roman distinction between *actio directa* and *actio utilis* to convince themselves that the co-existence of various "ownerships" in land was inherent in Roman law. It was thus that the lord's property right came to be known as *dominium directum* and the tenant's right as *dominium utile*. This distinction found its way into the Austrian Code of 1811, and also into other Codes, e.g. the Prussian Code of 1794. It was one of the minor merits of the French Revolution that owing to its—sometimes belated—influence the doctrine disappeared. It has left no trace in the Code Civil or in the modern German and Swiss Codes. The social phenomena which it tried to explain have been revived in Germany in modern legislation dealing with land settlement and homesteads—institutions which "point" beyond a purely capitalist conception of law.

(*67*) In this country the distinction between *dominium* and *jura in re aliena* is not as clear cut as on the Continent. The usufruct appears as—now, under the Law of Property Act, 1925, equitable—life tenancy, the leaseholder has a "legal estate", the mortgagee was, under the pre-1926 system of conveyancing, the holder of the fee simple, while the mortgagor merely had an "equity of redemption".

(*68*) It may be doubted whether Roman law "invaded" the countries in which it was "received". "Infiltration" might be a more appropriate word. It was "infiltration" in the sense in which the word was sometimes used in the late war. The process was not by any means peaceful, but nevertheless gradual and not "violent". See the survey of the process in Vinogradoff, *Roman Law in Medieval Europe*.

(*69*) The transformation of English law in the 16th, 17th and 18th centuries shows that, without any Reception, a legal system designed to meet the needs of a feudal society, can be adapted to those of commodity production. The most significant development in this country was that of the action of assumpsit which was used in order to create a modern law of contract capable of serving a capitalist economy. See Ames, *Lectures on Legal History*, pp. 129–166, Holdsworth, *History of English Law*, Vol. III, pp. 420–

423, pp. 429–453, Vol. VIII, pp. 1–98, Holmes, *Common Law,* Lecture VII.

(*70*) It has been pointed out in the Introduction that English law is still capable of doing so.

(*71*) This is still true of present English law, although, since 1926, only the fee simple and the leasehold have survived as "legal estates".

(*72*) This process of adaptation was mainly—though not by any means entirely—the result of the development of Equity. It was due to the development of equitable interests in land and in movable property that modern forms of investment became possible. Holdsworth, l.c., Vol. VII, pp. 82 *sq.*, Vol. IV, p. 476.

(*73*) In this respect a study of the use made by Soviet law of institutions developed under capitalism is most instructive. See Schlesinger, l.c., especially pp. 219 *sq.*, also pp. 137–139, 247 *sq.* The institutions of the law of corporations are used for the purposes of nationalisation in this country, e.g. under the Coal Industry Nationalisation Act, 1946.

(*74*) "The house will once again, Mrs. Dombey, be not only in name but in fact Dombey and Son," says Mr. Dombey to his wife after the birth of his son (Dickens, *Dombey and Son* O.U.P. ed. p. 20). In English, as in German, the term "house" is used to connote both the family and the firm. Renner refers to *Haus Schroeder,* Schroeder being the name of a commercial firm which is in the centre of a famous German novel: *Soll und Haben,* by G. Freytag.

(*75*) Had English law been capable of giving effect to the unity of the *universitas rerum,* the law of landlord's and tenant's fixtures, of *fructus naturales* and *fructus industriales* would not be in the confused and unsatisfactory state in which it now is (see *Benjamin on Sale,* 7th ed., pp. 181–200). The arbitrary and sometimes contradictory character of the decisions on what are landlord's and what are tenant's fixtures, and the almost incomprehensible casuistry developed around the questions "what is land?" and "what are goods?" is partly due to the fact that the law paid too much attention to physical connection with the soil and too little to dedication to an economic purpose. English law demonstrates the clash between the legal institution and its economic function more clearly than does French, German, or Swiss law. In these three systems the economic connection between objects dedicated to a common purpose is partly (though probably insufficiently) recognised. See Code Civil Art. 524: "Les objets que le propriétaire d' un fonds y a placés pour le service et l'exploitation de ce fonds, sont immeubles par destination." (This applies, inter alia, to the machines of a factory, though the principal application of the rule is in agriculture.) Similarly the conception of "accessories" in German law (Civil Code §§ 97, 98) and in Swiss law (Civil Code Art. 644).—In this country a contract of sale of land and a conveyance does not comprise these "accessories" (see sect. 62 of the Law of Property Act, 1925).—The Nazi Hereditary Farm Legislation tried to give effect to the "economic unity" of the farm, but this was coupled with the withdrawal of agricultural property from the credit system and with the well-known attempt to create a landless agricultural proletariat (the younger children) for purposes of settlement in conquered territories.

(76) In this country the place of this "share" is taken by the right to participate in the use of the "commons". The enclosure movement contributed to the transformation indicated by Renner.

(77) The Roman conception of the "*hereditas*" as an *universitas rerum* fulfilled Renner's postulate to a certain extent. It did so, however, merely with respect to the passing of property upon death, not with regard to transactions *inter vivos*.

(78) It must, of course, be remembered that any customary modifications of the law of property such as described by Ehrlich, l.c. pp. 486 *sq.*, are from the point of view of Renner's Austinian concept of law not "legal" institutions.

(79) The law of easements and profits *à prendre* cuts across the "isolation" of property objects. This is true of "acquired" as well as "natural" easements. It is true of the right of "ancient lights" as well as of the right of support. It is particularly true of the "way of necessity" the right to which, in this country, arises not by operation of law but as a consequence of an implied grant. All these are, in Renner's view, "complementary" institutions of property which form exceptions to its "isolation". See above, notes 22, 23.

(80) Renner's terminology suggests that he is inclined to adopt the views of Below, *Der deutsche Staat des Mittelalterns*, 1914, who insisted upon the application of the categories of public law to the feudal institutions of the Middle Ages. The "private law" or "public law" nature of feudalism was the object of a keen controversy in Germany. For a summary of the rich literature on the subject, see Below, l.c., pp. 1–112. Gierke was one of Below's principal antagonists. The situation in this country does not easily lend itself to this controversy. "In England, the strength of the monarchy, after the Norman Conquest, succeeded in reducing to very small dimensions the governmental aspect of feudalism; but the strong central court, which effected this result, made the feudal conception of tenure universal in our land law. The strength of the centralised institutions created by the Norman and Angevin kings made the English government the least, and the

English land law the most, feudal of any in Europe" (Holdsworth, *Historical Introduction to the Land Law*, p. 4). Maitland called feudalism "a denial of (the) . . . distinction" between public and private law (Pollock and Maitland, l.c. Vol. I, p. 230).

(*81*) In each of these respects the socialisation of consumption is, in this country, largely carried into effect. For vocational education see Education Act, 1944, s. 43, subs. 1. The county colleges maintained by the local education authorities will have to provide vocational training.

(*82*) Old age pensions, health insurance, and the national health service, are now destined to fulfil this function. National Insurance Act, 1946, and National Health Service Act, 1946. Renner's analysis is useful in that it shows how all this legislation is a belated—though necessary—concomitant of the destruction of the "house" community in the economic sense.

(*83*) Long after the journeyman and the apprentice had ceased to be members of the house community English law was still permeated with the spirit of the Elizabethan Statute of Apprentices of 1563. The Master and Servant Act, 1867, still gave the employer a criminal remedy for breach of contract. It was due to the pressure of the trade unions that the Employers and Workmen Act, 1875, gave full effect to the contractual nature of employment (see Webb, *History of Trade Unionism*, pp. 290 *sq*.). In all legal history there can be few examples of a "time lag" between economic and legal development as striking as this. It is equalled by the survival of the Prussian *"Gesinde-Ordnungen"* (orders referring to agricultural labourers) until 1918, when they were repealed by the first Proclamation of the Council of People's Commissars. See also note 107, below.

(*84*) It is less easily ascertainable in this country than on the Continent. It would overstrain the analogy between English and Continental developments if one were to argue that Edward I's Statute *Quia Emptores* of 1290 (which made land held in fee simple alienable and put an end to sub-infeudation) was the "moment of adaptation". The transformation of land law and of the law of contract was a gradual process extending over centuries. It is nevertheless true that the Statute of 1290 "set in motion a process by which, in course of time, the importance of merely tenurial principles has been immensely decreased" (Holdsworth, *Historical Introduction*, p. 107). In so far as English society ever conformed to the pattern postulated by Renner, this Statute certainly was an important phase in the adaptation of the law to its development.

(*85*) It is probably correct to say that none of the legal developments which, in this country, occurred between the middle of the

18th century (roughly the beginning of the Industrial Revolution) and the publication of the first volume of Marx' *Kapital* in 1867 affected the property concept fundamentally. The most significant enactment in land law from the social point of view was perhaps the Agricultural Holdings Act, 1851, which allowed an agricultural tenant to remove "fixtures". There were statutes of great legal importance such as the Prescription Act, 1833, the legislation of 1834 abolishing real actions and "fines and recoveries" and the Real Property Act, 1845. They facilitated alienation and simplified conveyancing, but they were final stages in the adaptation of land law to the needs of capitalist society (conceived in the reforming spirit of the Benthamite age), not developments away from the traditional property concept. They should be read in the light of Dicey's analysis of the "Period of Benthamism or Individualism" (*Law and Public Opinion in England*, Lecture VI).

(*86*) See for the relevant passage of the Code Civil the quotation in the Introduction.

(*87*) The provisions of the Prussian Code of 1794 were repealed by the Introductory Law to the German Civil Code which came into force on January 1st, 1900.

(*88*) See the quotation, p. 45 of the text.

(*89*) The Italian Code of 1865 might have been mentioned as a parallel enactment.

(*90*) The modifications continued or introduced by legislation outside the Codes themselves should, however, be taken into account. Throughout the 19th century, and especially during the second half of the century, there was, for example in Prussia, a steady stream of legislation restricting alienation and mortgaging by certain types of agricultural smallholders. This legislation remained in force after 1900 (Art. 62 of the Introductory Law to the German Civil Code). It was partly of a political nature—designed to promote the Germanisation of the Polish provinces of Prussia—but it served economic purposes as well.

(*91*) For quotation see the Introduction.

(*92*) This refers to Continental developments. In England the house for one family has, of course, remained far more common than either on the Continent or in the working-class districts of the Scottish cities. This point, however, would not seem to affect Renner's argument: the English working-class house is usually rented and not owned by its inhabitant.

(*93*) Renner thinks of a flat or tenement in Vienna, but could not the same thing be said of one of a long row of working-class houses in the East End of London or in Manchester?

(*94*) Even if we do, we are likely to own little of the "value" of "our" house. In this country Renner's analysis should be read with the paramount importance of the building society mortgage well in mind.

(*95*) Socially this is the least "favourable" case. It is probably more prevalent in Austria than in England.

(*96*) This is as true of England as it is of any Continental city. On both sides of the Channel the powerful movement for the acquisition of allotments has counter-acted this tendency. But this happened after Renner wrote his book.

(*97*) All this happened in this country much earlier than on the Continent. What Renner depicts is the effect of the Industrial Revolution.

(*98*) This would seem to neglect the important phenomenon of the small trader's "goodwill" which, in one form or another, is recognised by most legal systems as a personal asset capable and worthy of protection. The English principles governing the tort of "passing off" and the validity of contracts in restraint of trade are one example, French case law and Austrian and German statute law on unfair competition are others.

(*99*) Renner accepts the labour theory of value in full. It permeates much of his argument, but it does not touch the core of his analysis of the "functional transformation".

(*100*) In this country and in the United States it is certainly true that "public property is governed by the rules of private law". The legal nature of the ownership of the British coal mines remains the same under the Coal Industry Nationalisation Act, 1946, as before. This is not, however, universally true. It is not true in France, where public property is governed by the special principles applicable to *domaine public* (Berthélemy, *Traité Élémentaire du Droit Administratif*, Section III, chap. I). It should be a matter for serious consideration whether the rules of private law with regard to acquisition and alienation ought to remain applicable to nationalised property. Cp. the comments on this passage of Renner's book in the light of Soviet developments in Schlesinger, *Soviet Legal Theory*, p. 28. For the situation in America see Freund, *Administrative Powers over Persons and Property*, p. 8.

(*101*) It is unnecessary to enumerate a catalogue of laws from Town Planning Acts to Factories Acts, from exchange control legislation to agricultural legislation, in order to show that this statement is out of date.

(*102*) See, however, above, Note 63.

(*103*) See above, Note 41.

(*104*) In this respect the history of the Loi Le Chapelier of June 14th, 1791, is most instructive (see Thompson, *The French Revolution*, p. 169). Le Chapelier was moved by a genuine enthusiasm for individual bargaining. Workers' unions were suppressed in the name of liberty, equality, and fraternity. Eight years later Pitt secured the passing of the Combination Act. The ideology was very different indeed, the result much the same. Nothing can more vividly illustrate the contrast between the philosophical and juristic postulates of the Revolution and the reality of the world of facts in which they were translated into legislation.

(*105*) That Renner's remark about the insignificance of legal intervention during the early stages of industrial capitalism can be applied to this country, is obvious to every student of the history of factory legislation (see chaps. I and II in Hutchins and Harrison, *A History of Factory Legislation*). It was the period which Dicey described as the "era of legislative stagnation" (*Law and Public Opinion*, 1926 ed., p. 84).

(*106*) For descriptions see Ashley, *English Economic History*, Vol. I, chap. V; Trevelyan, *English Social History*, chap. I. For the connection with the development of the Poor Law: Jennings, *The Poor Law Code*, 2nd ed., pp. 1–2.

(*107*) The separation of the law of employment from the "law of persons" and the recognition of its contractual nature was, in this country, a very slow process. Blackstone's minute treatment of the law of master and servant in the Law of Persons (Commentaries, Vol. I, chap. 14), should be contrasted with the superficial mention the subject receives in the chapter dealing with contracts (Vol. II, chap. 30). Blackstone's chapter on Master and Servant illustrates the "time lag" between the developments of society and of the law. See also above, Note 83.

(*108*) It should be observed how Renner's description of the sociological background of the "*persona*" conception re-inforces the modern jurisprudential analysis of this concept as a creation of positive law. Both sociological and jurisprudential investigation lead to the result that the term "natural person"—as opposed to "artificial" or "juristic person"—has no place in a modern system of legal thought. It is, in fact, a heritage of the 18th century. Its close link with the natural law theories of the 18th century is shown by the manner in which Blackstone introduced it (1821, ed. Vol. I, p. 129): "Persons are also divided by the law into either natural persons or artificial. Natural persons are such as the God of nature formed us; artificial are such as are created and devised by human laws for the purposes of society and government, which are called corporations or bodies politic".

Section ii. THE DEVELOPMENT OF CAPITALIST PROPERTY
AND THE LEGAL INSTITUTIONS COMPLEMENTARY TO THE
PROPERTY NORM

I. PROPERTY AND THE CONTRACT OF EMPLOYMENT

THE subject-matter of the property-norm is generally an occupied item of nature, a corporeal thing. In its natural form it is technically subservient to man. In so far as it is not ready to be consumed, it is at first raw material or working tool, and in this form it enters the process of production.

The character mask of the property-subject is that of a person owning material goods. At the stage of simple commodity production the owner is at the same time a worker who enjoys the benefits of his labour. All economic character masks which later become distinct from each other, are still united within the same individual. The law which declares this individual "free" from all others, thereby gives him legal personality.

Side by side with the person who is also property-owner, there is the person who, equally free, possesses nothing. Formerly his character mask was that of beggar, he then develops into the legal type of pauper which soon becomes that of worker.

The Spanish beggars of the Middle Ages formed a chevaleresque order, they wore berets, daggers and guitars, they lived on the surplus product of the owners on the strength of the legal title conferred upon them by the Gospel. Since Paradise, labour has been the curse of possessions, but poverty gives a truly divine right to idleness. As we see, it was pleasant and honourable to be a beggar, and this character mask has been preserved till the present day in the venerable figure of the begging friar. But now the day of the lay-beggar is over, the poor are compelled to work; "pauper" and "worker" were still synonymous in the time of Adam Smith.[1] They enter the guild-master's workshop to obtain access to consumer goods. "Capitalist production only then really begins . . . when each individual capital employs simultaneously a comparative large number of labourers. . . . The workshop of the medieval master handicraftsman is simply enlarged" (*Capital* i, p. 311). A larger number of workmen is engaged, and property

---

[1] Man is a person not as a matter of course, but because the law has given him this status. A slave, though he is a man, is not a person. (*108*) on page 103.

which hitherto has fulfilled only the function of detention, suddenly assumes new functions.

a.   Property Becomes Power of Command

Journeymen and apprentices used to live in the master's household. Their relation was in the nature of a subjection determined by public law, on the lines of the Germanic *patria potestas*, which served the purposes of education, training and mastery of the craft, (*109*) and whose function therefore was to ensure the continuity of the working population. This relationship was abolished by the mere force of facts; it was replaced by the private contracts of *do ut facias*. The old regulation of labour is dissolved, and for a while there is no new regulation.

But the property-object (*res*) as it develops into and assumes the functions of capital, itself inaugurates a process of education for the owner no less than for the dispossessed. "We saw in a former chapter, that a certain minimum amount of capital was necessary, in order that the number of labourers simultaneously employed . . . might suffice to liberate the employer himself from manual labour, convert him from a small master into a capitalist, and thus formally to establish capitalist production. . . . We also saw that, at first, the subjection of labour to capital was only a formal result of the fact that the labourer, instead of working for himself, works for and consequently under the capitalist. By the co-operation[1] of numerous wage-labourers, the sway of capital develops into a requisite for carrying on the labour process itself, into a real requisite of production. That a capitalist should command on the field of production, is now as indispensable as that a general should command on the field of battle. . . . The work of directing, superintending and adjusting, becomes one of the functions of capital, from the moment that labour under the control of capital, becomes co-operative. Once a function of capital it acquires special characteristics" (*Capital* i, pp. 320- 1).

What is the essence of this power of command? It is based on contract. But so was the relation of the feudal lord to his vassal, yet this was essentially of a public nature. (*110*)   An element of domination is without doubt implied in this system of super-

---

[1] Marx distinguishes three stages in the development of industrial production: co-operation, manufacture and machinofacture (the factory system) and we shall adhere to his division.

ordination and subordination, and in spite of the form of contract it remains essentially a system of power.

The question is whether this control is still in essence the Germanic medieval *mundium*, that reflection of paternal power. Is it established in favour of the ruled or of the ruling, is it a government of protection or of exploitation? What are its essential features? "The directing motive, the end and aim of capitalist production, is to extract the greatest possible amount of surplus-value, and consequently to exploit labour-power to the greatest possible extent. . . . The control exercised by the capitalist is not only a special function, due to the nature of the social labour-process, and peculiar to that process, but it is, at the same time, a function of the exploitation of a social labour-process, and is consequently rooted in the unavoidable antagonism between the exploiter and the living and labouring raw material he exploits. . . . Moreover, the co-operation of wage-labourers is entirely brought about by the capital that employs them. Their union into one single productive body and the establishment of a connexion between their individual functions, are matters foreign and external to them, are not their own act, but the act of the capital that brings and keeps them together. Hence the connexion existing between their various labours appears to them, ideally, in the shape of a pre-conceived plan of the capitalist, and practically in the shape of the authority of the same capitalist, in the shape of the powerful will of another, who subjects their activity to his aims" (ibid. pp. 321-2).

In the eyes of the law, the property-subject is related to the object only, controlling matter alone. But what is control of property in law, becomes in fact man's control of human beings, of the wage-labourers, as soon as property has developed into capital. The individual called owner sets the tasks to others, he makes them subject to his commands and, at least in the initial stages of capitalist development, supervises the execution of his commands. (*III*) The owner of a *res* imposes his will upon *personae*, autonomy is converted into heteronomy of will.

Capital extends its scale, it expands beyond the sphere of the capitalist's personal control. "Just as at first the capitalist is relieved from actual labour, . . . so now, he hands over the work of direct and constant supervision, . . . to a special kind of wage labourer. . . . The work of supervision becomes their established and exclusive function" (ibid. i, p. 322).

We see that the right of ownership thus assumes a new social function. Without any change in the norm, below the threshold of collective consciousness, a *de facto* right is added to the personal absolute domination over a corporeal thing. This right is not based upon a special legal provision. It is the power of control, the power to issue commands and to enforce them. (*111*) The inherent urge of capital to beget constantly further capital provides the motive for this *imperium*.

This power of control is a social necessity, but at the same time it is profitable to the owners—it establishes a rule not for the purpose of protection but for the purpose of exploitation, of profit.

The subordination of the workers which at the same time effects their mutual co-ordination, (*112*) is a corresponding phenomenon. Is this co-ordination also based on contract? The workers are not asked whether their neighbour appeals to them, yet they are forced into close proximity and in this way they become united into an association of workers. (*113*) What is it that brings about this passive association of the workers? [1] What is it that correlates their functions and shapes them into a unified productive body? There is no doubt that these workers who contribute partial operations form a compulsory association according to all rules of legal doctrine. (*114*)

This association receives its individuality from the capital that collects the workers in one place and keeps them there. Just as the law is the norm for the citizens, so the plan, the plan of production, is the abstract and impersonal norm for this compulsory association, supported by the ultimate and most concrete authority of the capitalist, the power of an alien will. (*116*) Supervision is delegated to special functionaries, and thus relations of super-ordination and subordination are made into an organic whole.

Thus the institution of property leads automatically to an organisation similar to the state. Power over matter begets personal power. "It is not because he is a leader of industry that a man is a capitalist; on the contrary, he is a leader of industry because he is a capitalist. The leadership of industry is an attribute of capital, just as in feudal times the functions of general and judge were attribute of landed property" (ibid. i, p. 323).

---

[1] There has scarcely been any investigation of the legal nature of these associations which are essentially determined by compulsion and yet based upon free contract. A great change has been made in this respect by the law relating to Works Councils, where the attempt has been made to treat the community of the workshop on the lines of a corporation of public law. (*115*)

We see that even at the first stage of capitalism, that of co-operation, the old microcosm is replaced by a new one which derives its unity from capital, which here is the aggregate of the technical means of production, i.e. objects of ownership. These new organisations bring about a gradual transformation of man and matter, without any norm imposed by the state.

b.   Property Assumes the Function of Organisation

Industrial progress develops co-operation into primitive manu-facture. The differentiation of labour is reflected in the labour product. "The commodity, from being the individual product of an independent artificer, becomes the social product of a union of artificers, each of whom performs one, and only one, of the constituent partial operations" (pp. 328–9). "Individual" "private" property creates "unions of artificers" without regard to their wishes, without leave from the authorities; it lessens their personal freedom, and debases their inherited skill to the con-tinuous performance of partial operations. Such property encroaches upon the division of labour which has existed for centuries, on the one hand combining crafts that formerly were separated, on the other hand dissolving formerly undifferentiated crafts into individual partial operations.

". . . its final form is invariably the same—a productive mechanism whose parts are human beings" (p. 329). ". . . each workman becomes exclusively assigned to a partial function, . . . and for the rest of his life his labour power is turned into the organ of this detail function" (ibid. p. 330).

Property increasingly fulfils the function of capital, encroaching in actual fact on that freedom which in the eyes of the law is universal, by assigning to every individual a specific and strictly differentiated social function. As its subject-matter is concentrated into a microcosm or macrocosm of goods, property concentrates the workers and at the same time differentiates their work, it appropriates specialised labour to each of its constituent parts and it thus converts the labourer into an organ of capital for the whole of his life-time. Further, Marx shows that: "Manufacture, in fact, produces the skill of the detail labourer, by reproducing, and systematically driving to an extreme within the workshop, the naturally developed differentiation of trades, which is found ready to hand in society at large. On the other hand, the conversion of fractional work into the life calling of one man, corresponds to the tendency shown by earlier societies, to make trades hereditary . . . to petrify them into castes. . . . Castes and guilds arise from the action of the same natural law, that regulates the differentiation of plants and animals into species and varieties, except that, when a certain degree of development has been reached, the heredity of castes and the exclusiveness of guilds are ordained as a law of society" [1] (ibid. i, p. 331).

The evolution of the property object gives to property the power to create separate species within the *genus homo*, a power like that of an Egyptian king who establishes castes; yet the lawyer does not take cognisance of this supreme power. The evolution of property develops its special "hierarchy of labour-powers" (*Capital* i, p. 342), but this is a hierarchy for which no Canon Law has been developed by the experts.

The division of labour within the workshop, brought about by the system of manufacture, is established by the control of the employer who is the capitalist, at the very same time as free competition leads to an automatic and anarchic general division of labour within society among the employers. Therefore the owners and the dispossessed are organised according to two contrasting principles. "The division of labour in the workshop implies concentration of the means of production in the hands of one capitalist; the division of labour in society implies their dispersion among many independent producers of commodities. . . . Division of labour within the workshop implies the undisputed authority of the capitalist over men, that are but parts of a mechanism that belongs to him. The division of labour within the society brings into contact independent commodity-producers, who acknowledge no other authority but that of competition" (ibid. i, p. 349). "The same bourgeois mind which praises division of labour in the work-shop, life-long annexation of the labourer to a partial operation, and his complete subjection to capital as being an organisation of labour that increases its productiveness . . . denounces with equal vigour every conscious attempt to socially control and regulate the process of production, as an inroad upon such sacred things as the rights of property. . . . It is very characteristic that the enthusiastic apologists of the factory system have nothing more damning to urge against a

---

[1] We would draw our readers' attention to the confrontation of natural and social law which is so typical of this method of Karl Marx.

general organisation of the labour of society, than that it would turn all society into one immense factory. . . . In a society with capitalist production, anarchy in the social division of labour and despotism in that of the workshop are mutual conditions the one of the other" (ibid. p. 350).

We see that two "societies" are superimposed here, as they were in the feudal period. Compulsory associations according to factory law, the "copy-holders" of capital, form the base, the free market communities of owners form the higher stratum and above all stands the bureaucracy governed by the law of administration. (*117*) We are reminded of old times when the peasant lived according to manorial law, the owner of an allodium according to land law and the vassal according to feudal law. (*118*)

c. Property Dissolves the Old Social Order

The evolution of property does not rest, it is like a Chronos who devours—other people's children. The system of manufacture which as yet has no knowledge of machinery develops into the factory system (machinofacture). The property-object now absorbs not only physical but also intellectual labour, for it employs the brain worker. Just as muscular power is embodied in the labour-product, as it must be embodied if a tangible object is to achieve citizenship in the world of commodities, so the inventor's genius must be materialised, it must be embodied in the machine. And since this world is ruled by private property, the machine is forced into the Caudian forks, into the service of capitalism—it must become an object of property and in this capacity a value which begets surplus value. And were not the owners of the manufacturing enterprises entitled to appropriate the results of science? Had they not first dissolved muscular labour into mechanical functions, degrading man to a machine, so that later on he should learn to make machines?

Whereas during the period of manufacture, the traditional simple means of production, the legal 'res' confronted labour-power as ruling capital, large scale industry separated scientific labour from nanual labour, embodying the former in the machine, a concrete object of property. It is industry on a large scale "which makes science a productive force distinct from labour and presses it into the service of capital" (*Capital* i, p. 355). Our inventors of genius were foolish to imagine that labour-saving machines would diminish the suffering of mankind. No doubt it should have been so, for the machine really does save labour. How could the result have been different? But then—the machine became property, an object of ownership, and consequently assumed social functions at once. Would these be new functions, as the *res* was of a new kind?

"In its specific capitalist form . . . manufacture is but a particular method . . . of augmenting at the expense of the labourer the self-expansion of capital. . . . It increases the social productive power of labour . . . for the benefit of the capitalist instead of for that of the labourer. . . . It creates new conditions for the lordship of capital over labour" (ibid., p. 359).

The organisation of the control of labour by property had not been perfected. Artisans skilled in their trades still opposed their reduction to detailed functions of the productive mechanism. "Order was wanting in manufacture and 'Arkwright [1] created order' " (*Capital* i, p. 362). [2] The worker was still a master of labour, the labour process was centred around him, and the finished raw material, the tools which he employed, were means to an end. The inanimate property-object did not yet completely rule over the work of flesh and blood, "order was wanting". But now the *res* is transformed into the machine, into the automaton. "The automaton itself is the subject, and the workmen are merely conscious organs, co-ordinate with the unconscious organs of the automaton, and together with them, subordinated to the central moving-power" (ibid. p. 419).

Lo and behold! paradise grows out of chaos. "In these spacious halls the benignant power of steam summons around him his myriads of willing menials" [2] (ibid. i, p. 419).

"In handicrafts and manufacture, the workman makes use of a tool, in the factory the machine makes use of him. . . . In manufacture the workmen are parts of a living mechanism. In the factory we have a lifeless mechanism independent of the workman, who becomes his mere living appendage. . . . Every kind of capitalist production . . . has this in common, that it is not the workman that employs the instruments of labour, but the instruments of labour that employ the workman. But it is only in the factory system that this inversion for the first time acquires technical and palpable reality. By means of its conversion into an

---

[1] Arkwright, the inventor of the spinning machine.
[2] Ure, quoted by Marx.

automaton, the instrument of labour confronts the labourer, during the labour-process, in the shape of capital, of dead labour,[1] that dominates, and pumps dry, living labour-power. The separation of the intellectual powers of production from the manual labour, and the conversion of those powers into the might of capital over labour, is, as we have already shown, finally completed by modern industry erected on the foundation of machinery" (ibid. pp. 422–3).

The kind of subject-matter which is the object of the property-norm is irrelevant to the legal definition of property. One object is as good as another. The norms which make up the institution of property are neutral like an algebraic formula, for instance the formula of acceleration. But if one factor in this formula of acceleration is the avalanche, everybody is crushed, and if one factor in the property-norm which makes a person the owner of a thing, is the machine, generations are devoured. The development of machinery abolished the technical foundation for the division of labour which manufacture had brought about. Its typical hierarchy of specialised labourers was consequently replaced by a tendency to equalise labour, or to level it down in the mechanised factory. (*119*)

The artisan guarded the skill of his craft as his own "mystery"; his qualified and specialised labour was his social power, his pride, his bread. In comparison with this, the instruments of labour had scarcely any social significance. Albrecht Duerer's study was not very different from the workshop of a master house-painter. The worker of the manufacturing period was still an individualised worker, though capital in its initial stages made him join a co-operating group. Now capital blots out every individual trait, moral as well as technical. "Thus we see that machinery, while augmenting the human material that forms the principal object

---

[1] Dead labour is the result of previous work performed by living workmen. When this has materialised in the form of a concrete object, it is taken away from the worker and appropriated by the capitalist in his capacity of owner of material objects. Each labour product is, as it were, living labour in preserved condition, to be subsequently employed again and thus revived. The difference between manufacture and the factory system can also be described in the following terms: manufacture correlates various simultaneous labour processes, but the factory system correlates past and present labour processes in their order of time. The worker in the machine shop made looms, the worker in the spinning shop made yarns. To this product—dead labour— the weaver adds his work and produces textiles. Past labour does not immediately become related to present labour, looms and yarns are first appropriated by the capitalist whose own means of production they are, and thus they become instruments of control over living labour. It should be added that in every enterprise both principles are at work together; the decisive factor is which one is predominant.

of capital's exploiting power, at the same time raises the degree of exploitation" (ibid. i, p. 392). "Taking the exchange of commodities as our basis, our first assumption was that capitalist and labourer met as free persons. . . . But now the capitalist buys children and young persons under age. Previously, the workman sold his own labour-power, which he disposed of nominally as a free agent. Now he sells wife and child. He has become a slave dealer" (ibid. p. 393).

This piece of property called the machine, this organism of property-objects called the factory, are substituted, though only temporarily, for another legal institution, they take over the functions of paternal and conjugal power.[1] (*120*)

The evolution of property makes the *res* in the owner's hand "into systematic robbery of what is necessary for the life of the workman" (ibid. p. 426), it converts the property-object, machine, "the instrument of labour" into "a competitor of the workman himself" (ibid. p. 430), and into a powerful weapon of war for the repression of periodical revolts committed by workers against the autocracy of capital (ibid. p. 432), leading to "the economical paradox, that the most powerful instrument for shortening labour-time, becomes the most unfailing means for placing every moment of the labourer's time and that of his family, at the disposal of the capitalist for the purpose of expanding the value of his capital" (ibid. p. 406). (*121*)

Now we understand the implications of the general power of disposal which the legislator has given to the owner, we understand what it means that a person should have an all-embracing right over a corporeal object. But we are still far from our goal, for we have considered the *res* only at a certain stage, that of production, and only in a special form of economy. We adopt Marx's concise description of one function fulfilled by this legal institution:

"The technical subordination of the workman . . ., the peculiar composition of the body of workpeople . . ., give rise to a barrack discipline which . . . fully develops this before mentioned labour of overlooking. . . . The factory code in which capital formulates, like a private legislator, and at his own good

---

[1] The first restrictions to be imposed by society on property are in respect of this function, for it is the first to become evidently anti-social, it militates against the functions of ensuring maintenance of the population and leads to depopulation. The venerable paternal and conjugal power, established for a thousand years, becomes a curse to the wife and children whom it should protect.

will, his autocracy over his workpeople, unaccompanied by that division of responsibility, in other matters so much approved of by the bourgeoisie . . . [1] (*122*) is but the capitalist caricature of that social regulation of the labour process which becomes requisite in co-operation on a great scale, and in the employment in common, of instruments of labour and especially of machinery. The place of the slave driver's lash is taken by the overlooker's book of penalties" (*Capital* i, pp. 423-4).

At this stage it is useful to realise the original implications of the institution of property: it is not a mere order of goods. It is just in respect of the deliberate planned social distribution of goods that it first abdicates. It merely protects him who has possession by virtue of an unassailable title, but it does not distribute goods according to a plan. Contrast with this the law of property of the feudal epoch. How richly diversified was its catalogue of *jura in rem*. The property law of bourgeois society leaves the order of the goods to the goods themselves. It is only thus that they become commodities and capital, only thus that they organise themselves and accumulate in accordance with the specific laws of capitalist circulation. At this stage we see already that this anonymous and anarchical regulation of "goods" becomes control over men in their capacity as potential labour. We also see that in our time this factual regulation of "goods" presumes to dictate the social regulation of power and labour. We see further that this regulation of power and labour remains concealed to the whole of bourgeois legal doctrine which is aware of nothing but its most formal, general and extraneous limitations, viz. its foundation on the contract of employment. [2] (*123*)

Wage labour is a relation of autocracy with all the legal characteristics of despotism. The factory is an establishment (*125*) with its own code with all the characteristics of a legal code. It contains

---

[1] Special attention should be paid to Marx's mode of expression. It is excellent legal terminology. It shows that Marx must have thought out most precisely the mutual influences between law and economy.

[2] In the 25 years after the first publication of this study, especially after the World War, noticeable progress has been made and legal doctrine has taken an interest in the investigation of the relations of labour, though results are still inadequate. The relations of superordination and of subordination, the criminal code of the factory in particular, have not been fully appraised. Investigators of writ have raised the law relating to labour to the rank of a special study and some universities have established special professorships for it. The above references were fully justified 25 years ago when they were written, now they apply only to those "civil lawyers" who do not acknowledge the law relating to labour and to economics as independent sciences and disciplines, regarding them as illegitimate intruders. The main progress of legal doctrine in the last quarter of the century lies in the development of these two branches of learning. (*124*)

norms of every description, not excluding criminal law, and it establishes special organs and jurisdiction. (*126*) Labour regulations and the conventions valid within economic enterprises deserve just as well to be treated as legal institutions as the manorial law of the feudal epoch. This, too, was based upon private rule, upon the will of a Lord, one manorial custom differing from another only in details. Even if this difference had been so fundamental as to exclude all understanding and exposition on a common basis—and this cannot even be imagined—these institutions would still remain an integral part of the legal system of that period. The same applies to factory law, the general regulations of labour in economic enterprises. No exposition of our legal order can be complete without it, it regulates the relations of a large part of the population. If material differences were to prevent a general exposition, there would still remain the fundamental problem of the intrinsic nature of this right.

d. Property Becomes Control over Strangers

Once we have raised this question, all the fictions of bourgeois legal doctrine disappear, above all the distinction between public and private law. (*127*) The right of the capitalist is delegated public authority, conferred indiscriminately upon the person who will use it for his own benefit. The employment relationship is an indirect power relationship, a public obligation to service, like the serfdom of feudal times. It differs from serfdom only in this respect, that it is based upon contract, not upon inheritance. (*128*) No society has yet existed without a regulation of labour peculiar to it, the regulation of labour being as essential for every society as the digestive tract for the animal organism. The period of simple commodity production when in fact the working *persona*, the instruments of labour and the labour product merged into one another, was the only period in which the process of production and reproduction, the very life process of society, was independent of social consciousness. As an individual process, it remained private, not revealing any underlying correlations of power and labour. The co-operative labour-process, however, is social; in its very essence it cannot be private. The contents of the right have assumed a public nature, though legal doctrine still conceives of it in terms of private law. (*129*)

During Karl Marx's life-time the capitalist is still in full control, legislative, executive and judiciary, of his enterprise. (*130*) His power contains all the elements of state absolutism, mitigated only by the fact that it is founded upon a contract which can be dissolved by notice. Up to this period capital knows no "separation of powers". This purely legal limitation, however, becomes illusory, as soon as we conceive of capitalists and wage labourers confronting each other as classes. If we accept this, it becomes evident at once that the worker, though he can exchange one individual capitalist for another, cannot escape from the Capitalist. (*131*) There is no doubt that in the sphere of production the bourgeoisie as a class has absolute control of the non-propertied classes as far as the law is concerned. Restrictions of their power in fact are imposed only by bourgeois self-interest and fear of the "subjects of steam power". Such is the position at the height of capitalist development.

Since no society can live without the eternal and natural necessity of labour, it is a naïve conception that any society could exist without a regulation of labour, an organised power of disposal over the whole of its available labour-power. It is exclusively the merit of Marx to have discovered this hidden regulation of labour within bourgeois society, to have explored its nature and to have analysed its functions. The "natural laws" of society which normally achieve this regulation within capitalist society are sufficient only so long as labour-power remains actually chained to the *res*.

If a revolt of the workers loosens these chains, society throws off its mask of torpor. It suddenly becomes conscious of its mission to regulate labour. Then it applies direct and authoritative measures of coercion against labour in the form of laws. (*132*) "In the ordinary run of things, the labourer can be left to the 'natural laws' of 'production' " (ibid. i, p. 761). But whenever these laws fail, bourgeois legislation has recourse to direct force outside the economic field. [1] So, above all, at the stage of primitive accumulation. [2] It was only upon the completion of the capitalist order of economy that the wage-regulating laws were repealed. (*133*) "They were an absurd anomaly, since the capitalist regulated his factory by private legislation" (ibid. p. 764). The machine was Lycurgus, Draco and Solon at the same time, it converted labour into the actual appendage of capital, its psychological embodi-

[1] Note again the precise legal terminology.
[2] Ibid. Chapter XXVI.

ment, just as a building is an appendage of an estate in the eyes of the law. Occasionally the capitalist, that psychological incarnation of capital, even unblushingly asserts the proprietary rights of capital over labour-power" (ibid. p. 587). "I allow that the workers are not a property, not the property of Lancashire and the masters; but they are the strength of both; they are the mental and trained power which cannot be replaced for a generation; the mere machinery which they work might much of it beneficially be replaced, nay improved, in a twelvemonth. Encourage or allow (!) the working power to emigrate, and what of the capitalist?" (Potter, quoted by Marx, ibid. p. 588). Capital demands no less than that public authority should maintain the labour which it has appropriated, even if, owing to lack of raw material, the machines stand idle. It demands that the state should store labour in the work-houses, capital's general public reserve dumps. (*134*) If ever labour remembers its personal freedom in fields where it is manifest even to the most stupid brain that work is a function of the social body (e.g. in the railway industry or the provision trade), if labour makes use of this freedom by strike, then the bourgeoisie makes labour a military institution or replaces free labour by a labour organisation on military lines, achieving a direct socialisation of labour.[1]

New functions thus accrue to the legal character "person" who also has the economic character "proprietor". Now he regulates labour, ruling and exploiting. Property, from a mere title to dispose of material objects, becomes a title to power, and as it exercises power in the private interest, it becomes a title to domination.

At the same time the free person, the labourer with no property, becomes a subject *sui generis*, as history does not repeat itself. Among all those who have the power and are destined to be his master, he may choose the master who most appeals to him, but as a class the subjects are chained to the class of the masters.

We see that property at the stage of simple commodity production endows the worker with the detention of his means of production, making man the master of matter. Now property changes its function without a corresponding change in the law. It gives the legal detention of the means of production to the individuals who do not perform any labour, making them thus the masters of

---

[1] This is especially true in times of war as is shown by the laws relating to military and public services. (*135*)

labour. Property automatically takes over the function of regulating power and labour, and it becomes a private title to domination. The law endows this non-worker with the legal detention of the means of production, but in any society only the worker can actually hold them, as he must have them in his hands in order to work with them. Thus the law, by means of a complementary institution, the contract of service, takes actual detention away from the owner. The worker may mind the machine, but he must pay the price of submitting himself to exploitation. A permanent state of war between legal and actual detention is thus established. (*136*)

2.   THE MOST RECENT DEVELOPMENT OF PROPERTY AND LABOUR

A generation and a half have passed away since the death of Karl Marx, two generations since the first publication of *Das Kapital*. Yet his analysis of the transformation of property not only gives a complete picture of the phase which it had reached in his days, it extends much further.   Nevertheless, contemporary development, which has by no means remained static, has overtaken Marx's analysis and again transformed the substratum of the norms. Above all, much has matured which at the time of Marx could only be seen in its initial stages.   These two generations, however, have changed the world of norms much more than the world of the substratum. Although exposition and explanation of this transformation of norms is beyond the scope of this enquiry, we endeavour to outline it briefly in order to achieve a clearer understanding. (*137*)

"The most surprising fact is the lack of social observation. Millions of people live among changing conditions, they daily feel their practical impacts, yet their theoretical implications do not become conscious to them.   They think in concepts of a by-gone generation." [1]

In order to illustrate this transformation, as well as the contradictions implied in our social order, we consider the following two examples.

Upon its enclosed estate there stands the manor house of the old noble family, and the peasant's farm is surrounded by his own land.   Property is distinctly fenced off, notice-boards announce that it is "private" and that "trespassers will be prosecuted".   In

[1] Karl Renner: *Marxismus, Krieg und Internationale*, 2nd ed. Stuttgart, 1918, p. 51

contrast, let us consider the most striking example of modern development, a privately owned railway. We enter the station hall, but though this is registered property like the manor and the farm, it does not even come into our minds that we have entered somebody else's property. No one enquires who is the owner, his identity has become a matter of indifference. We go to the booking office. There, the lawyers assure us, we conclude a contract for a *facere*, not for a *dare*. But nobody else thinks of it in this way. (*138*) We get our ticket which the other party is obliged to give us, (*139*) there is no trace of bargaining, of freedom of contract, of conditions and terms; published bye-laws fix everything in advance. (*140*) We board the train and do not think for a split second that we have hired Mr. X.'s private vehicle, though lawyers may still construe it in this way. We know that we have acquired the privilege, conferred upon us by public law, to make use of a public utility, against payment of the usual fee which is also fixed or confirmed by public law, and that we have thus submitted ourselves to the public regulations of the bye-laws. The owner, Mr. X., has no significance whatever in any of these proceedings and more than that, he remains outside the sphere of our consciousness.

In the first case the substratum and the norm coincide at least as regards the main aspect. One's own property is clearly distinguished from that of other persons, property appears as what it is: as private. In the second case, on the other hand, property has become everybody's own; the owner himself, if he books a ticket for a journey, is now like a stranger. As far as the economic and social function of the *res* is concerned, the legal owner has become completely irrelevant. Yet he continues to perform an invisible part with which we shall have to deal later on.

In this instance it has become evident that private property has been transformed into a public utility, though it has not become public property. The old peasant farm and the old manor are nothing of the kind. This example leads us to suspect that rights of ownership have outgrown the limitations of private law. In this particular case this is so evident that even the law takes cognisance of it, by creating a number of norms, public and private, which convert property into a public utility. (*141*) The private character of property has been forced into the background by complementary institutions of public law.

But these new norms, which, as we have stressed repeatedly, belong to another branch of research, could not accomplish more than to give a precise legal form to what had existed in the world of facts long before they intervened. The specific features of a public utility were established in the substratum before the norm got hold of them. In innumerable other cases this change within the substratum has not been recognised or admitted, though property indeed advertises its new character of a public utility. (*142*) The cobbler's shop advertises itself as a "shoe-repairing service", thus declaring that the whole public acquires the right to its services against payment of the scheduled fee. This kind of shop sign is more than a joke, thousands of similar signs express a new public opinion vis-à-vis a gradual creation of new law. It is the profession of lawyers to disregard and deny this; for this very purpose they have been led for years through the labyrinth of Roman Law. (*143*) But let us leave the cobbler. We give our soiled linen to a laundering establishment and get their receipt in exchange. The two contracting parties, as a rule, do not even know each other's name, they never see each other. It is a mere fiction that a private "contract" is here agreed on, though it might be so "construed". (*144*) A peasant farm adjoining that mentioned in our example above may have become a dairy and thus an establishment that owes to the public certain services against payment of specified and advertised fees. The transformation of private property into public utility is completed in form as well, as soon as the licensing authorities make it obligatory to serve everybody and to exhibit a tariff of charges. (*145*) But even without this, public opinion regards every owner of such an establishment as under a legal obligation. (*146*) Private property has now become accessible to everyone, it is put at everybody's disposal. I think that this change is remarkable enough. During the war this already existing trend of development has suddenly become strikingly apparent. The sovereign owner of private property has suddenly, by one stroke of the pen, been converted into a subject who has public duties. The landowner must cultivate his land or some other person seizes it for cultivation, (*147*) he must sell, he must charge the controlled price instead of the market price, he must dispatch his corn to the railway or mill, and so forth.

All of a sudden it becomes apparent to us that property has developed into public utility. [1]

---

[1] The tenement house of the big city has long been an establishment in this sense of the term. It is property which in fact is meant for the use of other people (*Fremdtum*). The laws relating to rent do not keep pace with this development. (*148*)

This is an indication of the trend of the future development of legislation. It will not only shamefacedly hint at this new character of property by complementary institutions, the norm itself will openly reveal it, and all property-units which to-day already have become the substratum of public utility, will accordingly become establishments of public law. This is the first unavoidable step towards nationalisation of private property. Even more striking is the development which has taken place at the other pole of society, that of labour. It was not in vain that the workers, thrown together by the capitalists into compulsory associations, were in revolt for fifty years. According to Marx, and in fact during his life-time, the capitalist hired the individual worker on the labour market for a wage that was individually agreed and took him into the workshop. The labour relation in its entirety was based upon individual regulation. But to-day the position is different, thanks to a century of struggle.

The prospective employee registers with a labour exchange, which is either a private establishment or run by the state, a municipality or a trade union. (*149*) He is assigned to a job by rote. This state of affairs is unintelligible in an economy based upon freedom of contract, which can explain it no more than pure science can explain the working of a typewriter, which is a technical product. If the worker is accepted, at terms which are fixed beforehand and scarcely mentioned, he goes on the job. Formerly based upon contract, the labour relationship has now developed into a "position", just as property has developed into public utility. If a person occupies a "position", this means that his rights and duties are closely circumscribed, the "position" has become a legal institution in character much like the fee of feudal times. (*150*)   The "position" comprises the claim to adequate remuneration (settled by collective agreement or works rule), (*151*) the obligation to pay certain contributions (for trade unions and insurance), (*152*) the right to special benefits (sickness, accident, old age, death) and finally certain safeguards against loss of the position or in case of its loss. (*153*)

What is the meaning of this development from the contract of employment to the position of work and service? The private contract, by means of the complementary institutions of collective agreement, labour exchanges, social insurance and the like, has become an institution of public law. It is still largely determined by the private will of the individuals concerned, yet this influence

5

is continually decreasing, and the state element is almost of greater importance than the private element, the collective element more important than the individual element. (*154*) It predominates to-day, when the job is becoming the "established position". The development of the law gradually works out what is socially reasonable. Labour, in fact, never is and never was a merely private affair, it has always been public service. Only an economic science unrelated to the state has transformed and disfigured the social necessity of labour into the private pleasure of individual capitalists and workers whose relations are established by acts of exchange.

Yet it is true that this development to "establishment" and "position" has affected only a part of property and labour and even this only partially. The fundamental character of society is undergoing a process of change. The ultimate direction of this change is clearly determined and its results are unequivocal, but they have neither undergone theoretical analysis, nor have they entered common consciousness. Human society, unconscious or only half conscious of its own needs, drags itself forward, driven on by obscure urges. The achievements of the second half of the century, at which we have here been able only to hint, are so predominantly a change of norms that they need special exposition.

3. PROPERTY AND CONTRACTS OF ALIENATION

At the stage of simple commodity production, the city-dwelling owner's way of life is no longer one of closed domestic economics. Not only does he sell occasional surplus products but he works with a view to selling his produce. Even at this period the contracts of alienation are the complementary legal institutions for this method of economy.

But he sells only his own produce, he owns the means of production as his patrimony and as a rule, as an agriculturist, he produces even his raw material. The sale of his produce is nothing but the short final stage of his own long labours. From a modern point of view we would say that the sale serves mainly to realise the wage for his labour. If it were permissible to apply the later category of wages to this earlier period, we could briefly say that alienation is essentially realisation of the wage and that price is only wage in disguise. This is the function of alienation. But it is not wage only that is realised.

Production in most cases is immediate production for customers. As the product is directly transferred to the consumer, its whole value is realised in one transaction, and alienation thus realises the full results of labour. This establishes the distributing function of property at this period. The great advantage of property at this time is that it distributes the total annual labour product among the workers automatically and strictly in accordance with the labour involved. The order of distribution remains below the threshold of collective consciousness and is anonymous exactly like the order of labour. This automatic distribution by the institution of property, however, requires a host of complementary legal institutions, especially the large number of those institutions which regulate alimentation as between parents and children, husband and wife, descendants and ascendants; furthermore as between guilds and impoverished masters, and their widows and orphans; and many other institutions; and, finally, the provisions of the Poor Law. These institutions transferred to non-workers wholly or part-ly the surplus over the labourers' requirements for self-preserva-tion. Yet the full proceeds were in fact, though not by law, at first in the workers' own hands. In no society was there, nor could there have been, a right to the full proceeds of one's work, for at least the growing and the departing generations have to live on the labourers' produce. Surplus labour is a general social necessity and therefore it is not only in a capitalist society that it obtains. Necessary labour is a category not only of the capitalist system but of every system, for it represents the minimum of work necessary for the physical reproduction of the workers, whereas surplus labour is in most cases intended to provide for society a fund of reserve and accumulation. In capitalist society, on the other hand, it is leisure time for one class only that is produced; this is brought about by transforming the whole life-time of the masses into work-ing time, the workers doing extra work not directly for the whole of society but for the owners of the means of production, for private individuals. The social fund of accumulation and reserve is to-day appropriated by private individuals.

a. Older Types of Alienation

If realisation of the labour-product is the material function of property and of its alienation, the question arises, in which legal forms this alienation is carried out. In the beginning this is not done in the forms of the contract of sale. The customer bespeaks the work and may also supply the material; the act-in-the-law concerned is a sub-species of the contract of hiring (*locatio conductio*), viz. the contract of "work and labour" (*locatio conductio operis*), whereas it is the other sub-species, the contract of labour or employment (*locatio conductio operarum*) that is destined to become the typical act-in-the-law of the proletariat. (*155*) The fact that the price of the commodity is wage in essence though not in form, is brought to light by the legal construction where the artisan or peasant supplies the raw material but sells it (as is natural in a system of production direct for customers) to order only: the contract here is one for goods to be manufactured by the seller, (*156*) and forms the transition from the hiring of labour to the contract of sale. Sale of goods becomes the typical legal institution of the period of simple commodity production, (*157*) only when the raw material for the work is kept in store and the finished product is alienated without having previously been ordered. It is only in this type of contract that the wage-element of the price disappears from the legal form of the transaction, the price now being the equivalent of material and labour together. It is only in these circumstances that the price appears as the mere equivalent for the thing itself, the equivalent for labour having vanished in the eyes of the lawyers and consequently in the common run of economic thought which can never distinguish between legal form and economic substratum. Yet at this period the connection remains obvious, in spite of the legal form which disguises it, for the market remains local and easy to survey, likewise the number of producers. In spite of the price form, simple commodity production remains, from an economic point of view, production for customers. The social functions of property, especially that of distribution, remain the same, though a new complementary institution, (*emptio-venditio*) is beginning to serve it.

b.   The Contract of Sale and its Economic Function

The twin institutions of property and contract of sale, however, completely change in character as soon as the manufacturer or factory-owner takes his place in this legal relationship. The person changes his character mask, and the object changes its economic form.

During the process of production, the owner assumes a mask,

increasingly severe, sinister, and in the end almost despotic. Now as he leaves the intimidating and gloomy factory with his wares, his features unwrinkle, they become bland, modest and agreeable. The man who stands in the market with his goods, though the same person, now wears a disguise that changes his appearance beyond recognition, that of a "guardian of commodities". Every recollection of that lower sphere of production, the sphere of exploitation, of the *do ut facias*, of despotism, has vanished from the thoughts of the man, and the appearance of the commodity reveals no traces of it. The capitalist has now become, as the guardian of commodities, a republican, an equal amongst equals. He has dealings with his own kind only, with other guardians of commodities. It is true that at first as a vendor he is confronted by the money-owner, the purchaser. But as soon as he has converted his commodity into money, he assumes the rôle of the money-owner and becomes a buyer himself. Apparently in this sphere there is no room for inequality and social dependency. [1]

There is one person, however, who does not appear on the commodity market as a vendor—the worker; he belongs to another section, the labour market. He does not enter this realm of liberty, equality and fraternity as a vendor; [2] he has no *locus standi* in the market, his status vis-à-vis the commodity is like that of a copyholder vis-à-vis the system of feudal times. It is the employer who stands there in the worker's place, he appears as the producer, the product appears as his product. Labour-power is economically mediated. At the period of simple commodity production the commodity used to be in fact the product of the worker; labourer and owner were the same. It was a matter of course that the pro-

---

[1] Sale and purchase not only serve to bring about the circulation of the products of the enterprises, the commodities, they do not only serve the purpose which we have outlined above. An economic enterprise as a whole can be bought as a *universitas rerum*. A transaction of this kind has not only different economic functions (that of regulating succession, cf. Section vi), but its legal character is different, too; it demands special treatment even from the point of view of legal analysis. It does not only convey rights *in rem* upon the acquiring *persona* but makes him enter into all private powers and obligations as well as public duties and encumbrances. (*158*) Legal theory considers the sale of commodities as individual succession, and the sale of an enterprise as universal succession. (*159*) It goes against the spirit of language to speak of "succession" where merely a commodity changes hands, and we do not recommend this terminology. On the other hand, from an economic point of view, the acquisition of an enterprise by a person is not so much the acquisition of a *res* by another *persona* (exchange of objects), but succession of another *persona* to the position of governor over an enterprise conceived as static. In the first case it is the position of the *persona* that is changed, and it is therefore convenient to limit the term of "succession" to the second case. The transfer of the creditorship of an obligation against a price by way of assignment also requires treatment different from that of the sale of goods. (*160*)

[2] But only as a buyer of consumers goods.

duct accrued to him at this period; property had the function of guaranteeing to the worker the proceeds of his work. [1]

What is it that property realises when it is sold and how does this realisation take place? Two persons have been concerned with the *res*, the owner of the raw material and the stranger who works on it. To the lawyer it is an instance of *specificatio:* the non-owner converts the owner's property into a new object (*nova species*). In ancient Rome there was a long controversy between two rival schools of jurists, the Sabinians and the Proculians. Should the product fall to the owner or to the transformer of the material? [2] (*162*) In our case the right of the owner to appropriate the object could never be disputed, as it is tacitly acknowledged *ab initio* in the contract of employment. If the product which has now assumed the economic form of commodity is alienated, one person, the worker, has been compensated beforehand, and only the other person, the owner, performs the act of alienation. (*163*)

But what is the recompense of the worker, the copy-holder? As far as the legal aspect of the transaction is concerned, it is the wage. But the amount of the wage is no longer determined by the relations between worker, means of production and product, it is independent of the technical process, it bears no individual relation to the commodity. The wage is fixed outside the locality of the enterprise, far away on the market of hands and brains. It is not the wage that is realised by the act of alienation, not the proceeds of labour but something seemingly substantial, the value of the object. The elements of this value are nothing but concrete things: constant capital which has been advanced by way of fixed purchase price of the means of production, and variable capital which is the advanced price of labour. In the capitalist's calculation, these elements of value are not realised, they are simply refunded and restored to him. It is only from a general and social point of view that alienation is realisation of value. To the capitalist, on the other hand, it is realisation of the surplus value, the surplus over the value that has been advanced. It has now become the function of property and sale to realise this surplus value. (*164*)

Thus the owner alone enters the market with the product and pockets the surplus value that is contained in the product.

Thus property assumes the function of dividing the total annual

[1] At this stage of development, the right to the full proceeds of labour, for the first time an object of practical controversy, became a socialist slogan, only to vanish again later. (*161*)

[2] Gaius II, 79.

product into two parts: "The capitalist class is constantly giving to the labouring class order-notes, in the form of money, on a portion of the commodities produced by the latter and appropriated by the former" (*Capital* i, p. 580). This fund of victuals, the labour fund which the labourer requires for his subsistence and reproduction—this part of the total annual product assumes the form of variable capital. [1] The other part, the surplus value, remains in the hands of the capitalist class.

It is not the law or a legal privilege which endows property with this function of regulating distribution, but the quiet force of facts. Yet it is not a process against or outside the law, but a process which occurs on the basis of the very norms which in the past corresponded with the system of simple commodity production. The legal content of the right of ownership is neither enlarged nor restricted; nor is it abused. It is not even necessary to invent a new complementary institution to supplement the institution of property. There is nothing special in the power to alienate one's own property and to spend money as an equivalent for hired labour, nor is the power to hire out one's own labour against payment an abnormal exercise of the right of personal freedom. There has been no change in the legal content of either institution. "The original conversion of money into capital thus proceeds in strict accordance with the economic laws of commodity production and with the laws of property derived therefrom. Nevertheless, its outcome is (1) that the product belongs to the capitalist, not to the worker; (2) that the value of this product . . . is inclusive of a surplus value on which the worker has expended labour and the capitalist nothing whatever, but which nevertheless becomes the legal property of the capitalist; (3) that the worker has preserved his labour-power and can sell it anew if he finds a buyer. . . . In other words, the law is not broken, rather it is given the opportunity for perpetual operation" (*Capital* i, 18th German ed., p. 548). [2]

Thus, as soon as there has been a change of the actual substratum of the legal order, the legal institution reverses its original function without any active participation of the law itself. When

---

[1] It constantly flows back to the capitalist class, as soon as the worker appears as a buyer on the produce market and exchanges money for means of subsistence, and it is constantly re-advanced by the capitalist class to the workers. (Circulation of variable capital.)

[2] We would again draw the reader's attention to the legal precision with which this procedure is analysed. No other economist is equally precise. Karl Menger has always acknowledged this outstanding virtue of Marx.

the *res* has assumed a new character, when it has become capital, the law of property no longer safeguards the proceeds of labour for the worker. Now it has made a volte-face, it limits him to the labour fund, it absolves the owner from mankind's eternal need to work, and appropriates the surplus product for the owner. Property becomes a title to surplus value, its function becomes the regulation of distribution in a specific manner typical for this particular economic system and opposed to the earlier system.

At the initial stage of capitalist economy this function of the legal institution is readily recognised and openly admitted. "The natural produce of our soil is certainly not fully adequate to our subsistence. . . . A portion at least of society must be indefatigably employed. . . . There are others who, though they 'neither toil nor spin', can yet command the produce of industry, but who owe their exemption from labour solely to civilisation and order. They are peculiarly the creatures of civil institutions" (Eden, quoted by Marx, *Capital* i, p. 629).[1]

Because the aspect of property as a title to surplus value is fully revealed neither in the process of production nor in that of circulation, it remains hidden from the casual observer. Surplus value is created in the process of production, where it is not realised, and it is realised in the process of circulation, where it is not created. It resembles the *spurii* who to the law are fatherless, as the father cannot be ascertained by legal means. The only difference is that in this exceptional case the capitalist is glad to confess to a paternity for which he is not responsible.

c.   Purchase and Profit

On the commodity market, among equal sinners, every sinful origin is forgiven at once; on the contrary, the p∩rthenogenesis of the surplus value seems self-evident. Surplus value is not attributed to labour of any description, nor to a connection between labour and material, it is regarded as inherent in the object itself, inherent in capital. This completes the fossilisation of living labour in its product which now becomes the commodity. The labourer completely disappears from the calculations of the em-

---

[1] According to the theory of natural law the person with his property enters the social order for protection, so that his property is treated like an endowment of nature. Only the legal order, only organised society, creates property. It is quite understandable, though, why a bourgeois philosophy of natural law should enumerate property among the natural rights, conceiving it as prior to the legal order.

ployers of market status; in this higher sphere he is of no account. The market community is a self-contained society; human society as a whole does not enter the realm of its consciousness. Just as men and things are valued according to different standards in different social strata, so are commodities valued here. If man in general is valued according to his abilities, in bourgeois society he is valued according to his possessions. In the lower sphere man is judged according to what he achieves for others, in the upper sphere according to what he can achieve and afford for himself. Thus the members of the market community value commodities from different aspects, yet always within the limits of the general value. "However, the cost of the commodity to the capitalist and the actual cost of this commodity, are two vastly different amounts. That portion of the value of the commodity which consists of surplus value does not cost the capitalist anything for the reason that it costs the labourer unpaid labour. But on the basis of capitalist production, the labourer plays the rôle of an ingredient of productive capital as soon as he has been incorporated in the process of production. Under these circumstances the capitalist poses as the actual producer of the commodity. For this reason the cost price of the commodity to the capitalist necessarily appears to him as the actual cost of the commodity. . . . The capitalist cost of the commodity is measured by the expenditure of capital, while the actual cost of the commodity is measured by the expenditure of labour" (*Capital* iii, pp. 38–9).

At the stage of simple commodity production this special valuation coincides with the general valuation, for everybody owns roughly the same amount and has to work for himself. At the stage of capitalist production this is no longer true. The owner who does no work relates value and surplus value not, as hitherto, to labour but to possessions. Invested capital, constant and variable, seems to be a homogeneous whole: the cost of production pure and simple, the cost price of the commodity; as to the surplus-value, it appears as profit coming from nowhere, from the "market". The *res* assumes the form of cost price and profit, the *persona* dons the character mask of producer—such are their proper and respectable forms in this sphere. The rate of surplus value becomes the rate of profit.

There is no other link between the guardians of commodities than that of *do ut des*, I give—I take. Universal freedom, complete co-ordination, equality of citizenship has been established.

d.   Competition and Market

The free market community of capital owners, however, is nothing but the result of the division of labour within the whole of society [1] among independent commodity producers.

All partial production therefore is but a function of social production and for this reason it is necessarily determined by the whole as a part. Again, the type and extent of these partial productions is not determined by conscious rule of the common will, but by the natural law of *bellum omnium contra omnes*, by competition. This is not a case in which workers of different qualifications compete to obtain these means of production which each can use to the greatest advantage, but competition between those who alone have market status, i.e. capitals and their owners, for the only object in which they are interested, i.e. profit. For it is considered a matter of course that labour has become a mere appendage of capital; labour-power, moreover, is put into storage as the reserve army of the unemployed, ready to respond to every beck and call. The result of this competition with the tacit assumption of the dependency of labour is that the actual exchange of commodities is now no longer determined by value but by cost and profit. (*165*) But this does not prevent these profits from being surplus value. They are surplus value not only as to their nature, but also as to their quantity; for the total profit accruing to the capitalist class is limited and determined by the total surplus-value which is pumped out of the working class. Whereas the exchange of commodities in a system of simple commodity production is determined according to value, this exchange in a system of capitalist production is determined by profits, and in particular by average profits, within the limits of the general value.

The individual capitalist thus cannot fully enjoy his freedom in this republic of guardians of commodities, for "competition enforces the social character of production and consumption" (*Capital* iii, p. 228). He remains dependent upon the workers and all other capitalists, as there can be no exploitation below a certain limit, and no profits above a certain value, so that surplus profits which have been won by the greatest individual efforts are in the long run always reduced to average profits. What is more: "The capitalist who produces surplus value . . . is, indeed, the

---

[1] Which must be distinguished from the division of labour within a manufacturing unit.

first appropriator, but by no means the ultimate owner, of this surplus value. He has to share it with capitalists, with land-owners, etc., who fulfil other functions in the complex of social production. Surplus value, therefore, splits up into various parts" (*Capital* i, p. 576). The capitalist commodity-producer in the sphere of circulation encounters other capitalists who are not producers of commodities but wear quite different character masks. Like brothers, these capitalists later receive their share of the surplus-value which has been created in the inferno of the factory by methods far from fraternal.

It is therefore by no means easy to understand how property in conjunction with the contract of sale fulfils the function of dis-tribution. We could say that the proceeds of alien labour accrue to the owner-vendor, but the situation is too complicated to be described in such simple terms. Sale and purchase take place in a community which has been constituted by society as a fixed establishment, termed the market. This is something more than a social and economic institution, it is an association in the eyes of the law, even where it is not established as a corporation of public law like the stock and commodity exchanges. (*166*) It is a com-plementary institution of public law. This legal phenomenon, too, has not yet been adequately analysed.

e. The Merchant: His Economic Character Mask and His Legal Personality

Up to now our capitalist has worn a three-fold legal character mask. He first appeared on the stage as owner (*dominus*), then as purchaser of means of production and vendor of commodities (*emptor venditor*), and thirdly as a party contracting with labour, hiring human commodities (*conductor operarum*); in accordance with these three legal aspects of the person, the *res* has assumed three economic forms. First the owner disposes over money, then over means of production, and finally over merchandise. Step by step his property has assumed three different forms of capital. "Money capital, commodity capital, productive capital are not, therefore, terms indicating independent classes of capital, nor are their functions processes of independent and separate branches of in-dustry. They are here used only to indicate special functions of industrial capital, assumed by it seriatim" (*Capital* ii, pp. 59–60). "The capital which assumes these different forms in the course of its total process of rotation, discards them one after the other, and performs a special function in each one of them, is industrial capital" (ibid. p. 59). Capital is a unity embracing these three forms. "But in reality, every individual industrial capital is contained simultaneously in all three cycles" (ibid. p. 115). But the *res* as merchandise in the owner's hand soon gains independence; because of its special economic function, merchant-capital claims a special functionary and representative. This is the merchant who takes his place alongside the industrialist. (*167*)

In the hands of the merchant who disposes of it in a specific manner, the *res* plays a new part. "The function of selling it has been transferred from the manufacturer to the merchant, has been converted into the particular business of the merchant, while it used to be a function which the producer had to perform after completing the process of its production"[1] (*Capital* iii, p. 317). This, however, is not the historical sequence. Merchant-capital learned to become resigned to this position only after capitalist production had been fully developed, and only with regard to entrepreneurs or industrialists who actually produced by employing capitalist methods. (*168*) Here the relationship is as follows: "Commercial capital, then, is nothing but the commodity-capital of the producer, which has to pass through its transformation into money and to perform its function of commodity-capital on the market. The difference is only that this incidental function of the producer is now established as the exclusive business of a special kind of capitalists, of merchants" (*Capital* iii, p. 318).

What is it that gives commodity-capital this character of an independently functioning capital?

Once again a function has become independent and personified, and a new economic character mask has been created. This implies that a determinate type of capital has become independent as well—a capital completely remote from the sphere of production, yet clamouring for profit. Every connection with labour, with production, is apparently wiped out. The owner no longer transfers his object into the actual detention of the worker, he does not exercise his right of ownership by means of a contract of employment. He has no need of this complementary institution.

---

[1] The merchant who owns a stock of commodities, is a rather peculiar type of owner. In principle, he appropriates the product of other people, only to give it up immediately to yet others. Thus he disposes over property which is in essence *Fremdtum*, destined to serve others. Simple commodity production would call such practices wicked cheating. (*169*)

Indeed he no longer disposes of his own by any technical process, (*170*) not even indirectly, by intermediaries, or by "copyholders". His disposal is a mere act-in-the-law without any technical content or reference. Not even physical transfer is always necessary, the merchandise is stored in the warehouse, and ownership is transferred by warrant. (*171*) This type of owner buys in order to sell, a practice which from the point of view of the patrimony would have been regarded as wicked cheating, not as an economic procedure. Yet even this fulfils an economic function, for it brings about circulation and is, indeed, distribution. But all this takes place in a third sphere, where property circulates and is utilised without any intervention of labour-power, without even the recollection of labour of any kind, in a sphere where the rule of *do ut des* has become absolute. The *res* claims profit in the hands of the owner-merchant as well as in the hands of the producer, thus depressing the producer's rate of profit.

When the development has so far advanced, general civil law generates a special off-shoot, mercantile law, and the merchant as a person with specific legal qualifications becomes distinct from all other persons in civil law. (*172*) Many repeatedly occurring economic transactions are made into typical acts-in-the-law by special norms (mercantile transactions). To examine this development, however, we should have to digress, for it is a change in norms.

f. The Social Function of Commercial Business

Mercantile capital may lead to more harmful results in a system of simple commodity production than in a fully developed capitalist system. In simple commodity production it intrudes upon the herd of free and equal individuals with devastating results, and even to-day it acts in this way wherever the properties of small producers are managed by the owners themselves. Merchant-capital exploits both customer and producer. It gains control of production by making the producers dependent on it and by doing them out of the whole of the surplus value. (*173*) This mode of operation is a concomitant of transition. None the less, it does not of itself promote the revolutionary transformation of the old mode of production, rather it conserves the old mode and retains it as the basis of its own existence. In every case it obstructs the genuinely capitalist mode of production, and declines when the latter develops. Not transforming the mode of production, it merely depresses the position of the immediate producers, converting them into mere wage labourers and proletarians under worse conditions than those of the workers directly controlled by capital, and it appropriates their surplus labour on the basis or the old mode of production.

Here the merchant is the real capitalist who pockets the whole or the greater part of the surplus value. This form of capitalism does not expropriate, it only appropriates: it has no evolutionary effects but serves to petrify obsolete methods of production: it leaves the owner the title to possession but deprives him of the title to the surplus-value; it creates the hybrid character of an entrepreneur who yet is nothing but a labourer.

Thus this form of property—merchant and mercantile capital—frequently operates in a way different from that of industrial capital. As a result of industrial capital "the technical and social condition of the process, and consequently the very mode of production must be revolutionised, before the productiveness of labour can be increased. By that means alone can the value of labour-power be made to sink, and the portion of the working-day necessary for the reproduction of that value be shortened" (*Capital* i, pp. 303–4). Though fundamentally based on exploitation, industrial capital also constantly promotes organisation by increasing the productivity of labour and thus preparing a new order. Merchant-capital does not operate in such an unequivocal way. When it works with, or is ancillary to, industrial capital, it contributes extensively to economic development, but as soon as it gains the upper hand, it partly petrifies the old methods of production, and partly changes them: for it conserves the old relations of possession, but adapts to its own purposes the method of labour, converting it into sweated outdoor work which is so characteristic a feature of modern conditions. Marx refers to this merchant-capital which becomes industrial capital without being invested in factories [1] when he writes: "Besides the factory operatives, the manufacturing workmen and the handicraftsmen, whom it concentrates in large masses on one spot, and directly commands, capital also gets in motion, by means of invisible threads, another army—that of the workers in the domestic industries who dwell in the large towns and are also scattered over

---

[1] This is made possible above all by the contributions to the labour fund with which we shall deal later.

the face of the country. . . . The exploitation of cheap and im-
mature labour-power is carried out in a more shameless manner
in modern manufacture than in the factory proper. . . . The
exploitation is more shameless in the so-called domestic industry
than in manufacture, and that because the power of resistance in
the labourers decreases with their dissemination; because a whole
series of plundering parasites insinuate themselves between the
employer and the workman" (*Capital* i, p. 465). Thus merchant-
capital produces a second order of labour and hierarchy of
workers side by side with that obtaining in the factory, and this
second order is a serious obstacle to social enlightenment and
revolution; compared with industrial capital, its functions are
often antisocial to a much higher degree.   It even upsets the
regulation of distribution developed by the capitalist economic
system, or at best it retards this development.[1] (*174*)

Wherever the contract of sale appears as an institution complementary to property, the latter reveals its characteristic function
of distribution.   This function, however, is not inherent in the
institution of sale, and the sale is always only the exercise of the
right of ownership, a special way of using the object. An element
of capitalism is no more implied in the legal concept of *emtio-
venditio per se* than it is in that of *locatio conductio operarum*.[2]   The
legal form appears suspect only because it is nowadays a mere
means to a certain exercise of capitalist ownership. Property, and
in particular the property-object, is the basis of distribution. It
provides in general the title to surplus value and in particular the
title to profit. But property distributes not only the surplus value
but also part of the wages (as variable capital), it even realises for
the capitalist profits and wages which are not his due (in the form
of the price). Thus it creates relations of dependency which weigh
heavily upon some members of the capital-owning class itself.

[1] Far from forcing the operating modes of capitalism into a schedule, Marx examines
the specific effect for every kind of capital according to the different countries and
climates, different national characters, etc., as far as such exposition can be fitted into
the framework of a general theoretical treatise.   His task is limited by his specific
object, viz. the exposition of capitalist production at its climax, and he therefore
cannot dwell on hybrid forms; though he does not deny the powers of resistance and
longevity of these hybrid forms.   In particular, he pays no attention to the legislative
attempts aiming at their conservation, the so-called legislation for the protection of
the middle classes, for all this belongs to a later period. It creates institutions of public
law for the protection of traditional economic institutions against the onrush of
competition (licensing, certificates of proficiency, guild privileges, etc.). (*175*)

[2] A social criticism which rejects the contracts of sale and employment as un-
socialistic on the grounds that they serve capitalist exploitation, is quite mistaken. It
confuses legal form and social function. (*176*)

Later, we shall encounter the more typical instances of this relationship.

4. PROPERTY AND CONTRACTS OF RESTITUTION

Commodities of which the members of the economic community have constant detention, do not serve their proper purpose with the same constancy. Every form of economy knows dead use-values, but only in a society of private owners are these at the disposal of private individuals. In the period of natural economy, three institutions are predominant which temporarily endow one person with the detention of property owned by another person. (1) The deposit (*depositum*) is an agreement in favour of the owner who cannot provide a safe keeping for his goods and for instance gives his horse into a neighbour's keeping; (2) the loan for use (*commodatum*) is an agreement in favour of the recipient who uses the movable or immovable object without consuming it, for instance, if he borrows a horse from his neighbour for ploughing; (3) the loan for consumption (*mutuum*) is an agreement again in favour of the recipient who may consume the movable generic [1] object, for instance, if he borrows five bushels of seed corn which he returns after the harvest. At the end of the agreed period, the borrower must return either the same individual object or objects of the same *genus* in the same quantity and quality. At this stage of economic development, the transaction is gratuitous, (177) and its gratuitousness is recognised by law and rural custom. The prohibition of the charge of interest on money is only a special instance of the general legal principle. We shall here consider the development of these institutions only in so far as they are concerned with money, starting at the period when money first became their principal object.

a. Money, its Substratum and its Legal Norm

Money is a property-object, a thing assigned to a person. Nowadays its natural substance as a rule and primarily is coined metal, gold, silver, and the like. Chemistry describes the properties of the substances, metallurgy teaches the methods of alloying them and of coinage. We may therefore consider coined money first from its physical and technical aspect.

---

[1] Legal terminology has it that generic objects of a species are fungible, as equal amounts of the same *genus* can be substituted for each other, e.g. oxen, corn, money, etc.

The economic approach to money is based upon this aspect. (*178*) Money has a definite economic form and function. Precious metal, when it leaves the place of production, is a product destined for the market according to its origin, a commodity of a certain value, which value is economically determined. All tangible precious metal is part of the world market, it is a commodity, no matter whether its destination is the goldsmith, a chemical factory or the mint. The substance which operates as money must previously have been a commodity, it must have had value in order to become an adequate means of exchange for other commodities. The commodity form of precious metal, therefore, is the necessary substratum for the economic function of money.[1] The long historical development of exchange transactions gradually brought it about that coins of metal of a specific quantity and quality (one pound of gold of specified fineness) which are themselves commodities, assume the functions of serving as remuneration and of being an equivalent for all other commodities. In this respect we speak of a general equivalent form.

A buried pot full of coins is a hoard. Money is hoarded even if it is not really but only figuratively buried, viz. when the owner has put it by for some time without using it. In this case it is of no direct benefit to him, nor does it directly harm anyone else. Money is a hoard equally in the chest of the miser and in the safe of the entrepreneur so long as it is ready cash that is not employed but saved up for use later. (*179*)

Only when the coins are employed in sale and purchase, thus starting commodities on a process of circulation, does money assume the equivalent—or price-form (a pair of oxen costs one pound of silver)—only then does it become an economic means of circulation. Once this economic form (equivalent form) and function (means of circulation) have become historical and economic facts, they form the substratum of norms, a substratum on which the law can build. It is not the law which creates money, money is not a product of the law but a product of economics. (*180*) It is only later that the law becomes concerned with it, first declaring the prevalent custom, then stabilising quality and quantity, and perhaps regulating its production. An economic substratum which is already in existence, subsequently becomes

---

[1] Cf. the first chapter of Marx's *Capital*. Marx analyses in detail why and how far symbols and titles of money can replace money. But these exceptions do not contradict the rule that money must be a commodity before it can assume the specific functions of money.

the concern of the law or even of the state. Yet there remains always the reservation that a change in the substratum overthrows the norm, and that the norm which deviates from the substratum in an uneconomical way destroys the monetary character of the substratum. (*181*) The opposing tendencies, the struggle between economic substratum and legal norm can nowhere else be studied to greater advantage than in the case of money.

Precious metal as a commodity has become money. In the process of the circulation of commodities it has become the opposite pole of the commodity, apparently its counterpart, and yet essentially its equal. The old nature of a commodity comes to the fore immediately as soon as money of one kind (gold as against silver or copper) or of one national currency is compared and exchanged with money of another kind (or currency). Money becomes a commodity in the exchange business and thus it operates as money-changer's capital which is on a par with merchant-capital (*182*); money is the merchandise of this trade, a commodity of first-rate importance in international trade, a trade which is international and supra-natural, a trade that is not restricted by the laws of individual national states. (*183*)

We see that one natural object, like a versatile actor, appears in many parts. In a discussion of money it should first be made clear which rôle is referred to, and much damage is done in theoretical arguments by a confusion of the various rôles of money. Even socialists are not free from this error, if they regard money *per se* as an evil, rejecting it in all its functions, preferring to throw all coins into the melting pot to convert them into all sorts of practical objects. It is the function of money which is decisive. And here we cannot neglect to point out that, apart from its physical and technical form, which does not interest us, and apart from the three economic forms which we have already considered (hoarding, equivalent and commodity), money assumes a fourth form, that of capital. Once it has assumed this form, the character of the deposit [1] and of the loan [2] is changed and the contracts of restitution develop different functions. Formerly subsidiary institutions, almost without importance in a system of natural economy, they become regular methods for the use of property, its principal functions, indeed the very purpose of its existence. Property now serves no longer to be exploited in a natural manner but to be

---

[1] As *depositum irregulare*.
[2] We need not consider the loan here.

given away. Property which has no other purpose than to be taken away from the owner and to be given to another person, is worthless to all intents and purposes, that is unless this transfer itself becomes remunerative. As soon as the contracts of restitution become regular ways of exercising the right of ownership, they cease to be gratuitous: a Fall of which Canon Law knows nothing.

"Money . . . may be converted into capital on the basis of capitalist production. By this conversion it is transformed from a given value to a self-expanding, increasing value. . . . In this way it acquires, aside from its use-value as money, an additional use-value, namely that of serving as capital. Its use-value consists then precisely in the profit, which it produces when converted into capital. In this capacity of potential capital, of a means for the production of profit, it becomes a commodity, but a commodity of a peculiar kind. Or, what amounts to the same, capital as capital becomes a commodity" (*Capital* iii, pp. 397–8). Thus capital develops its own market, the *capital market*. It is the use-value of the capital function of money, of the function of ensuring a profit, which thus becomes part and parcel of the contract. *Interest* is a specific name, a specific compartment for that part of the profit which working capital must hand to the owner of capital.

Thus ownership of money enables the owner to seize in the form of interest a part of the potential profit accruing to the person who uses the capital. It is true that other commodities which fulfil the function of capital (industrial capital, commercial capital) can be lent or borrowed; the loan as an economic institution is not confined to money capital. But at the modern stage of development it is always the monetary value of the object or a certain amount of money which is regarded as the object of a loan.

b. Loan and Interest

Lending is mediated by an act-in-the-law which is neither sale nor purchase but *mutuum*, loan: the transfer of a quantity of fungible objects into the ownership of the recipient who is under obligation to return objects of like quality and quantity. The transfer of ownership, its loss on the part of the owner and its acquisition on the part of the recipient is unavoidable as far as the law is concerned. Even to-day this act-in-the-law *per se* is not necessarily a valuable consideration; on the other hand, the economic loan, under existing circumstances, is never gratuitous. The remuneration consists of interest. The act-in-the-law may

serve purposes which do not directly appertain to economics; as a
legal transaction it is individualised by its normative content, just
as are all other institutions of a developed legal system. (*184*)
Therefore, as far as the legal structure is concerned, it is not
essential that there should be remuneration for the loan or that its
object should be capital. It is only where the obligation has a
definite material content that it becomes the "interest relationship" from an economic point of view. "The juristic forms, in
which these economic transactions appear as activities of the will
of the parties concerned, as expressions of their common will and
as contracts which may be enforced by the law against some
individual party, cannot determine their content, since they are
only forms" (*Capital* iii, p. 399).

From an economic point of view, we are not now dealing with
an act of exchange, as a loan is not based upon mutual alienation.
When we pay money in exchange for a commodity, we alienate
the money and retain the commodity as its equivalent. We have
irrevocably given away what we formerly owned, but we may
dispose at once of the equivalent value. In the case of the lending
capitalist, on the other hand, the owner gives away his capital
without retaining anything, but he does not alienate his capital;
for it does not enter into commodity circulation, it is only transferred from the lender to the borrower and at the end of the agreed
period it is immediately re-transferred from the borrower to the
lender. This transfer and re-transfer is not a part of the real process
of circulation, it is merely a legal transaction by which the
capitalist-borrower joins the capitalist-owner so that both persons,
from an economic point of view, occupy the same place in the
process of commodity circulation. Capital that has been lent
fulfils a function in the economic process only once, just as a piece
of land is functioning once only, though a tenant may have joined
the landowner. Capital does not change its function, it only
changes hands: it is transferred from the non-operative capitalist
to the working capitalist. Similarly its restitution is not the result
of an economic process but simply the fulfilment of a contract.
We see that capital is here remote not only from production but
also from the circulation of commodities; [1] it takes part in a purely
legal process, the change of possession.

---

[1] We do not deny that capitals circulate to a certain extent; this process, however,
is not that of a circulation of commodities but a circulation peculiar to capital.
Similarly, it is not commodity circulation when landed property changes hands.

The lender's remuneration is part of the average profit. We have a distinction between capitalists as finance capitalists on the one hand, and as industrial and commercial capitalists on the other; and the actual separation of their economic functions, bringing about the conversion of one part of the average profit which gives rise to the economic category of interest. It is the control of alien labour and the claim to appropriate the results of this labour—the controlling and exploiting functions of property— which are transferred from the finance capitalist to the working capitalist. Where no alien labour can be appropriated, there is no interest (*Capital* iii, p. 419 ff.), as we saw in the system of natural economy, where the loan was gratuitous. That part of the average profit which remains to the working capitalist after he has paid out the interest, assumes a new character and name, it constitutes the *profit of enterprise:* the capitalist who works *without possessing capital* becomes in character and in name the *entrepreneur*. Employment of alien capital now becomes the rule and every working capitalist to a smaller or larger extent sets alien capital in motion. (*185*) As this innovation develops, the term "capitalist" disappears from common usage. Nowadays we commonly speak only of employers and employees. Only the entrepreneur, not the finance capitalist, really provides employment; he alone is the real promoter of the circulation of commodities and of production.

Where the credit system is fully developed, even an entrepreneur who works with his own capital calculates interest and the profit of his enterprise in separate accounts. The interest which he would have to pay to a supposed lender of his own capital, appears to him as a part of the product, as the part which is due to the ownership of capital as such, to the mere legal power of disposal. (*186*)   Conversely, that part of the earnings which accrues to the actively working capitalist he takes to be the entrepreneur's profit; in his estimation it derives from operations or functions which the capitalist performs personally, in the way in which he applies his capital. Profit, in fine, is attributed to the function of entrepreneur, and interest appears to the entrepreneur, the operating capitalist, as a result of the mere ownership of capital, of capital *per se*, a consequence of the title to possession quite unconnected with the reproduction of capital—interest appears as the fruit of capital irrespective of any function which it may fulfil. The profit of his enterprise, on the other hand, appears to him as the exclusive result of the function which he fulfils with his capital. Contrasting this function with the inactivity of the finance capitalist, the entrepreneur regards it solely as his own activity. This subjective conception is the necessary consequence of the fact that wherever in fact money is borrowed, the interest accrues to the inactive lender, and what remains of the average profit accrues to the borrowing entrepreneur (*Capital* iii, p. 439). As soon as both character masks are developed—finance capitalist and operating capitalist—even the capitalist who is his own entrepreneur separates, in his book-keeping as well as in his thoughts, the two functions which are united in his person.

In the sphere of interest, the fourth and highest sphere of economic life, the contrast between capital and wage labour is wiped out. Capital which bears interest is confronted not with wage labour but with actively working capital.[1] "Interest-bearing capital represents capital as *ownership* compared to capital as a *function*" (*Capital* iii, p. 446). In the hands of the owner it exists but has no function and only in the hands of the borrowing entrepreneur does it begin to operate. The entrepreneur looks upon the profit of his enterprise as it were as wages: in his relations with the creditor-capitalist he regards himself as a worker.

We see that in the market community, that republic of equals, the contrast between ownership and non-ownership is reproduced, though in a different form. In the mind of the operating capitalist the idea necessarily develops that the profit of his enterprise is wages for labour, for supervision, and that they are wages of a higher standard, first because they pay for more complicated work and secondly because the owner himself calculates his wage (*Capital* iii, p. 449). But in the first place interest is a relation between two capitalists, not between capitalist and worker, secondly supervision is something more than labour, and lastly the wage for supervision is distinct from the profit of enterprise.[2] Large business undertakings tend to separate administration as a vocation from the possession of capital. Thus interest-capital produces a managerial class which has no title to the capital to which it is assigned and yet fulfils all functions of the operating

---

[1] The reader should again pay attention to the astute distinctions of Karl Marx.

[2] "The labour of superintendence and management will naturally be required whenever the direct process of production assumes the form of a combined social process, and does not rest on the isolated labour of independent producers" (*Capital* iii, p. 451). Technical management is therefore in general socially necessary labour. Different is that kind of supervision which arises from the antagonism between capital and labour and belongs to the *faux frais* of capitalist production, on its debit side. (Cf. *Capital* iii, p. 453.)

capitalist. (*187*) These managers are not wage-labourers from an economic point of view, yet in the eyes of the law they live according to a contract of service, however this may be modified. (*188*) This complementary institution of property shows itself capable of serving at all stages of the hierarchy of labour, and thus the regulation of labour from a legal point of view is completely separated from the regulation of possession.[1] As soon as the salary for supervision is paid in full, or, where the entrepreneur acts as his own manager, as soon as it is taken into account as a separate item, that part of the earnings emerges which constitutes the profit of enterprise.

The entrepreneur or working capitalist is now confronted with the mere owner who does not engage in any kind of economic activity and yet plays his part in economic life. He is neither worker nor entrepreneur, neither manufacturer nor merchant, but he is superior to them all, to "serfs" and "citizens", to production and circulation alike.

Capital which bears interest is of course not an object without functions. It is the owner of property who does not fulfil any function. His right is a mere title to interest, a means to appropriate values and products without having to fulfil any individual function. (*189*) For a developed society of capitalists, this form of capital appears at first to be a tremendous improvement, but for human society in general it is exploitation, even in its mildest form. "Even in cases where a man without wealth receives credit in his capacity as an industrial or merchant . . . he receives credit in his capacity as a potential capitalist. This circumstance, . . . very much admired by the apologists of the capitalist system . . .

---

[1] The entrepreneur in the strict meaning of the word is a capitalist without capital, he fulfils the functions of capital, and the profit of his enterprise is his reward. The manager is not a capitalist, but for a salary he fulfils the function of a capitalist. The technical qualifications of both persons are the same, they are based upon economic abilities which in every economic system are as indispensable as they are rare. This is proved by the experience gained in the management of workers' co-operatives. The gift to appraise values and to organise, the art of giving orders and of managing men and things, the ability to make quick decisions are the result alike of natural endowment and of efficient training. We may justifiably call these gifts the qualifications of an entrepreneur, if we confine this term to the capitalist without capital of his own. Entrepreneur and manager socially stand on the same level, although the former is paid mainly with profit and the latter with a salary. This difference is levelled down if on the one hand a minimum of the profit is accorded to the entrepreneur by agreement in the form of interest, and if, on the other hand, the manager receives a part of the profit in addition to his salary. The splitting up of the surplus value which we have described above makes it possible to expropriate the greater part of the titles to surplus value without depriving a future economic system of the qualifications necessary for its organisation.

secures the supremacy of capital itself, expands its basis, and enables it to recruit ever more forces for itself out of the lower layers of society" (*Capital* iii, p. 705).

Finance capital demonstrates the distributory function of property in an ideal form, since in the hands of the owner the property-object fulfils no function whatsoever. In order to give an active detentor access to the property-object and thus to keep it functioning, the detention conferred by law upon the owner himself must be bought off for a ransom by private contract. Thus society always re-purchases indirectly, unconsciously, by private contract, what previously it had conferred freely, consciously, and by a sovereign act. Society constantly pays instalments on a fund of redemption, yet it can never finally redeem its goods. When every entrepreneur, even the acting one who does not borrow, comes to calculate the interest on every particle of his property, the general tribute of society to the creature of its own laws becomes clearly visible. Aristotle calls the tool a slave without a soul; the institution of interest makes it true to say that the free society of living people bears tribute to its lifeless slave.

c. The Social Function of the Credit System

It is not always true—especially not in the initial stages of capitalist development—that finance-capital operates (at least in the "republic" of equals, amongst the capitalists themselves) innocuously or even partly beneficially. Finance-capital usually starts as usury in a mild way, and with the progressive maturity of the capitalist economy it becomes, as *credit*, an organic institution of this economic system.

"Interest-bearing capital, or usurer's capital, as we may call it in its ancient form, belongs like its twin brother, commercial capital, to the antediluvian forms of capital" (*Capital* iii, p. 696). Where it predominates, its effects are analogous to those of merchant-capital in a society of independent producers. "Under the form of interest, the whole of the surplus over the necessary means of subsistence (the amount of what becomes wages later on) of the producers may here be devoured by usury (this assumes later the form of profit and ground rent). . . . Usurer's capital in this form, in which it appropriates indeed all surplus labour, of the direct producers, does not alter the mode of production. The ownership, or at least the possession of the means of employment by the producers . . . are its essential prerequisites. Here capital does not subordinate labour to itself directly, and does not confront the labourer as industrial capital, while usurer's capital merely impoverishes this mode of production . . . and at the same time perpetuates these miserable conditions" (*Capital* iii, p. 699).

"Usury centralises money wealth, where the means of production are disjointed. It does not alter the mode of production, but attaches itself to it as a parasite and makes it miserable" (*Capital* iii, p. 700). Not every form of capitalism, as we have seen, promotes evolution and improves organisation. Usurer's capital, in particular, uses capitalist methods of exploitation, without its mode of production (*Capital* iii, p. 782). It creates relations of social dependency (the Roman "*nexum*") compared with which the despotism of the factory is an idyllic shepherd's frolic.

The credit system with its numerous economic and legal institutions some of which are novel, gradually wins the day as a reaction of industrial and merchant-capital against usury. Usury is kept in bounds in part by this economic development itself and in part only by the intervention of the legal norm. The law intervenes by statutes controlling usury but also by the provision of new institutions for the organisation of a credit system: savings banks, mortgage banks, and the like. This control is no more nor less than the subjection of finance-capital and its devotees, the lending capitalists, to the conditions and requirements of the capitalist method of production itself, the requirements of the industrialists and merchants. (*190*) It is not human society as a whole which here subjects to its own requirements one form of capital; it is capitalist society which organises finance capital by means of a credit system, with banks of every kind and description, thus effecting its integration into society. On the whole, therefore, interest-bearing capital in the modern organisation of credit is adapted to the conditions of capitalist production, to the needs of its champions, the capitalists. Yet "interest-bearing capital retains the form of usurer's capital in its transactions with such persons or classes, or those in such circumstances, as do not borrow in the sense corresponding to the capitalist mode of production, or in which borrowing cannot take place in that sense. This applies to borrowing from individual want at the pawnshop . . . or to borrowing money on the part of producers who are not capitalist producers, such as small farmers, craftsmen, etc., . . . finally to borrowing on the part of capitalist producers, who still produce on such a small scale, that they approach those self-employing producers" (*Capital* iii, p. 705). Yet even where usurer's capital is controlled by institutions which provide for co-operative lending, it remains interest-bearing capital—its essential character is to be capital. Such capital, however, as we shall see, is capable of further evolution. For "it should never be forgotten, that money, in the first place . . . remains the basis from which the credit system naturally can never detach itself. In the second place, it must be kept in mind that the credit system has for its premise the monopoly of the social means of production in the hands of private people (in the form of capital and landed property), that it is itself on the one hand an immanent form of the capitalist mode of production and on the other hand one of the impelling forces of the development of this mode of production to its highest and ultimate form. The banking system, so far as its formal organisation and centralisation is concerned, is the most artificial and most developed product turned out by the capitalist mode of production. . . . It presents indeed the form of universal book-keeping and of a distribution of products on a social scale, but only the form" (*Capital* iii, p. 712).

Finance-capital, though it is partly integrated into society with regard to its functions (i.e. for one group of capitalists) remains private capital, whether it is held by the smallest savings bank or by the Central Bank. It is not appropriated for society as a whole but only for the capitalist class, which forms a part-society within the larger society. It is put at the collective disposal of this class in return for a tribute which the active entrepreneurs wrest from the labours of the workers, whether these are unequivocally wage-labourers or wear the hybrid character mask of independent producers.

Thus the property-object retains its capital function unimpaired, even under the auspices of companies and corporations. Yet by the development of interest-bearing capital to an organised credit system and that of corporate associations (discussed below), the owner is rendered completely superfluous. The finance capitalist no longer administers his capital for himself, nor does he even lend it out himself, for he deposits it in banks or invests it in joint stock companies and the like. Every function is carried out by persons in salaried positions, and wherever the development is sufficiently advanced ". . . only the functionary remains and the capitalist disappears from the process of production as a super-fluous person" (*Capital* iii, p. 456).

In interest-bearing capital the capitalist relationship has found its most remote and fetish-like expression. Capital now appears as a mysterious and original source of interest. The property-object pure and simple has become capital in its own right. [1] "The social relationship is perfected into the relation of one thing, viz. money, to itself" (*Capital* iii, p. 460). Ownership is reduced to a mere legal title. The owner of property does not cultivate his own, neither by work nor by any other activities. He exercises his right only by divesting himself of the *res* for a period; he uses the thing by abstaining from use; his ownership exhausts itself in its temporary transfer to another person; he is owner in ceasing to be so and in contenting himself with a personal title; he expropriates himself for the sake of a paper title and for private tribute. Thus he himself acknowledges the necessity of his expropriation, the fact that he fulfils no social function. Later we shall encounter another economic character mask, playing a similar part, in the person of the great landowner.

The occasional loan transaction, as it took place in the period of simple commodity production, usually accompanied by guarantees and pledges, has been developed into the completely organised legal institution of the credit system. This progress was achieved by powerful legislation in all countries, (*191*) in the main subsequent to the great codifications (Prussian Land Law, the *Code Civil*, etc.). We see the results of this legislation in mercantile law, in the law relating to bills of exchange and in the banking regulations. In essence these are only extensions of the existing law, which is based on property. I have dealt with the economic functions of these new legal institutions at greater length in my book, *Die Wirtschaft als Gesamtprozess und die Sozialisierung*, especially in the section relating to credit. As far as this legislation is change of norms, it falls outside the scope of this enquiry, but we can see even here that the complementary institutions of public law (public credit organisations, the Central Bank, mortgage banks and savings banks) are already indications of a new social order.

---

[1] Theories of capitalist economics are mainly concerned with this highest and most exalted form of capital. They disregard the living beings who set the object in motion. Trying to deduce the quality of capital from the thing itself, capitalist economics neglects the relations of capital to man and matter and can therefore only arrive at abstractions which are without value for a deeper understanding of economy.

5. LANDED PROPERTY AND ITS COMPLEMENTARY INSTITUTIONS

To the mind of the peasant, landed property as we know it belongs to the farmer as a matter of course, (*192*) as a necessary adjunct, in the same way as an arm or a leg is a bodily member of the individual. The peasant conceives of the relation between farmer and land as existing prior to the state and all law, not realising that it was only introduced by the legal system at a determinate and comparatively recent period of history, that it is conferred and maintained by the law and can equally be abolished by the law. To the peasant, state and law are institutions established only *a posteriori*, in order to protect the owner and his land. Land ownership has prejudiced the peasant mind in particular to such a degree that a thousand years in the history of the soil, when land owning was unknown, are completely erased from memory. To such an extent has the legal institution of the "own and patrimony" become part of the flesh and blood of the rural population. (*193*)

The purpose of landed property in the pre-capitalist era is to secure for the workers the disposal over the means of production, to put these into the hands of the producer, to secure for him the full proceeds of his labour, to safeguard the life of the next generation and to ensure, by the institution of succession, the continuity of labour and of consumption. The institution of land ownership is originally established fundamentally for the purposes of labour.

The norms which make up this institution, however, presuppose a monopoly of certain persons to consider certain portions of the globe as subject to their disposal, where their private wills reign supreme to the exclusion of any influence of other persons (*Capital* iii, p. 722). [1] Nothing is determined by virtue of the legal power of these persons to use or to misuse certain portions of the globe; the use of this power depends wholly upon economic conditions which are independent of their will (*Capital* iii, pp. 722–3). The legal institution which regulates the relations of wills is an empty frame to be filled only by the exercise of the right bestowed by the law; such exercise lies outside the realm of the norm.

---

[1] Listen to this apotheosis of land ownership: "The surface of the earth and all that is above or below, belongs to the owner, his realm extends to heaven and to the centre of the earth" (Gesterding, quoted by Krainz: *System des oesterreichischen allgemeinen Privatrechts*, 3rd ed., i, p. 537). (*194*)

A person acting as landowner usually also fulfils other functions, and conversely, a number of persons are actively concerned with the soil without being landowners. The unfree occupier of a rural *peculium* in ancient Rome had the functions of a landlord, although he was a slave, not even a person and far less a landowner. The landowner with his full rights, on the other hand, is subject to the state which, under all constitutions, has sovereignty over its territory. If we wish to study land ownership in its purest form, we must confine our observations to the property title, disregarding everything which can be derived from a *function* of the owner. As long as land ownership combines all the functions, our imagination fails. The old-fashioned peasant is simply unable to work out the elements of ground rent, interest and wage from the homogeneous price for his produce. Hence the confusing fact that those who are immediately and creatively concerned with the land, understand least of all what is really happening to them. For these people the fact and significance of ground rent is in most cases a sealed book. We could not even in theory pursue our investigation if economic development had never produced a landowner who was merely a landowner without fulfilling any functions. "It is one of the great outcomes of the capitalist mode of production, that it detaches property in land on the one side from the relations between master and servant (corvée, bondage, tithe), and on the other hand totally separates land as an instrument of production from property in land and landowners. . . . Private property in land thus receives its purely economic form" (*Capital* iii, pp. 723-4). This would have to be our starting point even if every landowner were personally to farm his land, thus uniting various functions in his person. It is impossible to understand hybrid types without reference to the elementary types.

a. Agricultural Lease

The landlord who leases out his land to tenants exhibits the function of land ownership at its purest. The ground rent is the form in which landed property is realised and utilised from an economic point of view. In this case the complementary institution is the lease; it differs from the loan *inter alia* in this, that the object remains the lessor's property, although detention is given to the lessee. [1] However, it is not only in the tenure of rural and urban land that ground rent emerges and becomes manifest. Land ownership, in the eyes of the law, is the power of disposal over a part of the globe, but from an economic point of view it is a title to rent. The institution of tenure exhibits a relationship where legal form and economic function coincide. The landowner draws the ground rent.

We have said before that the essential function of property is that of detention, securing the land, the object of farming, to the farmer. The lease, however, transfers the object into the detention of the non-owner, thus depriving property of this function of detention. [2] Thus the purest form of land ownership serves as our starting point.

In this form, property in land fulfils no productive function, its effects are purely distributive. (*197*)   It enables the owner to appropriate the surplus profit produced by the tenant. The part-owners of the globe thus "pocket a result of social development brought about without their help—*fruges consumere nati*" (*Capital* iii, pp. 726–7). The urban ground rent shows that the soil need not bear fruit in order to yield rent. Society which endows the owners with the property title, is here again compelled to buy it back from its own creature piecemeal, and for limited periods, paying a tribute in the form of rent. But "property in land differs from the other kinds of property by the fact that it appears super-fluous and even noxious, at a certain stage of development, even from the point of view of capitalist production" (*Capital* iii, pp. 729–30).

Above all every piece of land that is capable of cultivation is now occupied and assimilated. This occupation and assimilation requires the investment of capital in soil. Just as the rent is a tribute to the landowner, the owner of the *terre-matière*, so must the tenant who invests his capital in land, buildings and improvements calculate interest on this capital, the *terre-capital* which is incorporated in the land, in accordance with the laws of capitalist distribution. (*198*)   The ownership in buildings and the urban tenement lease, however, clearly show "the difference between

---

[1] It is solely the economic nature of the object which accounts for the fact that it becomes, in case of the loan, the borrower's property. The loan applies to a quantity of fungible things, generally money, viz. objects which have no economic individuality. Therefore, in the case of *mutuum*, the restitution of the same individual object is unnecessary and indeed impossible as far as the law is concerned. (*195*)

[2] The tenant enjoys also the protection of the law for his possession. (*196*)

real ground rent and interest on fixed capital incorporated in the soil" (*Capital* iii, pp. 728-9). Rural and urban leases show moreover that the alien capital incorporated in the soil "ultimately passes into the hands of the landlord . . . and that the interest on it helps to swell his rent" (*Capital* iii, p. 729) since the departing tenant, the "*superficiarius*", and sometimes also the urban tenants, leave their *terre-capital* with the owner. (*199*) This interferes with the law of capitalist appropriation; and the tenant capitalist is inclined therefore to avoid all improvements. Thus property in land restricts not only rational agriculture but also capitalist production on a higher level; for this necessarily depends on agriculture.

Disposal over land and soil is a necessary condition for agricultural labour, indeed for labour pure and simple, since a place is required for all production. If the entrepreneurs and workers do not own the land, they can only obtain detention of the soil by means of the lease. They must become tenants, even though the profit or remuneration which remains to them after deduction of the farm-rent may be much below the average agricultural income. Thus it is possible that a partial deduction from the average profit, from the normal wage or from both is hidden in the lease, quite apart from the ground rent due to the owner. In this case, the owner of landed property realises not only its due and proper rent, but also interest, average profit and even wages, without investing any capital, without taking an active part in production and without labouring. For "if the tenant pays a rent which is either a deduction from the normal wages of his labourers, or from his own normal average profit, then he does not pay a rent which is clearly distinguished from wages and profit in the price of his product" (*Capital* iii, p. 877).

All ground rent is surplus value, a product of social surplus labour. More than anything else, this fact offends the "common sense" of those who live on the land and work within their patrimony. Everything which is yielded by the soil must appear to them as the fruit of this soil only, and this is true, indeed, for the natural rent. But it is different in the case of the capitalist ground rent. "Common sense" neglects the fact that the produce must be taken away from the land and brought to market where it can be passed on to society. It is society which determines the price of the produce, yet this society has established by law a monopoly price of the land. It is society which has created this surplus value which the owner pockets as ground rent. It is typical of the capitalist ground rent that it is a *social surplus-value* which is appropriated by the owner. Yet the landowner is not always satisfied with the normal portion of the surplus value, he encroaches on the capitalist's pocket and takes a part of his average profit. Moreover, the landowner is not always satisfied with the surplus value alone, but encroaches upon the variable capital, thus diminishing the labourer's wages. Finally, he appropriates the constant capital incorporated in the soil. In such ways ownership in land draws the surplus revenue from the social fund of labour and accumulation, thus stunting, on the one hand, the life of the present generation, and on the other hand, the material development of the future.

b.   Urban Lease

When we say that property fulfils the function of distribution and so becomes a mere title to rent, we have dealt with but one aspect of its social significance. Landlordism in the cities shows the curse of property much more strikingly than landlordism in the country.

Every human being needs a place to live in, and the history of human habitations is the principal part of the history of human civilisation. It leads back into the pre-human period, a period of unconscious social existence when we all were a mere object of natural history. Even the animal world knows dwellings which sometimes are wonderful pieces of craftsmanship, like the bee-hive. The progress from the savage's cave to the nomad's tent and onward to the stone house of settled peoples has been long, marked by struggle and invention, and in its course the actual use of a dwelling has been developed by the norm into the right to a home. For countless centuries all external conditions of life were com-munal property of the tribe, whereas the dwelling had already become a "*suum*" in Ofner's sense, a *privatum* as contrasted with the public good. (*200*) But this private *suum* is not yet individual and private property. Over a long period the house (*domus*) belongs either to the *gens* or to the family; house connotes family; the master of the house (*dominus*) is in public law the head of a community, the household, which is perpetuated by the rearing of children and by succession: the household is conceived as being the real subject of the right to the house, and is represented by the house-father or *dominus* only as regards external relations. (*201*) For a long time the rights in all movable accessories to the house are vested in this house-community, until these chattels first become individual private property. It is only the civil law which disintegrates the household, since it abolishes the old character of a *universitas juris*. Now the household is replaced by a new legal construction, a combination of individual rights, and the house becomes as a rule the private property of one person, the *pater familias*. Family relationships are dissolved into individual institutions (father and mother: conjugal rights; father and child: paternal powers; ancestors and descendants: rights of intestate succession) which are also conceived of as individual rights. (*202*) The home, although it still serves as a communal organisation of many persons, becomes the private *suum* of one person, who may dispose of it freely *inter vivos*, even by testament, without consulting his fellow members. To this extent the home becomes private property.

It is quite obvious that, right from the beginning, even in the period of the "own and patrimony", the legal construction was in absolute contrast to the real function of the institution. The absurdity of the law was only mitigated by convention which in practice maintained the house-community, so that a really free disposal of the *dominus* over the *domus*, a disposal by sale or by testament against the wishes and interests of the other house members, was a rare exception. Moreover, such exercise of the right, should it occur, was generally condemned by the other members of the community. (*203*) A man's home is the centre of his life. In the period of the "own and patrimony" it was the universal centre of his whole existence, of his family life, of his production and consumption (cf. pp. 81 f.). But the capitalist economic order has destroyed the unity of this focal place. The workshop, the warehouse and the shop have been taken out of the house, and it is now technical convenience which determines their respective localities. The most favourable locality for the workshop is different from that for the storage and marketing of the finished commodity. As soon as the growing generation is educated in state schools outside the house, the home is reduced to a mere place of residence, which again has a most favourable locality. The simple word "house" has to-day a different meaning. It is a capitalist provision for the utilisation of a specific locality. It is either a dwelling house or a factory, a warehouse, a store or a school. As a rule it is neither private nor a *suum*. The present-day dwelling house is intended to serve as a lodging place for strangers, it is a "*Fremdtum*" (*204*)—nobody's own or *suum*. The factory serves to accommodate the masses of strangers at work within its gates. The school house serves all families at the same time. The saying "master in one's own house" is a ridiculous misunderstanding of the purpose of the house as we know it; for from the very beginning, it is built to serve other persons.

The locality has gained paramount and decisive importance in the capitalist economic order which is based upon the exchange of all products all over the world. This becomes first apparent in the struggle of the merchants for the market stand, then for the best, shortest and cheapest way to the market, and finally for the site most suitable for production according to the markets for raw material and produce. The better site yields a surplus profit to the occupier surpassing that of his competitors; it yields a rent. The authorities may grant concessions to occupy certain market stands against payment of a fee. Every possessor of a market stand can enter into the same transaction, now under private (instead of public) law, by letting the market stand.

The locality is a point of a line in space, it is completely insubstantial. It is not a product, not a good nor a value. It is of no more value than the turnpike of feudal times, by means of which levies were extorted from passing merchants. (*205*) The locality which in itself is but a geographical point, has become so important because the economic development of society has become so enlarged and distributed in space, that the traffic of men and goods has a special need for this locality. If the locality can be called a "product" at all, then it is a product of the society which surrounds it. It is society which gives value and importance to the locality, not the individual holder who owes his position to the mere chance of the law. The lucky holder may, however, exploit the importance of the locality created by society in an economic way by demanding from all passers-by a share of their profit. This share becomes a permanent rent, which can be capitalised and so has a price. The lucky holder may now give away or lease this geographical opportunity for pocketing a surplus profit, temporarily or permanently, or he may sell it for this price. But he always takes a share of the social product without taking a personal part in the economic process. Rent and price of a locality flow directly from national economics, unconnected with any functions.

It is rare for the locality alone to be let or sold, as happens in the instance of the market stand. As a rule, the equipment required for the utilisation of the locality, the selling booth or market stall, is also manufactured by capitalist methods: the site is built on and sold or let together with the building. For this purpose money must be invested to bring in that rate of interest which is locally or nationally customary. In the case of alienation, the capital for building must therefore be added to the price of the site, and in the case of letting, the interest on this capital must be added to the rent. The house built in this way is a capitalist enterprise for the exploitation of the invested capital and the realisation of the rent for the locality, and this applies to dwelling houses as well as to industrial buildings.

Urban house property thus becomes, by means of the lease as a complementary institution, a typical *Fremdtum*; this means that it is its economic destiny to fall wholly or partly into the detention of strangers so that nothing is left to the owner but a claim to tribute. The greed to snatch up valuable sites lets loose speculation in estates; the greed to exploit these sites to the limit accounts for the unhygienic methods employed in building capitalist tenement houses in the big cities. (*206*) Where there are, however, natural limits to the expansion of a site, or where the general social development is ahead of the building industry, these consequences of the fundamental laws of capitalism lead to the building and housing racket. Capital connected with land ownership is a handicap to social development, pocketing not only the surplus profits which arise from the locality, but also part of the normal profits of the factory owners and merchants, and a deduction from wages which is paid out in the form of rents that are too high. Therefore urban landlordism is inimical to development, it is a parasitical institution, even from a capitalist, not a socialist point of view. Within the last decade therefore legislation has been compelled gradually to restrict private building industries and private house-ownership by laws regulating the building trade. The economic development and state legislation account for the fact that the urban tenement house has more and more assumed the characteristics of a public establishment. At the same time central and local government authorities have increasingly substituted public for private building. Building societies have endeavoured to make the home, the rooms and their interior equipment, once again into a private *suum*, directly or indirectly, by the building of family and communal dwelling houses. [1] (*207*)

During the war 1914–18 the disadvantages of private house-ownership became so unbearable that in every country special legislation had to provide for protection of the tenants, thus depriving the owner of most outlets for the exercise of his right, or restricting this exercise. (*208*) The aggregate of these norms has given to the tenant a great number of privileges outside the law of contract, privileges which are protected by public law. (*209*) By this, as it were in a negative way, the tenant has acquired the positive right to a home, a new form of a right to a roof over his head which in the future will eventually replace private ownership of dwelling houses.

c.   Mortgage

Both rural and urban land ownership as a monopoly of the soil or site require for their exploitation additional capital (*terre-capital*) which need not always be in the hands of the landowner, as chance has made him. *Terre-capital* may be borrowed and incorporated into the soil. Then it merges with the land; its value becomes part of the price of the land. The "realty" is the fusion of soil and capital. Where the capital does not belong to the owner, a security becomes necessary. This need is met by the legal institutions of land registration, of a registered lien on the land, and of mortgage. (*210*)

The economic analysis of the institution of mortgage is most difficult, as property as a title to interest is strangely combined here with property as a title to rent. Where the lease system is

---

[1] It is natural that the housing question should play a predominant part in socialist literature. Older socialists see in the legal form of property an evil in itself and every form of communal property appears as progress to them. They stick to the form and neglect the function. In the economic process as a whole every good must in the end become a good of consumption. This may be enjoyed, like the pictures in a gallery, for instance, socially and communally. But in most cases consumption is an individual process. Therefore movable chattels, the objects of personal use, should be assigned to the individual as his *suum*. Then there will remain a sphere of private and individual "own", a personal realm where the community has no need to interfere and where the individual will consider interference by others undesirable. To this private sphere will also belong some means of production which by their nature make capitalist exploitation impossible, as for instance the professor's library, the artist's studio, perhaps the vine-grower's vineyard, and certainly the allotment garden. No doubt the individual home will also be in this sphere, and communal living will only be the exception (boarding school, etc.). Socialist criticism of every legal institution should consider its function, not the norms that make it up.

predominant in a country, it is the rule that the ground rent absorbs the interest and that the *terre-matière* absorbs the *terre-capital*. But in the case of a mortgage, finance capital subjugates the landed property. It has all the petrifying and pauperising effects of usury, so long as it is not controlled by credit institutions of public law. In the eyes of the law, capital is completely bound up with the soil. The title to interest, originally an ordinary debt, by virtue of the deed of mortgage becomes a right *in rem*; by way of foreclosure (forced sale) it may at any moment become property itself. If the credit system is organised, (*211*) it deprives the property in land of rent and interest and makes the landowner a mere entrepreneur, so that from an economic point of view he is like a tenant of his own property. (*212*)

What we have proved by the analysis of pure property in land, is valid also for its hybrid forms. In countries and provinces where historical development has led to a predominance of medium-sized property, the functions of the owner and tenant are combined, and where small-holders' property is the rule, one person is owner, tenant and labourer at the same time. So he might appear to gain in one character part, what he has lost in the other, and this was actually the case so long as the property did not change hands, by succession of sale, at the time when the capitalist development started. The revenue from one's own land, whether it is rent alone or interest or part of the average profit, or part of the wage for labour or a mixture of these elements, determines the price of land in accordance with the usual rate of interest. The farmer's purchase money contains an advance payment of this capitalised revenue. (*213*) "The expenditure of money-capital for the purchase of land, then, is not an instrument of agricultural capital. It is a proportionate deduction from the capital which the small farmers can employ in their own sphere of production" (*Capital* iii, p. 942).

Now there are three possibilities. (1) The farmer owns the whole purchase money as well as the capital required to run the farm, when he takes over the property. Then his three character parts of owner, entrepreneur and labourer cancel each other out, and he gains as owner what he loses as labourer or entrepreneur. (2) The farmer borrows the purchase money but owns the capital to run the farm. Then it is true that he is owner from the point of view of detention; from an economic point of view, on the other hand, he is not the owner. His property fails to be a title to rent, he is expropriated by finance-capital and becomes a mere detentor on behalf of finance-capital. Of course the whole of the purchase money is hardly ever given on credit; in the case of inheritance the successor always receives an hereditary portion. What is said therefore applies only to the balance of the purchase money, or to the compensation that is given to the heir's brothers and sisters in lieu of inheritance. The mortgagee therefore is owner from an economic point of view, as regards the title to rent, and the farmer who also has detention is owner in the eyes of the law. Here the relationship is nothing but a reversal of the relationship established by the lease, where the legal owner is also the economic owner and the tenant the detentor and cultivator. (3) The farmer owns the purchase money but not the capital to run the farm. He borrows the latter on mortgage and in the end the same relation is established as in case (2). Mortgage and lease therefore in most cases are nothing but two forms of the same thing. The farmer who has to-day possession in the form of the old patrimonial property, is often expropriated to the extent of the economic function of his property and he retains only detention of the means of production. (*214*)

Wherever there is no land ownership on a large capitalist scale, finance-capital takes the place of land ownership and thereby automatically appropriates the ground rent in the course of generations. We have already encountered finance-capital in this function: it does not develop new methods of production but petrifies old methods to which it attaches itself as a parasite. "Small peasants' property excludes by its very nature the development of the social powers of production of labor, the social forms of labor, the social concentration of capitals, cattle raising on a large scale, and a progressive application of science" (*Capital* iii, p. 938).

Property in land, whether in the form of large estates or of small holdings, is therefore not only antisocial but an obstruction to capitalism itself, preventing its complete emancipation from its prehistoric forms of merchant's and usurer's capital and obstructing its development into industrial capital. It is an obstacle to social development in general, at least so long as capitalist accumulation does not overcome it, or an association of producers does not, by the organisation of public credit, neutralise its bad effects, at least those which would injure their own interests.

For Note (*108*) Section ii see page 103.

(*109*) See for Blackstone's treatment of the law of master and servant as part of the law of persons above, note 107. For the Germanic *patria potestas* and its fate in this country: Pollock and Maitland, l.c., Vol. II, pp. 436 *sq.* For general descriptions of the Germanic *patria potestas*: Schröder- v. Künsberg, *Lehrbuch der deutsches Rechtsgeschichte*, 6th ed., Vol. I, pp. 71, 350; Hübner, *Deutsches Privatrecht*, § 90.

(*110*) For Renner's conception of feudalism see above, note 80. Feoffment is not, of course, a contract in any legal sense of the word. Renner's terminology seems to import modern ideas into medieval law. See, however, above, note 25.

(*111*) In this country the "works rule", i.e. the crystallisation of the exercise of the employer's command power is construed as a term of the contract of employment. English law which had been slow to separate the law of employment from the concept of status was particularly radical in giving effect to the contractual fiction. In Germany the Industrial Code (Gewerbe-ordnung) (§ 134 c) emphasised the character of the works rule as a source of law and the Works' Councils Act of 1920 provided (§ 78, § 80) that it had to be agreed between employer and works council or to be settled by arbitration.

(*112*) In this country legislation has not so far generally recognised the existence of this co-ordination. See, however, note 39, above.

(*113*) A striking illustration for the compulsive character of this community is afforded by the doctrine of common employment according to which an employee cannot recover damages from the employer for negligent acts committed by a fellow-servant, provided the work is of such a character that the negligence of one workman creates a special risk to the other. This doctrine—laid down in 1837 [*Priestley v. Fowler*, 3 M and W 1] and nowadays severely criticised by the Courts (see, e.g. Lord Atkin and Lord Wright in *Radcliffe v. Ribble Motor Services*, [1939] AC 215)—was and is justified as an "implied" term in the employee's contract of service by which he is said to take upon himself this special risk. It is, as was argued in *Radcliffe v. Ribble, supra*, "based on industrial and social conditions which have changed", but, since the House of Lords is bound by its own decisions, not liable to be abrogated by the action of the Courts themselves. The rule is thus another example for the phenomenon analysed by Renner that a norm can survive the change of its substratum. Its abolition has now been recommended in the Final Report of the Departmental Committee on Alternative Remedies (Cmd. 6860).

(*114*) On compulsory associations see the Introduction. Apart from local government bodies, institutions such as marketing boards established under the Agricultural Marketing Act, 1931, can be mentioned as examples. It should be noted that Renner calls the workers "a compulsory association according to all rules of *legal* doctrine". His analysis is here not confined to the social function, but extended to the normative structure itself.

(*115*) See note 39, above.

(*116*) The compulsory association which Renner discusses has its "norm", and that norm has its sanctions. The primary sanction is, of course, the employer's power of dismissal, but there are subsidiary sanctions—fines, claims for damages, etc. The "law making" character of the employer's command powers emerges clearly from the Truck Act, 1896. Section 1 of this Act provides a —somewhat rudimentary—codification of basic principles of a "criminal law" and of a "criminal procedure" for the workshop. In theory all this belongs to the law of contract, but that is only a disguise for a regulation of the employer's law-making power. The Truck Act prescribes a certain form for criminal legislation (notice or writing signed by the workman), it gives effect to the rule "*nullum crimen, nulla poena sine lege*" (the acts and omissions with respect to which the fine is to be imposed and particulars from which its amount can be ascertained must be specified in advance), and it also prescribes a certain form of "sentence" (specification in writing of the act for which the fine is imposed and of its amount). The employer's "legislative" power itself is only restricted and formalised, not abolished by this statute.

(*117*) "The law of administration"—*Amtsrecht*—does not mean "administrative law" in the now accepted sense of that word, but only that part of it which concerns the status of the public servants. It thus comprises the principles of local government law regulating the appointment, rights and duties, and dismissal of local government officers as well as the rules and practices governing the status of civil servants of the central government.

(*118*) The distinction between the custom of the manor and the law of free feudal tenure requires no comment, but "we can hardly translate into English the contrast which Germans draw between *Lehnrecht* and *Landrecht*" (Pollock and Maitland, l.c., Vol. I, p. 235). *Landrecht* is the general law of the land, including the law of free (allodial) property not comprised in the feudal nexus, *Lehnrecht* is the law of feudal tenure. It is thus that the distinction is used in the foremost sources of German law of the 13th century, the *Sachsenspiegel* and the *Schwabenspiegel*. In this country "every acre of land had been brought within (the) . . . scope (of dependent and derivative tenure), so that the English lawyer can not admit even a bare possibility of land being holden of no one" (Pollock and Maitland, l.c., p. 234). In England *Landrecht* and *Lehnrecht* are one. "Our *Landrecht* is *Lehnrecht*; in so far as feudalism is mere property law, England is of all countries the most perfectly feudalised. But this truth has another aspect:—our *Lehnrecht* is *Landrecht*; feudal law is not a special law applicable only to one fairly definite set of relationships, or applicable only to one class or estate of man; it is just the common law of England. The extensive application of the feudal formula . . . which is characteristic of England, and which perhaps was possible only in a conquered country, must have impaired its intensive force" (l.c. pp. 235–236).

(*119*) It is difficult to accept this statement in the light of modern developments. A glance at any "piece rate statement", say, in the cotton spinning or boot making industries, will convince the reader that mechanisation leads to an increase and not to a decrease in the number of specialised functions.

(*120*) That this is a valid observation on the conditions revealed, say, by the Report of Sir Robert Peel's Committee of 1816 (see Hutchins and Harrison, l.c., ch. II), can hardly be denied. Provisions of enactments such as the Children and Young Persons Act, 1933, and the Education Act, 1944, which partly prohibit and partly regulate the employment of children, must be understood as part of modern family law.

(*121*) The regulation of hours of work by legislation or collective agreements was the earliest and remains the most notable restriction of the command power which is the concomitant of the ownership of means of production. It is thus of more than symbolic sigificance that the Hours of Work (Industry) Convention, 1919 (International Labour Code, Art. 97 *sq.*) was the first major measure to be passed by the International Labour Organisation. The central importance of the "normal working day" as a substitution of collectively agreed or statutory regulation for dictated collective regulation is stressed and succinctly analysed in Webb, *Industrial Democracy*, pp. 327 *sq.* (1926 ed.)

(*122*) See note 116, above. Note that, under the Truck Act, 1896, legislative, judicial, and executive power are all vested in the employer. Apart from the special provisions mentioned in note 39 above the "*séparation des pouvoirs*" in the factory has, in this country, been the achievement of collective bargaining, not of legislation. See, e.g., the Agreement in the Engineering Industry of 1922 (Milne—Bailey, *Trade Union Documents*, p. 163), and the Agreement on Production Committees in the Engineering Industry of March 18th, 1942. For a general survey see *Industrial Relations Handbook* (H.M. Stationery Office, 1944), pp. 107–116.

(*123*) The emptiness of the lawyer's conception of a "contract" cannot be sufficiently emphasised. The employer's power to direct, the worker's duty to obey, to submit to the imposition of fines, to dismissal without notice on various grounds, are all "implied terms" of the contract of employment. The Courts have, in this country as elsewhere, and sometimes more so than elsewhere, used the technique of "implying" contractual terms as a disguise for the exercise of their own law-making power. What is, in fact, judge-made law often appears as the effect of the "implied intention" of the parties. This is a general phenomenon, not by any means confined to labour law. Much of what elsewhere was the result of legislation (e.g. with respect to the duties of a seller of goods, the effect of impossibility of performance, etc.) was in this country introduced by "implying" that the parties had "willed" it. In labour law the legally "implied" intention often bears no relation whatsoever to the real intention of the worker. The "order of labour" of modern society was based on the "implied intention" of those under its sway, a revival of the *contrat social* in a new setting. "You always can imply a condition in a contract. But why do you imply it? It is because of some belief as to the practice of a community or of a class, or because of some opinion as to policy, or, in short, because of some attitude of yours upon a matter not capable of exact quantitative measurement, and therefore not capable of founding exact logical conclusions" (Holmes, "The Path of the Law," 10 *Harvard Law Review* 457, at p. 466). See also Llewellyn, "What Price Contract—an Essay in Perspective" (1931), 40, *Yale Law Journal* 704, at p. 731, and Dicey, *Law and Opinion*, p. 152.

(*124*) The "law of labour", as here understood, is mainly the law of labour disputes, of collective bargaining, of conciliation and arbitration, and of workshop organisation. This discipline—"collective" labour law—has been much developed both on the Continent, and, largely as a consequence of the National Labor Relations Act, 1935, in the United States. It has not yet received a full systematic treatment in this country, partly owing to the fact that much of what was done abroad by legislation was in this country achieved by collective bargaining, a subject which the legal profession has so far regarded as lying outside its province.—"Economic Law" is the sum total of those principles which regulate competition and either establish or restrict monopolies. There are, on this subject, scattered remarks in the books on the law of contract (restraint of trade) and tort (conspiracy), and also a few monographs (e.g. Haslam, *Law Relating to Trade Combinations*, and Dix, *Law of Competitive Trading*), but—in the absence of legislation like the American Anti-Trust Laws or the German

Kartellverordnung—nothing like the voluminous literature existing in America and on the Continent. There is, however, in addition to the legal literature, some discussion of the legal problems in works such as Piotrowski, *Cartels and Trusts*, and Levy, *Retail Trade Associations*.

(*125*) See the quotation from Gierke's *Genossen schaftsrecht* in the Introduction. The concept of an *"Anstalt"*, a legal person which is not a corporation, but a segregated portion of public administration, is unknown in this country. Its place is taken by the "public corporation". The National Coal Board, established by the Coal Industry Nationalisation Act, 1946, is an *Anstalt* in this sense. For a classical definition see Fleiner, *Institutionen des deutschen Verwaltungsrechts*, § 19, 8th ed., p. 322.

(*126*) See notes 111, 114 above.

(*127*) The separation between public and private law (see note 7 above) of which (see note 80) feudalism was innocent is itself a product of the capitalist age. Continental scholars are continually baffled by the problem whether, e.g., the collective agreement is a public law or a private law contract. Like feudalism all institutions "pointing" beyond capitalism are a "denial" of the distinction between public and private law. For the difficulties encountered by Soviet jurists in their attempts to fit the institutions of a socialist economy into the dichotomy of public and private law see Schlesinger, l.c., e.g. p. 205, p. 252.

(*128*) In 1940 Lord Atkin, in *Nokes v. Doncaster Amalgamated Collieries Ltd.*, [1940] AC 1014, said that there was "ingrained in the personal status of a citizen under our laws. . . . the right to choose for himself whom he would serve, and that this right of choice constituted the main difference between a servant and a serf". From a legal point of view the "right of choice" is the essence of the distinction between serfdom and service. The lawyer ignores the question, to what extent economic conditions permit the servant to exercise this right.

(*129*) Or, to use Maine's formula (*Ancient Law*, Pollock ed., p. 174), what outwardly appears as "contract" is in essence a matter of "status". The *legal* development from contract to status has often been discussed (e.g. by Dicey, *Law and Opinion*, Lecture VIII).

(*130*) Marx died in 1883, the first volume of *Das Kapital* was published in 1867. In this country, the "legislative" power of the entrepreneur was no longer unrestricted at either of these dates. Much social legislation (including the Ten Hour Act, 1847) had been passed since 1832. Renner's statement applies with much greater force to Germany. The major enactments for the protection of women and children were passed in 1869 and in 1891, but, of course, industry developed in Germany far later than in this country.

(*131*) This sentence postulates the existence of a competitive economy. In many instances the worker cannot nowadays "exchange one individual capitalist for another". If the word "employer" is substituted for the word "capitalist", this is even more obvious, and becomes increasingly obvious with the nationalisation of many branches of economic activity. In modern industrial relations this means that the "shop agreement", i.e. the collective bargain concluded by one employer with a union or unions is becoming increasingly prominent, at the expense of the agreement concluded by an employers' federation. It also means that the size of the bargaining unit on the workers' side must be large, and that inside the unions power is apt to shift from the periphery to the centre. Except in the case of certain very highly placed technical and commercial employees it does not, however, affect the essence of the labour relationship. In their case it should lead to an increased emphasis on the protection against "restraint of trade" clauses formulated in decisions such as *Morris v. Saxelby*, [1916] 1 AC 688.

(*132*) The German or Austrian reader of this sentence was inclined to think of events more recent than the massacre of Peterloo of 1819, the application of Pitt's Combination Acts, the suppression of Owenite unionism among the Dorchester labourers, the suppression of the Paris working class in the "June battle" of 1848, or even the Commune of 1871. The calling out of troops against strikers was no uncommon event in the Germany of the concluding decades of the 19th century, the most notorious example was the coal miners' strike of 1889.

(*133*) The provisions for the fixing of wages in the Elizabethan Statute of Apprentices, 1562, and the 17th century legislation (1 Jac. 1 ch. 6, 16 Car. 1, ch. 4) which extended it to labourers were not repealed until 1813 (53 Geo. 3, ch. 40). The Act of 1813 was preceded by the decision in *R. v. Justices of Kent* (1812), 14 East 395, in which it was held that the fixing of wages was in the discretion of the justices and that mandamus would not lie to compel them to do so. (See Slesser and Baker, *Trade Union Law*, 3rd ed., p. 7.) It would, however, be wrong to think that these wage fixing provisions had remained part of the living law until 1813. Although a survey of the 18th century development (see Slesser and Baker, l.c.) shows that instances of their application were perhaps more numerous than is sometimes assumed, Adam Smith's statement that in 1776 the fixing of wages had "gone entirely into disuse" (*Wealth of Nations*, Bk. I, ch. x, quoted Webb,

History of Trade Unionism, p. 49, note 2), is thought to be broadly correct.

(*134*) The Minority Report of the Poor Law Commission of 1909 shows that, at that time, the workhouse had long ceased to play the role ascribed to it by Renner. The "General Mixed Workhouses", described and condemned by Sidney and Beatrice Webb in Part I, Chapter I of the Minority Report, were no longer reserve depots of the able-bodied unemployed. Of 250,000 inmates (Part I, p. 6) something like 10,000 (Part II, p. 36) were healthy and able-bodied men, and the figure of 5000 for London was described by the Webbs as "a phenomenon quite new and unprecedented, we believe, during at least half a century".

(*135*) The acceptance of the Essential Work Orders by the working class in this country and by the trade unions, shows the distance we have travelled since this sentence was written. For a clear and succinct survey of the development of labour direction in the Soviet Union, see now E. H. Carr, *The Soviet Impact on the Western World*, pp. 48 *sq.* It shows how, in the Soviet Union as elsewhere, war (civil and external) and labour compulsion were inter-connected. The 1936 Constitution enacted the right to work, but not a "duty to work" in a legal sense. The voluntary character of the contract of employment was—temporarily—jettisoned under the stress of impending war in 1940 (see Schlesinger, l.c., p. 219, pp. 221–222). In view of the achievement of full employment this "voluntary" character was more than a legal figure of speech.

(*136*) On detention see above, note 45. According to English law, as pointed out above, a servant is not in "possession" of his master's goods (Pollock and Wright, *Possession in the Common Law*, pp. 56, 58). Holmes, *Common Law*, pp. 227–228, was of the opinion that this "anomalous" rule was one of the "incidents" of the servant's "status". "It is familiar that the status of a servant maintains many marks of the time when he was a slave. . . . A slave's possession was his owner's possession on the practical ground of the owner's power over him, and from the fact that the slave had no standing before the law. The notion that his personality was merged in that of his family head survived the era of emancipation." (See the remarks above, notes 83, 107.) Pollock, l.c., p. 59, doubted the correctness of Holmes' explanation.

(*137*) The reader may use the following pages as a footnote to, and in parts as a refutation of, Dicey's Introduction to the Second Edition of *Law and Opinion* (written in 1913). Renner shows how the development of what Dicey calls "collectivism" cannot be understood without taking into account the change in the function of property to which it was a response. Renner's words were written in 1904. That the "substratum" has changed almost beyond recognition since that time is certainly true, but the main lines of the development were continued and not broken. The new element is the extent to which, especially under the impact of the Great Depression and of the Second World War, norms have been enacted which have changed the substratum.

(*138*) See the Introduction.

(*139*) The principles of the common law and those of the Railway and Canal Traffic Act, 1854, do not permit a common carrier of goods arbitrarily to refuse a consignment, and, since the decision of the Court of Appeal in *Clarke v. West Ham Corporation*, [1909] 2 K.B. 858, a similar principle has applied to the carriage of passengers. This phenomenon of the "compulsion to contract" may be of increasing importance in the development of the law. It generally applies to statutory monopolists such as public utility companies. Nevertheless the lawyer continues to insist on the existence of a contract. If I make a contract for my own transportation by railway, it may be said of myself and of the railway company: "Quamquam coactus, voluit". The "will" to contract is here a mere figment of the law. For the compulsion to supply which is imposed upon public utility undertakings: see, e.g. Gasworks Clauses Act, 1871, s. 11, s. 36; Waterworks Clauses Act, 1847, s. 53; Electric Lighting (Clauses) Act, 1899, s. 27 *sq.*

(*140*) E.g. the Standard Terms and Conditions of Carriage by Railway, laid down by the Railway Rates Tribunal in 1927, or— in the case of a carriage of passengers—the Railway Companies' Bye-Laws of 1926 which were made by the companies as delegates of legislative power under the authority of the Railways Clauses Act, 1945, and of the Regulation of Railways Act, 1889. It is interesting to note that even a bye-law by the making of which the railway company exceeded its legislative power may nevertheless apply as between passenger and company owing to a tacit incorporation of its content in the contract (*Butler v. M.S. and L. Ry. Co.* (1888), 21 Q.B.D. 207). Railway bye-laws, amongst other institutions, should discourage an attempt to insist upon a rigid distinction between public and private law in England.

(*141*) The first Housing Act was, in this country, passed in 1866: the Artisan's and Labourer's Dwellings Act, 31 and 32 Vict. c. 130. The first Rent Act was the Increase of Rent and Mortgage Interest (War Restrictions) Act, 1915. The first town planning measure was passed in 1909 (Housing, Town Planning, etc., Act). Safety provisions for factories, mines, ships, go, of course, back into the 19th century. The voluminous body of Public Utility Legislation which regulates maximum dividends, prices, etc., is one of the oldest and most important examples of this development. A Continental lawyer of the old school would be hard put to it to say whether gas, water, and electricity undertakings are institutions of "public" or of "private" law.

(*142*) In one important respect the English law of negligence has ignored the changed function of property. It is still the law that, as a matter of principle, an "occupier" of land can do with the land as he pleases. His liability to indemnify a person who has entered the premises for injuries suffered owing to the unsafe character of those premises cannot therefore be based upon a general duty of the occupier to safeguard the public against injuries. It must be founded upon the individual relationship between the occupier and the injured person. It is only this relationship which gives rise to a "duty to take care". The extent of the occupier's liability depends on the purpose for which the injured person had entered the premises: was it by right, e.g. under a contract, was it at least in the occupier's own interest, or was it by virtue of a "bare licence" to enter? In every single case these questions must be asked and answered. As long as the premises are a *suum*, "private" property in a social and not only in a legal sense, this rule fits a definite objective in accordance with the character of its substratum. When, however, the substratum changes and what is legally "private" is in fact dedicated to general use, i.e. "socialised" in this specific sense, the function of the unchanged norm has been transformed, a transformation produced by that of the property-object and by nothing else. To apply these rules of the law of negligence to a farmhouse or a private dwelling house occupied by one family is one thing,—to apply them to a railway station, to a public park, or even to a block of flats is, whatever the Courts may say, another. That the liability of a railway company to a man injured by the unsafe condition of a station should depend on whether he was there in order to wait for a train or to buy a newspaper at a bookstall, is grotesque. That the application of the rule to tenement buildings can work results little short of disastrous is shown by the case of *Fairman v. Perpetual Investment Building Society*, [1923] AC 74.

(*143*) Or, might we not say, of the common law? How much understanding for the changing function of the law do our students—whether university, bar, or law society—derive from their training in contract, tort, and real property?

(*144*) See, on "standard contracts" the Introduction and Prausnitz, *The Standardisation of Commercial Contracts in English and Continental Law*, 1937.

(*145*) In this country there are no general provisions enabling the Board of Trade or any other authority to enforce against retail traders either a duty to sell or a duty to exhibit prices. The common law imposes a duty not to withhold his services upon the common carrier and upon the innkeeper. Railway companies must give full publicity to their charges (see, e.g., the "rate book," which must be kept at every station under the Regulation of Railways Act, 1873), and road passenger transport undertakers may be—and usually are—compelled to exhibit a tariff of their fares by virtue of their road service licence under the Road Traffic Act, 1930.

(*146*) That at common law a shopkeeper cannot be compelled to sell any of the wares exhibited in a shop or shop-window—even if the price is marked on them—is a rule every law student has to learn at the beginning of his course on contracts. From a practical point of view, it would be impossible to "construe" the display in the shop window as an "offer" to contract which would become binding when "accepted" by the customer. The law regards it as a mere "invitation" to make offers, and it is the customer who is considered as making an offer, which the shopkeeper is free to accept or not to accept. This is a simple practical expedient—legally explained with the help of the presumed "intention" of the shopkeeper—used to obviate the difficulties which might otherwise arise from a repeated selling of the same article. Experience shows that, as a rule, the student who is invited to assimilate this principle has to overcome a considerable psychological resistance. This resistance arises from an inarticulate feeling that the shop-keeper is, as it were, an agent of a "public" process of distribution, and cannot arbitrarily grant or withhold his services. Not to "serve" the customer, though it would be possible to do so, appears not only as an act liable to disappoint legitimate expectations, but somehow as a conduct at variance with the public function the retail trader professes to exercise. There is a contrast between the law and a conception of fairness which arises from the awareness of a public function which common sense finds it difficult to reconcile with the legal form in which the function is exercised.

(*147*) The war of 1939–1945 gave rise to similar legislation in this country. The supervision and the powers exercised by the War Agricultural Committees have been taken over in a modified form by peace-time legislation. (See Part II of the Agriculture Act, 1947.)

(*148*) The Housing Acts and the Rent Acts are going some way towards giving legal expression to this "public" character of tene-ment property. The interpretation which the Housing Acts have received in the Courts illustrates the difficulties which must arise when the law tries to combine the institution of private property with the conception of public function. The duties imposed by the Housing Act upon the landlord have been pressed into the framework of the law of contract with the result that the object of the legislation has often been frustrated. See Jennings, "Courts and Administrative Law—The Experience of English Housing Legislation", 49 Harvard Law Review 426, especially pp. 436-8, and Plummer, "Some Aspects of the Law of Landlord and Tenant", 9 Modern Law Review 42, especially at p. 45. The landlord's statutory duty to keep small houses and flats "reasonably fit for human habitation" (Section 2 (1) of the Housing Act, 1936, reproducing similar provisions in the Acts of 1909 and 1925) appears in the Act as an implied condition of the contract. ·The unfortunate habit of giving to legal duties the appearance as something "willed" by the parties, rightly castigated by Prof. Llewellyn (see the Article quoted above, note 123), was here adopted by the legislature itself. It is quite clearly an expression of a hesitation to recognise that the relationship between landlord and tenant is open to regulation in the public interest. The public interest which intervenes in order to eliminate the results produced by the inequality of bargaining power between landlord and tenant, is concealed behind a fictitious intention of the parties so as to save the face of the law of contract. In this particular case the results were disastrous: the Courts have held that a third party—e.g. the tenant's wife or child—being a stranger to the "contract", cannot recover from the landlord damages for breach of this statutory obligation (*Ryall v. Kidwell and Son*, [1914] 3 K.B. 135). In the past the Courts have done a great deal to whittle down the protection given by this statute: thus they have given the narrowest possible meaning to the words "fit for human habitation" (see, e.g., *Stanton v. Southwick*, [1920] 2 K.B. 642; *Morgan v. Liverpool Corporation*, [1927] 2 K.B. 131), and they have held that the landlord of a tenement house is under no obligation to keep the staircase in repair (*Dunster v. Hollis*, [1918] 2 K.B. 795). The decision of the House of Lords in *Summers v. Salford Corporation*, [1943] A.C. 283, and especially the speech of Lord Wright, inaugurates a new approach (see note by Unger in 5 Mod. L. R. 266.) There are few examples more apt to illustrate Renner's point that the normative structure of private law—here the contractual nature of the landlord-tenant relationship—and the social substratum, the nature of the tenement house as a public "establishment" (*Anstalt*) are bound to get into conflict. The contractual nature of the landlord's duty was recently emphasised by the House of Lords in *McCarrick v. Liverpool Corporation*, [1946] 2 All E.R. 646.

(*149*) The Employment Exchanges, first set up in this country under the Labour Exchanges Act, 1909, have never had—apart from war-time legislation—a monopoly of finding jobs for workers or workers for jobs. They are supplemented by voluntary institutions, but the practice, widespread on the Continent, of setting up voluntary labour exchanges by collective agreement, does not seem to exist in this country. (It is not mentioned in the Ministry of Labour Report on Collective Agreements of 1934.)

(*150*) This is only another way of formulating the development from contract to status. It is easy to exaggerate the parallel between modern labour law and medieval feudal law. The recent decision of the Court of Appeal in *Hivac Ltd. v. Park Royal Scientific Instruments Ltd.*, [1946] 1 All E. R. 350, is a welcome and necessary reminder of the difference between the employee's duty of fidelity and the feudal tenant's duty of fealty.

(*151*) Since English law has not accepted a universal principle by which the employee or workman is legally entitled to the rights provided for him in a collective agreement, this statement requires a qualification. It can be applied to English conditions if and in so far as a minimum wage provision applies, e.g. under the Wages Councils Act, 1945 (which has taken the place of the Trade Boards Acts, 1909 and 1918), under the Agricultural Wages Acts, 1924 and 1947, under Part III of the Road Haulage Wages Act, 1938, or under the Catering Wages Act, 1943. It can also be applied to those cases in which, by express statutory provision, the content of a collective agreement has been made compulsory, either directly or through the medium of an Order of the Minister of Labour, or of an award of the National Arbitration Tribunal or of the Industrial Court, e.g. under the Cotton Manufacturing Industry (Temporary Provisions) Act, 1934, under the Conditions of Employment and National Arbitration Order, 1940, under Part II of the Road Haulage Wages Act, 1938, or under sect. 19 of the Wages Councils Act, 1945. In view of the voluntary observance of minimum wage clauses contained in collective agreements and in awards made by voluntary conciliation and arbitration machinery or under the Conciliation Act, 1896, and under the Industrial Courts Act, 1919, Renner's statement has a far greater factual validity in this country than a mere perusal of statutes and orders would reveal.

(*152*) The juxtaposition of—statutory—insurance contributions and—voluntary—trade union subscriptions shows that, in Renner's view, this transformation of the employer—employee relationship is only partly the result of a "legal" development. Present developments in this country show another significant phenomenon—partly "legal", partly "voluntary"—which reinforces Renner's contention: the "guaranteed" week which shifts the risk of impossibility of performance to some extent from the employee to the employer was inaugurated by statutory rules: the

Essential Work Orders. In spite of the disappearance of this war-time legislation the principle is kept alive in the form of voluntary agreements. Minimum wage fixing authorities, e.g. wages councils, are now generally empowered to fix "remunerations" and not, as in the past, time rates and piece rates (compare, e.g., sect. 10 of the Wages Councils Act, 1945, with sect. 3 of the Trade Boards Act, 1918). Under the Wages Councils Act, 1945, and under the Holidays with Pay Act, 1938, they are also authorised to fix holidays and holiday remuneration. All these developments, together with the steady growth of collective bargaining, contribute to the transformation indicated by the author. The "decasualisation" of labour operates in the same direction (see, e.g., the Dock Workers (Regulation of Employment) Act, 1946).

(*153*) English law has not, so far, given effect to the principle that an employer must pay compensation to an employee whom he dismisses arbitrarily. As long as he gives the customary or contractual notice, the employer is at liberty to deprive the employee of his position without assigning any reasons and without being compelled to justify the dismissal. Even in a case of unjustified dismissal without notice, the maximum amount the employee can recover by way of damages is represented by the wages or salary he would have obtained during the period of notice. (*Addis v. Gramophone Co.*, [1909] A.C. 488). The French Courts began about 1850 to develop the theory of "*rupture abusive*" or "*résiliation injustifiée*" or "*sans justes motifs*", which led to the enactment of the statute of December 27th, 1890, by which damages could be claimed for unilateral dissolution of a contract of employment. This was subsequently replaced by the more specific enactment of July 19th, 1928 (Code du Travail Art. 23, § 5) which expressly refers to "*résiliation abusive*" and authorises the Court to inquire into the "*circonstances de la rupture*". (See, for this development—highly significant from the point of view of Renner's thesis—Jean Vincent, *La Dissolution du Contrat de Travail*, Paris, 1935, pp. 461 *sq.*) The Weimar Republic—Works Councils Act, 1920, sect. 84—linked the idea of the "right to the job" with the statutory workshop organisation. The Nazis—Law for the Organisation of National Labour, 1934, sect. 56—maintained the right to compensation for loss of position, although they abolished the works councils.

(*154*) An English reader may be inclined to take exception to this formulation. In this country collective regulation was much less closely linked with state intervention than on the Continent. The transformation discussed by Renner was primarily the result of autonomous trade union action, the "law" being a passive spectator. On the Continent the legal enforceability of collective agreements stimulated the growth of collective bargaining and, with it, of trade unionism. In Britain the collective agreement has, to this day, remained an "unenforceable" "gentlemen's agreement". While it is true that, owing to collective bargaining, and, partly of course, owing to statutory regulation too, the "job" was, in many cases, transformed into a "position" (notably in the "sheltered" industries), it is in no sense correct to say that the contract of employment has become an "institution of public law". The difference between the legal developments in Britain on the one hand and, say, in France, in Germany, or in Austria on the other, reflects the histories of the various working class movements: in this country trade union organisation came first, and the political movement much later, on the Continent the sequence was the reverse. The distinction loses much of its significance if one accepts Ehrlich's definition of law, and his concept of "social sanction" (see ch. iv of his *Fundamental Principles*).

(*155*) *Locatio conductio operarum*, "*louage des gens de travail qui s'engagent au service de quelqu'un*", "*Dienstvertrag*", broadly corresponds to the contract of employment of English law. *Locatio conductio operis*, "*louage des entrepreneurs d'ouvrages*", "*Werkvertrag*", is roughly the equivalent of the English contract for work and labour. In this country the measure of control exercised by the "employer" is the chief criterion of the distinction. "The power of control which the master enjoys over the work of his servant is the decisive factor distinguishing the servant from an independent contractor" (Batt, *Law of Master and Servant*, p. 1). If the employer is only entitled to order the work, to say *what* is to be done, there will usually be a contract for work and labour, but if he also controls the "*how*" and "*when*", the mode of performance, the Courts will be inclined to hold that there is a contract of employment. On the Continent this criterion is not always applied, and, in German law, a distinction is drawn between "guaranteeing a result", and merely promising services (which, in turn, may be "dependent" or "independent" services), but, disregarding details, *locatio conductio operarum* may be said to fulfil the functions of the contract of service, and *locatio conductio operis* that of the contract for work and labour.

(*156*) A contract by which a person undertakes to manufacture goods from his own material and to transfer the finished goods to another person (*Werklieferungsvertrag*) is, according to English law, as a rule, a contract of sale, and not a contract for work and labour (Sale of Goods Act, 1893, sect. 5). There are marginal cases (see, e.g. *Robinson v. Graves*, [1935] 1 K B 579) in which the element of personal skill so much outweighs that of the value of the material that the Courts will classify the contract as one for work and labour. If the person who has ordered the goods has supplied the material, English law (like Continental law) refuses to call the transaction a contract of sale. The contract for the manufacture of goods out of material supplied by the manufacturer—the most important type of contract in an industrial community—is treated as a contract of sale in French Law (Cass. Civ. 20. 3. 1872, Dalloz 72. 1. 140) and in German law (Civil Code, § 651). This corresponds to the view which prevailed among the classical Roman jurists (*Gajus* III, 147) and which was adopted by Justinian (J. 3, 24, 4; D 19, 2, 2, 1; 18, 1, 20; 18, 1 65). Roman law thus provided (as so often) an ideal conceptual framework for the juristic analysis of developing capitalist institutions, but English law responded to the needs of a similar situation by reaching similar conclusions in its own way (see *Benjamin on Sale*, 7th ed., pp. 165 *sq.*)

(*157*) Since—see the previous note—modern Continental systems, like English law, treat a contract for the manufacture and delivery of goods as a contract of sale, the law does not *in practice* differentiate between the delivery of goods to order and the delivery of goods manufactured with a view to sale in a market. Nevertheless, the system of the Continental Codes reflects the difference between the two situations. The contract for the sale of goods to be manufactured from the vendor's own material, though treated like a sale, appears in the French Code Civil (Art. 1787), in the German Civil Code (§ 651) and in the Swiss Law of Obligations (Art. 365) in the sections dealing with "work and labour", while in English law it appears in the Sale of Goods Act. The systematic arrangement of the Continental Codes still shows traces of the transition from simple commodity production to industrial capitalism. This had little, if any, influence on the practical application of the law of sale to these contracts.

(*158*) The transfer of a business enterprise *en bloc* may, in a given case, involve a sale of goods, e.g. that of the vendor's stock in trade. Although the legal principles governing sale of goods would apply to the rights and liabilities of the vendor and purchaser of the stock in trade, English law does not—any more than do Continental systems—regard a business enterprise as "goods" within the meaning of the law of sale. The central feature of a transfer of a business is the sale of the goodwill, and this is not governed by the Sale of Goods Act. It is, on the other hand, clear that English law has never succeeded in developing the legal conception of a business enterprise as an *universitas rerum*, as an entity of assets and liabilities capable of being transferred *uno actu*. Nor is there any need for such a development under modern conditions. Owing to the spreading practice of incorporation of business entities as limited companies, the transfer of rights and liabilities can be brought about by a transfer of shares. For the amalgamation of companies English law (Companies Act, 1929, sect. 154) provides a form of "universal succession", and income tax law (Income Tax Act, 1918, Schedule D, Rule (Cases I and II) 11) makes special provision for the succession to a business.

(*159*) On the Continent the transfer of a business is, in some respects, sometimes treated as a case of "universal succession" to assets as well as liabilities. See, e.g., sect. 25 of the German Commercial Code, by which a person who acquires a commercial enterprise by transaction *inter vivos* and continues it under its old firm name is liable for the debts contracted by the previous owner for the purposes of the undertaking. For an analysis of the "enterprise" as a legal entity and for the influence of Roman and medieval law on its development see Oppikofer, *Das Unternehmensrecht*, 1927.

(*160*) The assignment of a debt is something essentially different from a transfer of tangible goods. The English Sale of Goods Act (see sect. 62) does not apply to a contract by which a creditor "sells" a debt to a third person. The law governing the contract for the sale of "choses in action" has not been codified in this country, nor has it received the comprehensive treatment by learned writers which was accorded to the sale of goods. The French (Art. 1689 *sq.*) and German (§ 437) Codes deal with it in connection with the Sale of Goods. From a legal point of view, the sale of a debt is clearly distinguishable from the sale of a tangible movable object, but the two types of transaction have far more in common than has either with the sale of an undertaking as a whole. Both are, in Renner's terminology, an acquisition of an object by a new subject, neither is "succession" in the economic sense.

(*161*) This refers to the movements amongst journeymen and labourers in the 14th century and after, for which see Webb, *History of Trade Unionism*, pp. 2, 3; Brentano, *Geschichte der wirtschaflichen Entwicklung Englands*, Vol. I, pp. 285 *sq.*; Ashley, l.c. Book II, ch. II, §§ 34–36, pp. 98 to 124.

(*162*) The famous controversy whether a thing manufactured out of another man's material belonged to the manufacturer or to the owner of the material was possibly influenced by the impact of different schools of philosophy upon the two "schools" of lawyers (see Jolowicz, *Historical Introduction to the Study of Roman Law*, p. 385, n. 5). Later jurists solved the dispute by a compromise which was adopted by Justinian: if the new *species* was capable of being reduced to its constituent elements, it belonged to the owner of the material, otherwise to the manufacturer (J. 2, 1, 25). The modern Codes make the destiny of the new *species* dependent upon the question which is the more valuable, the material used or the work done upon it. In the former case the new thing belongs to the owner of the material, in the latter to the manufacturer. Justinian's criterion of "reducibility" was abandoned (Code Civil Art. 570, 571—with a bias towards the owner of the material; German Civil Code § 950—with the opposite bias in favour of the manufacturer; Swiss Civil Code Art. 726—holding the balance between French and German law). English law has never solved this problem. At the end of the 15th century there was a tendency to adopt the Roman compromise solution (Holdsworth, *History of English Law*, Vol. VII, p. 496), but, in the course of the 16th century, the common law seems to have "departed from the Roman rule—the test being not, as in Roman law, whether or no a new species has been made which cannot be resolved into its component parts; but whether the maker previously owned a principal part of the material" (Holdsworth, l.c., p. 497). Here the matter was allowed to rest. In view of the "remedial" structure of English law, the question who was the owner did not require a practical answer. Enough that the owner of the material has, in any event, an action for damages for conversion against the manufacturer who had used it without being entitled to do so. The question whether he can demand the new thing *in specie* is a "matter of judicial discretion unfettered by any general principles", but "it may be assumed that in all ordinary cases the Court will be guided by the relative values of the interests of the rival claimants" (*Salmond on Torts*, 10th ed., p. 316). It is thus impossible to draw from English law a parallel illustration for one of the most startling phenomena of modern legal history: viz. that the Roman or modern Continental principles of *specificatio* were never applied to the industrial workman. The mere idea that he, like the independent artisan, might acquire ownership in the products of his labour was so absurd that it did not occur to the lawyers. Renner's explanation—the use of an "implied term" in the contract of employment—may be of some assistance in so far as the problem is one of positive legal doctrine. It fails to account for the absence of a discussion of the problem in 19th century Continental doctrine. There was, it is submitted, a subconscious feeling that the relation of dependence between employer and workman excluded the application of a doctrine designed to meet a situation arising between equals. The tacit elimination of the doctrine of *specificatio* from the employment relationship was difficult to reconcile with the fiction of equality, but a perfect recognition of the sociological nature of the modern contract of employment as a relation of subordination. It may be capable of an explanation similar to that given by Holmes (*Common Law*, pp. 227, 230) for the common law doctrine that a servant has no possession in the goods held by him on behalf of his master: a dim realisation of the economic essence of the relationship pushing aside the legal ideology of the "free contract" (see for a discussion of this problem, Sinzheimer, *Grundzüge des Arbeitsrechts*, 1925, p. 151).

(*163*) The most obvious and important modern illustration for this phenomenon is the vesting of patents for inventions made by an employee in the employer.

(*164*) Renner's analysis of the employment relationship retains its importance irrespective of the validity or otherwise of the economic theory of value with which it is connected in the text.

(*165*) The contrast between the legal sphere of the "market" and the legal sphere of the "factory" corresponds to that between free feudal tenure and villeinage. A clear-sighted non-Marxist Continental student of the social structure of English law found a corresponding dichotomy in the structure of the English Courts. Max Weber (*Wirtschaft und Gesellschaft*, p. 470) points out that "the administration of justice by *honoratiores* sometimes shows a dual face, according as to whether the typical legal interests of the class of *honoràtiores* itself are concerned or those of the classes dominated by them. English justice, for example, was strictly formal in all matters coming before the central Courts. But as administered by the justices of the peace, in matters concerning the every day disputes and wrong-doings of the masses it was informal and 'Kadi' justice to a degree entirely unknown on the Continent". The law of matrimonial separation as administered in the Magistrates' Court and in the High Court furnishes examples.

(*166*) Stock and produce exchanges are, in some countries, the object of exhaustive legislative regulation and close supervision: see, e.g. the German Exchanges Law of May 27th, 1908. Legislative control extends to the organisation of the exchanges, admission to membership, discipline, and the functioning of the exchange (including permission to deal). The "market" is thus an institution of public law. "Market police" is, of course, a legal phenomenon known to Roman law as it is to most modern systems. The presence or absence of such institutions of administrative law is, however, irrelevant from the point of view of Renner's argument. This is equally applicable where, as in this country, the stock exchanges—this is not true of the insurance exchanges governed by the Lloyds Acts, 1871 and 1911—rest on an entirely customary basis, and where legislative market regulations appear either in general statutes such as the Sale of Goods Act and the Food and Drugs Act or in judge-made law, e.g. with regard to passing-off.

(*167*) The legal concept of the "merchant" who is subject to a special "mercantile law" is, on the whole, alien to modern English law. There is not, in this country, a special body of principles governing "mercantile" as distinguished from "civil" sales, "mercantile" as distinguished from "civil" partnerships, etc., and the law of negotiable instruments as well as the law of bankruptcy applies to non-merchants as well as to merchants. All this is to some extent different on the Continent. There are, in this country, a few vestiges of a genuine "law merchant" in the Continental— and in the old English—sense: e.g. the provisions of the Factors Act, 1889, concerning mercantile agents, those of the Sale of Goods Act, 1893, (sect. 14), imposing special liabilities on habitual dealers, and the law of cheques (Bills of Exchange Act, 1882, sect. 60, and sects. 73 *sq.*) which apply to bankers only. Otherwise "mercantile" or "commercial" law is not a conception forming part of the substantive law of England. It is of importance as part of the law of procedure, in the sense that it constitutes the sum total of those causes arising out of the ordinary transactions of merchants or traders which may be assigned to the list of cases heard by a King's Bench judge in charge of the "commercial list" and to which a simplified procedure can be applied. It is also important for academic purposes as a teaching subject and as a topic for text-book writers. The "law merchant" became in this country the general law of the land.

(*168*) Renner does not analyse the next stage of the development which, in the era of monopoly capitalism, has led to a re-union of the producing and trading functions. The "central selling" organisations of German syndicates, trade organisations, etc., are described in Warriner, *Combines and Rationalisation in Germany*, pp. 82 *sq.* For a survey of the parallel development in Japan see Brady, *Business as a System of Power*, pp. 89 *sq.* For the elimination of wholesale trade in certain branches of German industry by "works trade" (Werkhandel), see Levy, *Industrial Germany*, especially pp. 197–200.

(*169*) For an account of the common law principles with regard to "forestalling", and of the 16th century legislation against forestalling, regrating and ingrossing, see Holdsworth, *History of English Law*, Vol. IV, pp. 375 *sq.*

(*170*) The manufacturer disposes of his property by changing the physical substance. The exercise of the right is consummated in a technical process: the conversion of raw material into a finished product. The merchant exercises his right of property by a legal process: purchase and sale. From his point of view the institutions of private law, and especially of the law of contract, occupy a central position in the organisation of his enterprise. From the point of view of the manufacturer as such the only legal institutions which go to the root of the organisation of his business are those referring to employment and those of patent law. It is therefore understandable that, in this country as well as on the Continent, "mercantile law" was a well developed discipline long before the very term "industrial law" had ever been heard of, and that, in this country, "industrial law" connotes what should be—and what in America is—described as "labour law".

(*171*) The law of "documents of title" is particularly highly developed in this country (see Purchase, *The Law Relating to Documents of Title to Goods*). Renner mentions warrants, but the most important type of document of title is the bill of lading. The central importance of documents of title is illustrated by the Factors Act, 1889, and that of the bill of lading in particular by the Bills of Lading Act, 1855, and by the Hague Rules, embodied, in this country, in the Carriage of Goods by Sea Act, 1924. The machinery of the finance of international sales transactions hinges to a large extent upon the existence of documents of title. See for descriptions and for legal analyses of documentary credits: Gutteridge, *The Law of Bankers' Commercial Credits;* A. G. Davis, *The Law Relating to Commercial Letters of Credit.*

(*172*) See note 167 above. One may, perhaps, say that in the most advanced capitalist economies the legal "character-mask" of the "merchant" disappears when the special "legal qualification" of being a "merchant" is abandoned, and the law merchant merges in the general law.

(*173*) The exploitation of home-workers and of out-workers by manufacturers and—Renner's main point—by contractors has, ever since 1864, been a main theme of British social legislation (see Hutchins and Harrison, l.c., p. 154, p. 170, p. 180, p. 207, and *passim*). The principal enactments now in force designed to meet these conditions are Sections 110 and 111 of the Factories Act, 1937. Under these provisions the duty to keep "lists of out-workers" in certain specified trades and the prohibition against the giving out of work to be done in unwholesome premises are imposed not only upon the occupier of a factory, but also upon contractors. The "particulars" clause of the Factories Act (sect. 112) is another enactment designed to prevent the exploitation of home-workers. The first English minimum wage statute, the Trade Boards Act, 1909 (now replaced by the Wages Councils Act, 1945), was passed to a large extent with the same object in view.

(*174*) It is perhaps true to say that the economic conditions of certain colonial areas, e.g. West Africa, provide contemporary examples for this phenomenon which has largely disappeared from the European scene?

(*175*) Licensing legislation, the requirement of concessions, of proficiency certificates, etc., may, of course, serve a large variety of purposes. It may serve public health and morals, e.g. liquor trade licencing; safety, e.g. proficiency certificates for masters of ships, managers of mines, etc.; the prevention of overcrowding on the roads, e.g. goods vehicle licences, etc. Among the numerous cases of concessions, licences, etc., required for a large variety of trades by German law (mainly under the Industrial Code of 1869), there were some clearly designed to protect a group of small traders against competition, e.g. chimney sweeps and owners of milk bars. With the same object in view co-operative shops were forbidden to sell to non-members (Law of May 20th, 1898, sect. 8). For a full survey of surviving private monopoly rights in Prussia see Dernburg, *Preussisches Privatrecht*, Vol. II, § 303).

(*176*) Both forms of transactions form part of Soviet law. A transaction between two state-owned concerns may take the form of a sale. After the nationalisation of the railways in this country a contract for the carriage of coal for the National Coal Board will not be legally different from a contract between a private trader and a private carrier, although it will be concluded between two public corporations.

(*177*) The contracts which Renner discusses under the heading of "contracts of restitution" belong either to the category of "bailments" or to that of "loans for consumption". *Depositum* and *commodatum*, whether gratuitous or for reward are, in English law, bailments. "Bailment is the delivery of goods to another, other than as a servant, for some purpose upon a condition, express or implied, that after the purpose has been fulfilled they shall be re-delivered to the bailor, or otherwise dealt with according to his directions, or kept till he reclaims them" (Chitty on *Contracts*, 19th ed., p. 630). The bailee may be entitled to use the thing, but he is not entitled to consume the substance, he has to restore the thing itself, not merely its value. "Loan for consumption", and, in particular, "loan of money", is not to-day regarded as a bailment (see, however, for the medieval law, Pollock and Maitland, l.c., II, 169). In this country the law of bailment developed outside the law of contract, it belonged—and, up to a point, still belongs—to the law of property and possession. The history of the law of bailment is older than that of the law of contract, and the principles governing the liability of a bailee were developed along lines very different from those which led to the modern law of contract (see Holmes, *Common Law*, Lecture V; Holdsworth, l.c., Vol. VII, pp. 450 *sq.*, Plucknett, l.c., p. 421).

(*178*) The economist's conception of "money" does not coincide with the legal conception. The lawyer regards as "money" only those physical objects which have been designated by the state as means of payment and units of measurement. A credit balance on current account may be treated as money for certain purposes, e.g. for the interpretation of a will (see *Perrin v. Morgan*, [1943] A.C. 399), but not in the general legal sense of the term. Money is not, in any legal sense, a "commodity", and where coins are used as a commodity (e.g. by a collector of curiosities), they are not functioning as "money" (as, e.g., in *Moss v. Hancock*, [1899] 2 B. 111). See Mann, *The Legal Aspect of Money*, pp' 5 *sq.* Foreign money may, however, be a "commodity". See below, note 182.

(*179*) The only way in which money—in the legal sense—can nowadays be lawfully used for "hoarding" purposes, is the hoarding of bank-notes, i.e. the accumulation of money-tokens without intrinsic value. That this does not "directly" harm anyone else may be true, if stress is laid on the word "directly". It is "indirectly" harmful owing to the potentially inflationary effect of a rapid realisation of the accumulated purchasing power.

(*180*) This view of the relationship between money and the law was (and is) accepted by a number of lawyers. It was the view of Savigny (*Obligationerrecht*, p. 407) and it is the view of Prof. Nussbaum (*Money in the Law*, p. 5). During a period of stability of monetary values, especially under a regime of a widely accepted gold standard, the lawyer will not usually find it necessary to examine the validity of the thesis that it is "recognition" by the community and not the action of the state which endows the monetary tokens with their quality to be means of payment and units of measurement. The principle of "nominalism", i.e. the legal rule that a debt expressed in a given currency can be discharged by the repayment of a number of units of that currency equal to the number of units advanced to the debtor, is of little more than theoretical importance as long as the purchasing power of a given currency in terms of gold does not move beyond the upper and lower "gold points". In our own time, however, this principle of nominalism has become a matter of the greatest practical significance. Savigny's anti-nominalistic view is to-day universally rejected, and, as Dr. Mann (*Legal Aspect of Money*, pp. 10 *sq.*) has convincingly demonstrated, it is difficult, if not impossible, to explain the nominalistic theory on the basis that money is anything but the creation of the law. The lawyer does not presume to dictate to the economist a theory of money, but he must insist on being allowed to have his own view of what money is. He is constrained to accept Knapp's State Theory of Money, whatever may be its merits from the point of view of economic analysis.

(*181*) The intrinsic value of the physical substance of the money tokens is, of course, legally irrelevant. Not even Savigny advocated a legal theory of "metallism". According to him the "value" of money as a measurement of obligations was determined by the exchange price (*Kurswert*), i.e. by the value which "public opinion attributes to a given kind of money" (l.c. pp. 432, 454). This view, now generally abandoned and rejected by the English Courts (*In re Chesterman's Trusts*, [1923] 2 Ch. 466), was the legal reflection of the free interchangeability of currencies which prevailed in the 19th century. It would have meant that the nominal amount of a debt expressed in a currency undergoing a depreciation between the time of the making of the contract and that of its discharge would have been automatically adjusted to the new "exchange value" of the monetary unit. Deliberate devaluations such as occurred in this country in 1931 and in America in 1933 would have missed their purpose (unless accompanied by a rule introducing a *cours forcé*). No special legal principles or statutory enactments would have been required to introduce a measure of "revalorization" of debts in countries going through a catastrophical inflation such as Germany. The norm that one Mark (the equivalent of one Shilling) was equal to one Mark (the equivalent of one billionth part of one Shilling) was not, as a norm, "overthrown" by the change in the substratum, though, in the economic sense, it finished by "destroying the monetary character of the substratum". The change in the substratum ultimately enforced the creation of a new norm, viz. a new monetary unit.

(*182*) Foreign money is a "commodity" according to English law, precisely in the sense in which Renner uses the term (see, e.g., *per* Lord Macmillan in *Marrache v. Ashton*, [1943] A.C. 311). It is, however, "money" all the same, in the sense that it can be used as a standard of measurement for a monetary obligation (see, e.g. Sections 3 and 9 of the Bills of Exchange Act, 1882).

(*183*) This sentence shows to what extent Renner's—like Savigny's—view of the legal theory of money was conditioned by the economic facts of the pre-1914 era. It is only necessary to mention the Exchange Control Act, 1947, designed, *inter alia* to perpetuate with certain modifications the restrictions imposed by British law (the Defence (Finance) Regulations) upon the international trade in sterling. Gold clauses (and other similar devices) have been used to evade the principle of nominalism, and to overcome the control of the exchange value of currencies by the laws and administrative practices of individual states. The Joint Resolution of Congress of June 5th, 1933, declared such gold clauses to be illegal and void as being against the public policy of the United States.

(*184*) The contract of loan is, perhaps, the most "adaptable" of all legal institutions. It serves an all but infinite variety of economic objectives. A credit balance on current account is, from the legal point of view, a loan given by the customer to the banker, and—certain exceptions apart—governed by the same principles as a loan given by a father to his son to help him to finance his training or establishment in business. To the lawyer a debenture-holder's investment in a company, a transaction between a moneylender and his client, a bank overdraft, and a building society's advance on the purchase price of a house, are all "loans". Even the money "advanced" by a holding company to its subsidiary is, legally speaking, a "loan". The concept of "loan" is one of the most highly abstract conceptions of the law, one of the clearest instances that legal notions may be quite valueless from the point of view of an understanding of the economic substance which underlie their application. It is not very surprising that the number of concrete legal rules governing loans of money is small if compared with those, say, of the law of sale, carriage, or insurance. In Chitty on *Contracts* the discussion of loans covers 13 pages as against 66 pages devoted to sale of goods, in Smith's *Mercantile Law* the contract of debt is dealt with in 18 pages, that of affreightment in 76. The Continental Codes show similar relations between the sizes of the titles devoted to loans and of those dealing with sales and other commercially important contracts.

(*185*) A history of the use of the word "capitalist" since, say, 1850, might be a revealing contribution to political science. In the middle of the 19th century it was still the equivalent of "entrepreneur", and it is thus used, e.g., by John Stuart Mill (see, e.g., *Political Economy*, ch. iv, § 1). To-day it means either "investor" or the political antipode of the "worker". A business man or manufacturer might object to being called a "capitalist", and resent the alternative innuendoes of lack of personal productive effort or of a certain political attitude he may not share. A similar investigation into the English words "labourer" (nowadays connoting lack of skill or training), "workman" (technical, economic, legal, denoting function), and "worker" (political, sociological, denoting class) might be equally fruitful. The "capitalist" was at one time the antipode of the "workman", to-day he is the antipode of the "worker".

(*186*) The calculation of interest on self-invested capital is of legal significance wherever the capital outlay made by an entrepreneur determines either the amount of compensation payable to him (as in the case of sect. 18 of the Coal Industry Nationalisation Act, 1946) or the level of remuneration he may lawfully demand for goods or services supplied by him (as in the case of the railway "standard revenue" under sect. 58 of the Railways Act, 1921). The difference between interest as a legal claim and interest as an accounting device is obscured in the case of holding companies. In their case interest, e.g. on loans granted to subsidiaries, appears outwardly as a legal claim while it is, in fact, interest on self-invested capital. The accounting requirements of the Companies Act, 1947 exclude such "capital" from the "investments" required to be set out (First Schedule, Part II A 1 (2) in conjunction with sect. 125 of the Companies Act, 1929).

(*187*) The development of English company law and practice reflects the transformation of the relationship between investor and manager. The board of directors which, under the English system of company law, manages the business of the company, was originally intended to be a superintending rather than a managing body. "Management," the conduct of the day-to-day business, would have been in the hands of salaried servants without any influence on major policy. "Direction," i.e. decisions on business policy and supervision of the working of the business would have been the sole task of the board of directors, who would have represented the interests of the shareholders who had elected them. It was only in 1929 (sect. 139 of the present Companies Act) that the appointment of directors became compulsory for public companies. Previous company legislation, down to and including the Companies (Consolidation) Act, 1908, was still content to consider the election of directors as a work of supererogation, something that could be left to the enlightened self-interest of the shareholders themselves. In fact, the appointment of directors had, of course, become a common practice. Yet, even the present Companies Act does not say *expressis verbis* that the board of directors is entrusted with the management of the company (although Table A, Nos. 67, 68, does so), and, where the Act mentions the "remuneration" or "emoluments" payable to a director (as, e.g., in sect. 128, see also Table A, Art. 69), it contemplates directors' fees only, and either implicitly, or, as in sect. 128, subs. 3, expressly, excludes the salaries paid to a managing director in his capacity as "a manager, i.e. as a person" who holds any salaried employment or office in the company". The Report of the Cohen Committee on Company Law Amendment (Cmd. 6659) notes (No. 89, p. 46) that "in recent years there has been a growing tendency to include in boards of directors men who hold managerial positions in the company". The board of directors is another legal institution which, without any decisive change in its normative structure, has completely transformed its social function, exclusively owing to the change in its "substratum". Supervision and policy-making, divorced from the routine practice of management, and exercised by persons who consider themselves as the shareholders' representatives vis-a-vis the managers, becomes impracticable with the growing size and complexity of modern business. As a rule, he who "manages" must "direct", and he who wants to "direct" must "manage". In fact, company boards nowadays usually include managing as well as non-managing directors. With the development of the modern relation between shareholder and company, it becomes increasingly untrue that the managers are "assigned" to the "capital". In the majority of cases it is the board of directors, and through it, the group of managers, which, in fact, controls the distribution of profits, the handling of reserves, the issue of new capital. The board is more likely to control the shareholders' meeting, than vice versa. If one refrains from drawing exaggerated conclusions in the political field one may in so far agree with Mr. Burnham that in company practice there has certainly been a "managerial revolution". For America the classical text on this problem is Berle and Means, *The Modern Corporation and Private Property*, especially Book I, ch. v. The authors analyse that revolution which has "divided ownership into nominal ownership and the power formerly joined to it". This power, "control", may be "control through almost complete ownership", "majority control", "control through a legal device" (such as holding companies, non-voting stock), "minority control", or "management control". In the present context the discussion of "management control" (pp. 84 *sq.*) is of particular interest.

(*188*) This is not always, and, perhaps, not even usually true of an English managing director. He may and does usually have, a contract (in the form of a separate document) with the company, but some of his rights (e.g. those giving him security of tenure) are often written into the constitution of the company, i.e. into its Articles of Association. This dual root of a managing director's rights illustrates the hybrid character of his position. As happens so often, legal problems of great difficulty have arisen out of a situation in which the substratum has outgrown the norm. In this case the norm, or rather normative practice, is the autonomous corporate legislation of the company itself. The company cannot by contract fetter its own *pouvoir constituant*, i.e. it can, by a special resolution passed by the shareholders' meeting, abrogate the rights of a director laid down in the Articles, despite any provisions of its contract with the director,—a principle clearly adequate as long as the "directors" are nothing but supervising agents paid by fees, but difficult to reconcile with the idea that *parta sunt servanda* where the director concerned is a salaried employee. The Courts have thus been driven to the inevitable, but rather desperate, conclusion that an alteration of the Articles, though lawful and valid, may nevertheless constitute a breach of contract entailing liability for damages. The difficulty (which is well illustrated by the recent decision of the House of Lords in *Shirlaw v. Southern Foundries (1926) Ltd.*, [1940] A.C. 701) arises from the continuance of the practice to write the terms of tenure of a director into the Articles, a practice which it is at variance with the employer—employee relationship now commonly existing between a company and a (managing) director.

(*189*) This theme is more fully developed—from a non-Marxist point of view—by Tawney, *Acquisitive Society*, especially ch. v (d) ("The Tyranny of Functionless Property").

(*190*) The most important "new institutions for the development of a credit system" were, of course, the public or semi-public banks of issue. In this country the legislation referring to the Bank of England and to the note issue (from the Bank of England Act, 1694, to the Bank of England Act, 1946) is the most important type of legislation relevant in this context. That concerning building societies and savings banks, i.e. institutions not directly serving the needs of manufacturers and farmers, but the provision of credit for private building and the safeguarding of personal savings, is discussed at p. 147 (see note 191). The classical country of a general banking legislation, extending beyond the range of banks of issue, is the United States, where banks of all kinds have been subjected to administrative regulation of a far reaching kind, both on the state and on the federal level. In New York State this legislation began as early as 1838. The wide regulative and supervisory powers vested in the Superintendent of Banking extend to "personal loan companies" and savings banks. (See Freund, *Administrative Powers over Persons and Property*, § 191.) The federal control powers exercised over "national banks" are vested in the Comptroller of the Currency and in the Federal Reserve Board (ibid. § 192). On the Continent, and especially in France and in Central Europe, banking legislation was mainly concerned with banks of issue—in Germany the Reichsbank was first organised by a law of March 18th, 1875, and its notes were made legal tender by a law of June 1st, 1909. The law of 1875 also regulated private banks of issue of which four remained in existence after 1906. At least as important and, perhaps more interesting from the point of view of Renner's argument, are those laws which concern the organisation of co-operative credit for farmers, artisans, and small manufacturers (e.g. The Raiffeisen Banks, see German Law on Industrial and Provident Societies of May 20th, 1898), and, above all, the public and semi-public agricultural credit institutions and the mortgage banks which played and play so prominent a part in the economic life of many Continental countries and for which provision has been made in this country by the Agricultural Credit Act, 1928. In France the Credit Foncier was established by Decree of February 28th, 1852. More than eighty years earlier, in 1770, the first Prussian *Landschaft* (for Silesia) had been founded, to be followed by many others in the course of the succeeding decades. These agricultural credit institutions made investment credits accessible to the landowners. In their more developed form (inaugurated in 1843) they acted as mortgage creditors and issued negotiable bonds secured by the mortgages (Pfandbriefe) which were held in high regard as gilt-edged securities. These *Landschaften* are perhaps the best illustration for Renner's contention that this "controlling of the credit system" serves the interests of those groups of capitalists, who are the borrowers. In this case organised credit (from which the small peasants were excluded) helped to conserve the large landed estates in Prussia. In the judgment of Prof. Aereboe, (*Agrarpolitik*, p. 521), without the *Landschaften*, "Prussia would never have become the ill-balanced land of large estates which in fact it is to-day". More significant even from a general economic point of view were the mortgage banks of the Crédit Foncier type, regulated in Austria by a law of 1874 and in Germany by a law of 1899. These banks (which were precluded from doing other business) gave mortgages on urban and rural property and, like the *Landschaften*, issued negotiable bonds which were "trustee securities". Their importance in the development of the large cities of Central Europe was very great indeed. Some of their functions are in this country performed by building societies. (For a full survey see Hedemann, l.c., pp. 194 *sq.*) In Austria and in Switzerland the state itself acted as "mortgage banker" on a large scale. The Austrian "Länder" and some of the Swiss Cantons established public corporations not working for profit and intended to promote the granting of credit on real estate in town and country (for details, Hedemann, p. 210).

(*191*) The first comprehensive codification of commercial law (including negotiable instruments), was Louis XIV's Ordonnance du Commerce of 1673, followed by the Ordonnance de la Marine of 1681. The Code de Commerce dates from 1807. The Prussian Code of 1794 dealt with commercial law (including bills of exchange). The National Assembly of 1848 passed a law on bills of exchange for all Germany and Austria which was introduced by all the states concerned. In 1861 the German Confederation submitted to the member states a draft Commercial Code which most of them accepted and which was in force in Austria until the 1930s. In Germany it formed the basis of later legislation.—For banking legislation see the previous note. The most important legislation in this country relevant to the concluding sentence in the text—apart from the Building Societies Acts, 1874 to 1939—are the Trustee Savings Banks Act, 1863, the Post Office Savings Bank Act, 1861, and the Savings Banks Act, 1929.

(*192*) This peasant mentality which looks upon ownership in the soil as a necessary element of the peasant's life is very prevalent in France, in Austria and in Southern and Western Germany. What was to a large extent the result of the assertion of "natural rights" in the French Revolution has itself become, in the minds of its beneficiaries, a *droit de l'homme*, something preceding the law and superior to it. It is difficult to over-estimate the psychological intensity and the political influence of this mentality.

(*193*) The Nazis—of whom it is sometimes wrongly asserted that they were inimical to private property—made it their business to foster this ideology of peasant proprietorship. The Hereditary Farm Law of September 29th, 1933, was designed to give it further strength. Darré, at that time the Nazi Minister of Agriculture and the chief promoter of the "blood and soil" propaganda, said in a preface contributed to a semi-official text-book on the law: "The Hereditary Farm Law puts an end to the peasant's fate—which has always menaced him in the past—of living in perpetual anxiety lest he might lose *his* farm and *his* soil". It "is the only possibility of *tying the soil inseparably to the peasantry and to preserve the farm for him* (*sic*) *and his grandchildren for times eternal*" (Saure, *Reichserbhofgesetz*, 6th ed., 1941, p. 11). The law discouraged tenant farming.

(194) The principle "cuius est solum, eius est usque ad coelum et ad inferos" is not, in this form, to be found in the Roman texts, although it represents Roman law (Buckland and McNair, l.c., p. 78). It is certainly English law (see Salmond's *Law of Torts*, 10th ed., p. 203, note (c)), French law (Code Civil Art. 552, al. 1: "La propriété du sol emporte la propriété du dessus et du dessous"), and Austrian law (Civil Code, § 297). The most modern and best drafted European Codes have abandoned it: Art. 667 of the Swiss Civil Code restricts the landowner's property in the spaces above and below. It exists only "in so far as there exists an interest in its exercise". German law (Civil Code, § 905) is similar to, but not as clear as, Swiss law.

(*195*) In this country the difference between an action for the recovery of a specific thing and an action for the recovery of a sum of money developed but slowly in the 13th century (see Pollock and Maitland, l.c., Vol. II, p. 173, p. 210).

(*196*) This means that the tenant can assert his possession against any one who tries to disturb it, irrespective of the question whether or not the interferer has a better right to possession. Possession as such is protected against interference even on the part of a person with a better right because such a right should be asserted in the Courts. This form of "possessory action" protecting the possessing person for the sake of his peace, not for the sake of his right, derives from Roman law (the possessory interdicts. Gaj. 4, 138 *sq.*; I. 4, 15; D 43, 16; D. 43, 17), and has found its way *via* the canon law (actio spolii) into some of the modern Continental systems (German Code, §§ 858 *sq.*, Swiss Code Art. 926 *sq.*). It should not be confused with the protection of the right to better possession (by which the possessor defends not merely his peace, but his title, which may, however, be short of property). This is the essence of the action of trespass in English law, and—historically—the outcome of medieval, not of Roman developments. The modern Continental tenant is certainly a possessor who can defend his possession, whilst the Roman *conductor* was a mere detentor and could not rely on the possessory interdicts.

(*197*) This is certainly true where the landlord is an "absentee" residing in London or Vienna, while the rent which is collected on his behalf is earned in Ireland or in Bohemia. The actual conditions of the Austro-Hungarian monarchy favoured absentee landlordism, in a sense the monarchy as a political institution was based on it. Renner's statement also applies in full to those cases in which the landlord resides in the manor house without taking any part in the activities of his tenants. Where—by direction, supervision, or advice,—he participates in the management, property has still a mainly "distributory" function, but is not devoid of all productive function.

(*198*) See the Introduction for a remark on the different conditions generally prevailing in this country. Where the landowner supplies the *terre capital*—entirely or in part—he is also less likely to allow his property to acquire merely "distributory" functions.

(*199*) It was in order to remedy this state of affairs that, in this country, the Agricultural Holdings Acts were passed. Since 1875 the outgoing tenant has been entitled to compensation for improvements. This right, greatly enlarged under the present provision—Section 22 of the Agriculture Act, 1947—cannot be contracted out. In addition compensation for disturbance is payable (sect. 30) unless the landlord has given notice for certain specified reasons. A right to compensation for improvements (and a right to compensation for goodwill) is also given by the Landlord and Tenant Act, 1927, to tenants who use the premises for the carrying on of a trade or business or of a profession. No statute protects the tenant of dwelling room who has invested money in improvements. The rule that, on termination of the lease, all that is connected with the soil, is forfeited to the landlord, operates here in all its stringency.

(*200*) The "*suum*" is the house, the property of the "familia", i.e. in communities governed by the patriarchal principle (like the Roman and Germanic communities) of the *pater familias* who exercised the *manus*, the *munt* over the rest of the family. Hence the Roman conception of *sui heredes*, i.e. heirs taking directly from their *pater familias*. This "*suum*" is the nucleus and origin of all those forms of communal life which Gierke characterised as *Herrschaftsverbände* (*Genossenschaftsrecht* I, 89; II, 134). We can see it most distinctly in Rome. It is generally assumed—and this is Renner's point—that this *suum*, the house and its contents, was already set apart at a time when agricultural land was still communally owned by the tribe, the clan, the *Sippe*, or the village community, as was the case with the Germans in Caesar's and Tacitus' day, as may have been the case with the Romans and Greeks during an age of which we know nothing or little, and as was certainly the case with the Russian *Mir* until the Stolypin agrarian reform of 1903. The Soviet Kolkhos is organised on a similar principle of separating a *suum* from the communal property (see Webb, *Soviet Communism*, l.c., p. 276).

(*201*) This is the quintessence of Maine's famous analysis of the early family (see, in particular, *Ancient Law*, ch. vi). Of the "Patriarch" (later the pater familias) he says (Pollock. ed., p. 197) that he had extensive rights, but that "it is impossible to doubt that he lay under an equal amplitude of obligations. If he governed the family, it was for its behoof. If he was lord of its possessions, he held them as trustee for his children and kindred. He had no privilege or position distinct from that conferred on him by his relation to the petty commonwealth which he governed. The Family, in fact, was a Corporation; and he was its representative or, as we might almost say, its Public Officer. He enjoyed rights and stood under duties, but the rights and duties were, in the contemplation of his fellow-citizens and in the eye of the law, quite as much those of the collective body as his own". Maine goes on to analyse and illustrate the connection between these primitive "corporate entities" and the *sacra*, both in Roman and in Hindu law. (See also Vinogradoff, *Historical Jurisprudence*, Vol. I, pp. 224 *sq.*). Similarly Mommsen, after having described the unlimited property right and the *manus* vested in the *pater familias*, points out that the *patria potestas* is "as it were of a representative nature". Its rationale is to be found in the need for a unified representation of the unity of the house (*Römische Geschichte*, Vol. I, p. 60). Prof. Jolowitz says (*Historical Introduction*, p. 129) that "in its main conclusion . . . Maine's view is still the prevailing one". Gierke's view of the ancient German family and of the *mundium* is precisely the same (*Genossenschaftsrecht*, Vol. I, p. 15).

(*202*) It may be doubted whether legal historians will accept without demur the statement that it was only the "civil law" (bürgerliches Recht—the Usus Modernus Pandectarum) which dissolved family relationships into individual institutions. Should it not be said of the whole course of Roman legal history from the Twelve Tables to Justinian that, in the spheres of family law and the law of inheritance, it was one continuous process of dissolving the "unity" of the primitive family of the *Jus Civile?* Did not this process begin when the *consensus* marriage supplanted the ancient form of marriage with *manus* (in Republican times) and when the law of *dos*, a purely "individualistic" phenomenon, took the place of the old property right of the *pater familias* in the belongings of the married women who were members to the "family"? Was it not further promoted by the institution of the *peculium* which, in fact, though not, until Justinian, in the full legal sense of the word, created an "individualistic" relationship between *pater* and *filius?* Was it not, finally, consummated by the supersession of the agnatic by the cognatic tie in the law of inheritance? In the Germanic world, the "community" idea survived the Middle Ages and, partly, even the Reception. It left its traces in the (theoretically) long continued principle of the *munt* exercised by the husband over his wife (it is still present in the *Sachsenspiegel*; see Hübner, *Deutsches Privatrecht*, § 93, 3rd ed., p. 544, note 3), and, above all, in the manifold forms of *régimes matrimoniaux*—communities of goods, husband's right and duty to enjoy and administer his wife's property, etc.—which are part of the modern Continental systems. Nevertheless, even in the Middle Ages, the relationships between father and child, husband and wife, etc., began to be viewed as separate institutions (see Hübner, l.c., p. 515), and, in this country, in the absence of a *patria potestas* in the Roman sense or of a *munt* over the married women (Pollock and Maitland, l.c., II, 437), this tendency was even more pronounced. That the disintegration of the family as a legal unit was, on the Continent, promoted by the twin agencies of Reception and Capitalism can hardly be doubted. That it had been prepared by pre-Capitalist and pre-Reception developments should be admitted.

(*203*) It was not only public opinion, but, for centuries (and, in some respects to the present day), the law itself which restricted such transactions. In many parts of Europe the next-of-kin had a right to avoid transactions *inter vivos* by which the owner disposed of property in favour of strangers. This *Jus Retractus (Retrait, Näherrecht)* referred mainly, but not exclusively, to land. It was of Germanic origin, though influenced by Byzantine institutions which had taken root in Southern Italy. In the 18th century it came to be considered as a mere burden upon the freedom of disposition. In Austria the Emperor Joseph II began to abolish it in 1787, the French Revolution did the same for the *"retraits"* in France (Decrees of 1790, 1792, 1794), and, in the course of the 19th century, they also disappeared in Germany. They have left a trace in modern French (Code Civil Art. 841) and German (Civil Code, § 2034) law in the form of the right of pre-emption given to a co-heir with regard to any other co-heir's share in the inheritance. (For details, Gierke, *Deutsches Privatrecht*, Vol. II pp. 766 *sq.*, Hedemann, l.c., pp. 40 *sq.*). More important are the legal limitations of the freedom of testation itself which, in some form or other, exist in all Continental systems (for a brief survey see 1 *Modern Law Review*, p. 304). The best known example is the *"réserve légale"* of French law (l.c. Art. 913). In this country an inadequate limitation of freedom of testation was introduced—largely on the New Zealand pattern—by the Inheritance (Family Provisions) Act, 1938. Among the upper and upper middle classes the practice of family settlements took to some extent the place occupied by statutory or customary restrictions of the freedom of testation elsewhere.

(*204*) The German word for ownership (property) is *Eigen-tum* ("Own-dom"). Renner coins the word *Fremd-tum* ("Strange-dom") to mark the contrast between the house, the *"suum"*, which serves its owner and his family, and the house which, as tenement building, as factory, or as school house, serves the use of others.

(*205*) In this country turnpike rights as well as rights to hold fairs and markets are of a purely private nature. See, for market rights, Law of Property Act, 1922, sect. 138, and 12th Schedule.

(*206*) From the point of view of a modern industrial community, and especially from that of the working class, the two most important institutions of private law—apart from marriage—are the contract of employment and the landlord-tenant relationship. These two complementary institutions of property have been the main instruments for the exercise of its command power. The bulk of social legislation centres round these two institutions. While, however, labour law has been supplementary—especially in this country—to the modification of the employment relationship brought about by trade union action, the law of housing, town-planning, and rent control was unable to look for support by voluntary action. The working class developed efficient organs of self-protection in so far as the worker as a producer was concerned, but—since co-operative action hardly extended to this field—it was unable by its own effort to counteract the tendency of capitalism described by Renner in the present chapter.

(*207*) It need hardly be pointed out that the building society movement is more developed in this country than in most other countries. It would, however, be somewhat fanciful to describe building societies as autonomous institutions of the working class, comparable to trade unions or co-operatives as expressions of the will to counteract the effects of capitalism. In a very limited sense they have restored the "*suum*", but, as pointed out in the Introduction, it is, from the point of view of a functional analysis, undesirable to draw too sharp a line between rent and mortgage interest.

(*208*) Exactly the same thing happened in this country. The long list of Rent Restriction Acts begins with the Increase of Rent and Mortgage Interest (War Restrictions) Act, 1915, and ends—for the time being—with the Furnished Houses (Rent Control) Act, 1946. They have created what the lawyer calls a "statutory tenancy", a landlord-tenant relationship established by law, in spite of the absence or expiry of a contract. In other words: where they apply, they have seriously curtailed the landlord's right of eviction and given to the tenant a modicum of security of tenure. In addition they have also introduced a control of the maximum amount of rent. It should also be noted that, where social legislation is involved, the (often fortuitous, but to the traditional private law vital) distinction between rent and mortgage interest is brushed aside. Social legislation, like revenue legislation, must consider economic substance rather than legal form, and thus sometimes retrospectively casts a light upon the social function of the private law institutions with which it deals. Rent legislation—and the same is true of some other parts of English social legislation—proves that "*rien ne dure que le provisoire*". As Mr. Megarry points out (*Rent Acts*, 2nd ed., p. 1), these statutes were, at first, "regarded as mere emergency legislation, but latterly they have been recognised as forming a more enduring part of the present social structure".

(*209*) These norms are, in this country, not only to be found in the Rents Acts (see previous note), but also in such provisions as sect. 2 of the Housing Act, 1936, which compels the landlord to keep working-class premises in repair so as to maintain them in a state fit for human habitation. See note 148, above.

(*210*) Renner presupposes a system of compulsory registration of mortgages. In this country—broadly speaking—only the registration of puisne, i.e. second and later mortgages is compulsory, the first mortgage is usually effectuated by handing over the title deeds (Land Charges Act, 1925, Sect. 10). It is different in those areas in which the Land Registration Act, 1925, applies.

(*211*) What seems to be contemplated, is not so much the organisation of credit through mortgage banks, building societies, insurance companies, etc., as the development of modern mortgage law itself, with its effective threat of foreclosure and forced sale.

(*212*) From the point of view of its economic function the mortgage is as colourless as any other legal institution. This, it is suggested, is one of the subjects which might be fruitfully developed with the help of Renner's method. The uses to which the mortgage is put are as manifold as those of the contract of sale as the contract of loan. From the mortgage securing a series of debentures issued by an industrial concern carried on in the form of a company to the one encumbering a farm in favour of the vendor as a security for part of the purchase price, from the building society mortgage to that which secures a bank overdraft, there are hosts of economic varieties of this ubiquitous legal institution. Renner discusses only two of these varieties: the mortgage securing a loan granted to an agricultural entrepreneur, and that imposed upon a peasant's farm as a security for part of the purchase price. He discusses these types of mortgages from the point of view of the mortgagor, but refrains from analysing the effect which, for example, the investment of large capitals in agricultural property has from the point of view of the mortgagees: the creation of antagonisms and solidarities between bank capital and agricultural interests (important in the recent history of the United States), the crystallisation of typical attitudes towards monetary policies, etc. The economic functions of the mortgage as a safe investment—a trustee security in this country, a savings bank investment on the Continent—and its history would be an interesting topic of investigation. In every respect urban, rural and industrial mortgages, mortgages for investment and mortgages destined to secure short term loans would have to be kept apart. Such an investigation would perhaps yield the result that only certain types of mortgages have the economic effect described by Renner, and that, e.g., a mortgage granted to an urban estate company by an insurance company (like the one discussed by the House of Lords in *Knightsbridge Trust Ltd. v. Byrnes*, [1940] A.C. 613), bears none of the characteristics ascribed to the mortgage as such by Renner. The temptation to treat the mortgage as if it was a socially uniform institution has had its effect on the doctrine of "clogging the equity of redemption" in English law. It is only

7*

recently that the Courts have begun to differentiate, and to realise that this 18th century doctrine designed to protect the mortgagor against exploitation cannot be usefully applied to all mortgages. The general approach of the English Courts to the mortgage as an institution is much less unlike Renner's than one might have expected.

(*213*) It was to counteract this tendency that the Weimar Republic enacted the Settlement and Homestead legislation of 1919 and 1920 which had been foreshadowed by Prussian (and other) legislation in the 19th century. The procurement of easy credits by public or semi-public authorities for the acquisition of land by settlers was one of the central features of this legislation. See the Agricultural Credits Act, 1928, mentioned above, note 190, and Part IV, especially Sect. 54, of the Agriculture Act, 1947).

(*214*) Renner does not indicate the economic and social effect of the concentration of mortgagee interests in the hands of a small number of large investors, such as the British insurance companies, the Crédit Foncier in France, the mortgage banks in Germany, the "*Länder*" mortgage institutions in Austria (see note 190, above). While these institutions have done much to suppress the grosser forms of usury, they have—partly by virtue of express legal enactments—to a large extent assumed control over the mortgagor's management, so much so that it sometimes amounts to a system of "tutelage" (Hedemann, l.c., p. 214). The total volume of this "institutional credit" is far in excess of individual mortgages, both in Austria and in Germany (though not in France). This concentration of mortgages is, of course, coupled with a wide diffusion of the economic benefit of the mortgages in the form of negotiable securities issued by the banks.

Section iii. Capitalist Property and Its Functions

In its legal aspect, the change from simple commodity production to capitalist methods shows as we have seen, above all a highly developed differentiation of property-objects. The old patrimony was a universality of objects of all kind, a *universitas rerum* with a uniform general method of functioning. As a rule it comprised a piece of land with the buildings appertaining thereto, and an aggregation of means of production, consumption goods, commodities and money. This totality offered to one *persona* all the means of labour and existence and nearly complete independence; in its legal fate it was undivided. (*215*) It was transferred as a legal unit to a new *persona* by settlement *inter vivos*, (*216*) and by inheritance *mortis causa*.

a. Dislocations in the Substratum. The Capitalist Function of the Property-object

Nowadays, however, every part—land, house tool, commodity, money—has its separate fate and assumes its specific function. Formerly the person of the owner gave unity to the totality. An expropriation of the primary owner becomes necessary in whole or in part when this totality is dissolved. The owner is now restricted to one character part and retains only goods of one kind. The remaining objects, which now are free, are appropriated by other persons. But when the owner brings them to the market and alienates them in the forms of private law, he realises their price and retains their value in the form of money. If he invests the proceeds, he may thus enlarge his specific enterprise by adding newly acquired property of the same species. This process of specialisation and differentiation of the articles involves a certain loss. If this loss is left out of consideration, the owner afterwards still possesses the same aggregate of assets as before, still the same value, though he possesses different and specialised objects. He has become, as it were, a specialist: factory-owner, merchant, gentleman of independent means, landlord of rural or urban property, or tenant. So long as we confine our attention to the mere process of differentiation and the subsequent process of accumulation, the owner does not become necessarily richer or poorer. Expropriation and appropriation supplement each other, they cover the same ground, they result in a change of value. If such a change of value should occur, it is not caused by alienation and acquisition, since normal trade consists of the transfer and return of equivalents. Increase and destruction of value are not brought by a legal transaction which at the utmost makes them apparent: they have other causes.

But now the property-object has become specialised and assumes specific functions. As we have shown, in the hands of the owner, it becomes in turn a title to power, to profit, to interest, to profit of enterprise, and to rent. And this is capital or an equivalent of capital. Accordingly, the object of the right of ownership is now industrial capital, merchant capital, money-changer's capital or landed property (fulfilling no function), and in each of these forms it has different functions which imprint a distinct character mask on the owner. The thing which from an economic point of view has become converted into capital, remains, as an object, unchanged; the change is due to a changed function, to wit, to rule over a whole society of individuals (wage-labourers, debtors, the market, etc.) and to make them tributary to the owner. The title to surplus, which is directed against others on behalf of the owner, is attached to the thing in its capacity as a social object.

At the same time the legal institution of ownership loses independence and self-sufficiency. Only by being constantly in association with other legal institutions can ownership now fulfil its function; whereas the simple commodity producer came into contact with the object directly, as a person, without intervention of third parties, engaging only occasionally in ancillary transactions. This typical connection with complementary institutions: the connection of property with the contract of sale, the contract of loan, the contract of service and the contract of lease, brings one object into the simultaneous detention of a score of individuals, a detention which is partly actual and partly legal. An object which according to the law is private, becomes in fact a communal object of society which is subject to the technical disposal of a smaller or larger number of persons and, by means of the market, subject to the economic disposal of the whole of society. The social aspect of an object that in itself is simple becomes complicated; various social relations are centred in it; it reflects its human surroundings like a spherical mirror; like a miraculous sponge it sucks in sweat and tears and sweats out drops of gold. It becomes the fetish CAPITAL.

It is the variety of functions which the object assumes in accordance with its individual detentor which accounts for the variety of relations between object and individuals. A piece of land is an instrument of labour to the worker, it is title to profit to the tenant, title to rent to the landowner and title to interest to the mortgagee, [1] all these at the same time. In general terms, the object of ownership is nothing but a technical tool to the wage labourer who gives it value but receives nothing in exchange; but to the capitalist owner it is title to surplus value, in the hands of the non-owner it has the function of production, and in the hands of the owner merely the function of distribution. This function of distribution is the indestructible function of property. The capital function pure and simple of the object of ownership is to be title to surplus value. The economic and social function of the legal institution of property is precisely defined by the concept of capital function. Such is its innermost and indestructible core.

b.   Economic and Legal Property

Our investigations so far have shown the capital function linked to the property-object. Like every right *in rem*, the legal relation of ownership connects two opposite poles, *persona* and *res*. The owner as the subject of this legal relationship apparently becomes the bearer of a determinate social function, in this instance the capital function, only by means of the object. Now there are certain legal relations, like the loan, which transfer the object into the temporary ownership of another person, the debtor, but leave the capital function with the original and final owner, the creditor. From a legal point of view, however, the holder of an I.O.U. is owner merely of a piece of paper (*217*)—the legal form and the economic effect do not fully coincide here. The legal owner, the person who has the absolute detention of the object, does not always or necessarily realise the title to surplus value, the capital function, for himself. As nowadays quite a number of persons are concerned with the *res*, the economic relation of these persons *inter se* is more important than their legal relation to the *res*. The

---

[1] The evolution of property by means of its complementary institutions revives the legal situation in old Germanic law that more than one person can have *gewere* (seizin) in the same object.

mortgagee, the merchant, etc., can appropriate the full surplus value without being owner in a legal sense. We can even imagine that under exceptional circumstances, the workers in an undertaking by virtue of their detention of the equipment can temporarily deprive the entrepreneur of the whole profit. [1] The legal form is here entirely overwhelmed by the force of its economic substratum. Thus the confusing relation is established that economic property, the essence of which is the capital function, need not necessarily coincide with the legal property and in a number of cases cannot do so. (*218*)

Consider, for instance, a mine which is run by a joint stock company. Everybody will say that the mine is owned by the shareholders, that it belongs to the controlling shareholder X, and so forth. Seen with the eyes of the law, however, this shareholder owns only the share certificate, (*219*) and has also a claim against the undertaking given to him by company law, which is attested by this document. Thus the legal construction differs from the facts. (*220*) For this juridico-economic composite of facts the term of economic ownership has been suggested. I admit that this term is contradictory and, at first glance, confusing. (*221*) The noun describes a legal category and the adjective qualifies this by reference to a non-legal category. Yet I make use of this term because it reflects the intrinsic contradiction of the actual development. At the initial stage of the capitalist epoch, ownership is the power to dispose both over the natural substance of the good in a technical way, and over its existence as an object of value which is inherent in its existence as capital. These two kinds of disposal can become separated. The tenant and the wage labourer dispose of the good only in a technical and natural way, the landlord and the factory owner dispose of it as regards its function as value and capital. The fact that all goods are objects of ownership accounts for and determines this last function. It is this economic function which, as the specific function of property, remains in the hands of the capitalist, so long as the connection is maintained by an act-in-the-law (loan, deposit, etc.), even in the case in which the good is legally transferred into another person's ownership. As the capitalist exercises the specific functions of the owner, we may well call him the economic owner, and thus give adequate

---

[1] Assuming that the employer is bound by contract under a high penalty to deliver at short notice at a fixed price, the workers may have come to know the position and may force him to pay exorbitant wages.

expression to the result of a contradictory development. (*222*)

As soon as the capitalist development is completed, the norms of legal rules as well as the decisions of the judges take note of this new function of the property-object. As a rule, a claim for restitution or damages no longer regards the object as a simple article with its price of production, but as a yield-producing value. (*223*) The property-object is no longer a mere preserve of stored labour performed in the past but an assignation to surplus value which is to be appropriated in the future. Even the law treats the capital function as a special quality of the object.

2. THE FUNCTION OF ACCUMULATION

We now have an understanding of how the property-object has developed into capital. We know by what economic forces and legal institutions it has acquired this function as its indestructible core. This change of function, to stress its most important aspect, has transformed ownership for the purpose of labour into ownership for the purpose of exploitation. The question now arises how this functional change further affects capitalist society. It might be only a solitary phenomenon, running its course in time and never repeating itself. Therefore we have to examine whether these functions have an inherent capacity for their own continual reproduction, so as to assist the continual reproduction of society in spite of their effects, which are in many instances anti-social.

It is a merit of Marx's system which has not been sufficiently acknowledged that he regards the economic process not only as it is at any given moment, i.e. as a static, comprehensive unity, but that he investigates its dynamics, its continuity in time and history. We mentioned this point above when dealing with Otmar Spann. Human economy must be perpetual and self-reproducing like the life of the species. Every element used and consumed in economy must always replace or reproduce itself. This reproduction must take place on an ever increasing scale, in view of the constant increase of population and the constant advances in civilisation. (*224*) Here is a fundamental question of economics which has never been answered more comprehensively than by Karl Marx, neither before him nor since.

Formerly we have concentrated on the appearance of the objects once they have become capital; we were not concerned with the property relations in the continual process of reproduction. We shall now see that the capital function is particularly enhanced by this process.

a. Distribution as a Function of Capital. The Specific Capitalist Manner of Appropriation

As we have shown above, property in the hands of the non-owner fulfils the function of production, but in the hands of the owner it has merely the function of distribution. It is the latter which has become the very essence of property. Property is responsible for the distribution of society's annual total product among all those concerned with production and circulation, which distribution takes place quite automatically, without intervention of a central social will. In a system of natural economy the house serves for use (*usus*) and the land yields fruit (*fructus*). In the steady economic process of that period nature herself showers her fruits (*fructus naturales*) (*225*) upon man, and society distributes them directly in accordance with customary or enacted law. The law assigns the feudal dues to the landlord and the tithe to the church, and leaves the remainder to the cultivator of the soil. To this extent the *fructus* accrue to the owner directly and automatically, even during this period.

The industrial capitalist who causes his workers to produce at his machines finished goods (textiles) from his raw materials (yarn), appropriates the finished goods. We cannot compare this procedure with the harvesting of fruits; moreover, the textile cannot be regarded as the fruit of the yarn. From the price of the textiles sold the owner first recoups himself for the cost of the yarn (circulating capital), then he writes off factory and machinery (constant capital) and recoups himself for the wages he has had to pay (variable capital): what then remains of the price after these deductions is his, he re-appropriates it anew. This procedure is no longer a gathering of fruits; it can be compared with the Roman *specificatio*, yet it is not the same. (*226*) It is the capitalist manner of appropriation, a specific mode of property acquisition. The worker acquires his property, the wages he takes home, by an act of contractual performance. As this form of property acquisition is very frequent, this also should be enumerated as among the legally recognised modes of acquiring property. The merchant capitalist, the lending capitalist, the landlord, all these draw the proceeds from their own property-object in a manner which constitutes a mode of acquisition distinctly authorised by the law. The Roman school gives all these proceeds the convenient name of *fructus civiles* or "civil fruits", treating them as analogous to the natural fruits, on the basis of the old "own and patrimony". (*227*)

If we survey cursorily the whole of the economic process, we see that products and goods are in continual motion, incessantly changing place and hands, until they come to one individual in whose hands they remain for the time being. How is this flow of goods distributed among the individuals? Part of the annual produce, the labour fund (variable capital) has gone to the workers, the remainder has become amalgamated with the property-objects, yet this residue is not entirely an increase of produce or "*fructus*". Goods are consumed, even destroyed, in the process of production and they must first be replaced. Thus the means of production, the constant capital, must reproduce itself, just like the labour fund which on its part reproduces the working class. If there is to be economic continuity, constant and variable capital must at least be reproduced. The quantity of produce sufficient for this is the necessary product of social labour. It is product but by no means yet *fructus*. This necessary product merely guarantees simple reproduction, it does not create an income for the capitalist: this can only derive from the social surplus product. In capitalist society, the surplus product or surplus-value is distributed among the capitalists as a form of dividend proportionate to their respective shares in social capital. Thus surplus value appears as average earnings accruing to capital. Yet this average profit is again split up into profit of enterprise and interest, and as such may accrue to capitalists of different kinds. This appropriation and distribution of the surplus value or surplus products, performed by capital, is further limited by ownership of land. "Just as the active capitalist pumps surplus labour and with it surplus-value and surplus produce in the form of profit out of the labourer, so the landlord in his turn pumps a portion of this surplus-value, or surplus product out of the capitalist, in the shape of rent" (*Capital* iii, p. 955).

Property therefore is a general title to surplus-value in the social process of distribution; it is assignation to appropriation of the proceeds of alien labour. But there can be no right to the full surplus value for the individual capitalist in a capitalist society, just as in a socialist society there is no right to the full proceeds of one's labour. The title to surplus value assumes the character of a title to profit, to interest, to profit of enterprise, and to rent. None of these titles is absolutely rigid and distinct from the other (*228*)—we have seen that the title to interest, for instance, can swallow up profit and rent. Thus property, in distributing the social surplus value and assigning it to the various groups of capitalists for the purpose of appropriation, reproduces not only the working class but also the capitalist class; which realises the surplus title for itself and thus appropriates the product of surplus labour as "*fructus*".

b.   Accumulation as a Function of Capital

The surplus value assumes the form of a revenue arising out of capital as a periodical increase of the capital value.   If this revenue only serves the capitalist as a fund to provide for his consumption; if he simply consumes his revenue, he cannot enlarge his undertaking, and simple reproduction will take place. "If this revenue serve the capitalist only as a fund to provide for his consumption, and be spent periodically as it is gained, then, caeteris paribus, simple reproduction will take place" (*Capital* i, p. 579).   But the capitalist is neither willing nor always able to consume the whole of his revenue, he re-invests a larger or smaller part productively.   Thus he fulfils the function of enlarging the social process of production and reproduction.   As a private person he fulfils the task which in other social systems is performed by the community (for instance the common clearing of new land by the tribe).   This partial reconversion of the surplus product into instruments of increased productivity, the so-called accumulation, is a phenomenon common to production in all periods and under all forms of human organisation, but it is not always and not necessarily performed by capitalist methods.   "In economic forms of society of the most different kinds, there occurs not only simple reproduction, but, in varying degrees, reproduction on a progressively increasing scale.   By degrees more is produced and more consumed, and consequently more products have to be converted into means of production.   This process, however, does not present itself as accumulation of capital, nor as the function of a capitalist" [1] (*Capital* i, p. 609).

---

[1] Accumulation is not the same as saving. The latter is either economising, i.e. reasonable disposition of income or proceeds over longer periods and therefore creation of reserves for the purpose of consumption, or accumulation, i.e. the reconversion of the proceeds of production into capital for the purpose of increased production. The worker can and should dispose economically but he is unable to accumulate.

Private property therefore takes over this function of accumulation as well. Thereby it becomes an agent in the revolutionary transformation of society. It is not as the man who "lives and lets live", as a consumer of surplus value, as the celebrated hero of the petty bourgeoisie and the servant class, as a "gentleman", that the owner performs his economic function as a capitalist. (229) "Except as personified capital, the capitalist has no historical value. . . . And so far only is the necessity for his own transitory existence implied in the transitory necessity for the capitalist mode of production. But, so far as he is personified capital, it is not values in use and the enjoyment of them, but exchange-value and its augmentation, that spurs him into action. Fanatically bent on making value expand itself, he ruthlessly forces the human race to produce for production's sake, he thus forces the development of the productive powers of society, and creates those material conditions, which alone can form the real basis of a higher form of society. . . . Only as personified capital is the capitalist respectable. . . . So far, therefore as his actions are a mere function of capital —endowed as capital is, in his person, with consciousness and a will—his own private consumption is a robbery perpetuated on accumulation" (*Capital* i, p. 603).

Accumulation of capital thus means the re-conversion of surplus value into capital, constant and variable, a fund for production and a labour fund simultaneously (*Capital* i, p. 594). Accumulated values which have been appropriated out of the unpaid labour of one's workers are first invested either in one's own undertaking which is thus extended, or, as loan or deposit, in undertakings owned by others. But the surplus value continues to flow. Accumulation demands ever new spheres for the investment of capital. If it is invested in colonies on a world-wide scale, it appears that its function to develop production is suspended in the mother country. Capital then operates as merchant capital and interest-bearing capital only from the point of view of a single nation, thus petrifying and conserving under certain conditions older methods of production. Merchant capital and interest-bearing capital accumulate on their own, but their function of exploitation is strictly limited, as they are unable to increase the productive power of labour. They can only accumulate in new spheres of exploitation. Sooner or later they must become reconverted into industrial capital in order to revolutionise those branches of production where the development has been retarded.

As the whole world is nowadays open to the investment of American and European capital, nothing seems more understandable than that the countries where capitalism originated, and all purely local and national branches of production, enjoy a period of protection, a "close time", as it were. We continually export a large part of our fund of accumulation and additional accumulated labour-power. If within the last five decades this export had not taken place, Europe would to-day be a socialist commonwealth.

The whole evolutionary power of property becomes apparent only in its function of accumulation.

3. EXPROPRIATION AS A FUNCTION OF CAPITALIST PROPERTY

It is accumulation, and accumulation alone, that enhances the function of appropriation assumed by capital to such an extent that it destroys property, expropriates other owners and appropriates the ruins of their property. Capitalist appropriation is fundamentally appropriation of the surplus value, it is accompanied by expropriation as a paramount effect of the accumulating process. This has completed the dissolution of the original "patrimony", and is thus accomplished by a process which does not run counter to the positive law, but on the contrary is based upon the very law which regulates simple commodity production, i.e. upon lawful contracts and lawful property. (*230*) Here we shall first deal with the fundamental form of appropriation, the appropriation of the surplus value.

Mere appropriation would not necessarily bring about a change in the relations of possession, if the surplus value were immediately consumed. Accumulation, however, must have this effect. It is this accumulation which produces that reversal of the function of property without any change in the positive law which becomes so striking a phenomenon. "In so far as each single transaction invariably conforms to the laws of the exchange of commodities, the capitalist buying labour-power, the labourer selling it. . . .it is evident that the laws of appropriation or of private property, laws that are based on the production and circulation of commodities, become by their own inner and inexorable dialectic changed into their very opposite. The exchange of equivalents, the original operation with which we started, has now become turned round in such a way that there is only an apparent exchange. This is owing to the fact, first, that the capital which is exchanged for labour power is itself but a portion of the product of others' labour appropriated without an equivalent; and, secondly, that this capital must not only be replaced by its producer, but replaced together with an added surplus. The relation of exchange subsisting between capitalist and labourer becomes . . . a mere form, foreign to the real nature of the transaction, and only mystifying it. At first the rights of property seemed to us to be based on a man's own labour. At least some such assumption was necessary since only commodity owners with equal rights confronted each other, and the sole means by which a man could become possessed of the commodities of others, was by alienating his own commodities; and these could be replaced by labour alone. Now, however, property turns out to be the right, on the part of the capitalist, to appropriate the unpaid labour of others or its product, and to be the impossibility, on the part of the labourer, of appropriating his own product. The separation of property from labour has become the necessary consequence of a law that apparently originated in their identity" (*Capital* i, pp. 597–8).

Thus a change of functions can reverse the social effects of a norm.

We have seen that not every form of capital, especially not that of merchant and usurer's capital, appropriates the means of production for itself. We have seen that interest-bearing capital can preserve legal property in land and yet may seize the economic property, the title to rent. Capital as such, however, even to-day always appropriates the social surplus product, and after a certain stage of development it cannot *make use* of this surplus product without dispossessing formerly independent owners, thus converting them into proletarians and exploiting them as new wage labourers. This is Marx's "expropriation" which we have now to consider as an ancillary form of capitalist appropriation. This development may proceed slowly, it may temporarily be not intensive but extensive in space, yet it is unavoidable. It gradually reverses all functions of property without changing its legal character. [1]

---

[1] "The mode of appropriation can be completely revolutionised without affecting at all the law of property corresponding to commodity production. The same law that ruled in the beginning . . . when the producer owned his product and could increase his wealth only by his own labours, is valid in the capitalist period as well, when the wealth of society becomes more and more the property of those who can afford to appropriate again and again the unpaid labour of other people.

"To the extent that simple commodity production develops into capitalist production in accordance with its own immanent laws, the laws of property turn into the laws of capitalist appropriation" (*Capital* i [German ed.], p. 550 ff.).

Capitalist expropriation and appropriation as an economic process is one of the principal agents of capitalist development. It is, of course, not legal expropriation pure and simple, as the lawyer would understand the term. Even the wage labourer who has no property either before or after the labour process, is not legally expropriated: he is only put into a position where he can neither appropriate nor accumulate, since the capitalist appropriates and accumulates the monetary value of his surplus product. The emphasis therefore lies on capitalist appropriation. Capitalists will expropriate other capitalists only in so far as either lack of opportunities for investment or lack of wage-labourers stands in the way of the appropriating tendency; and capital that has been accumulated and is not employed, clamours for investment. Accumulated capital makes room for itself by force. "As simple reproduction constantly reproduces the capital-relation itself, i.e. the relation of capitalists on the one hand, and wage-workers on the other, so reproduction on a progressive scale, i.e. accumulation, reproduces the capital-relation on a progressive scale, more capitalists or larger capitalists at this pole, more wage-workers at that" (*Capital* i, pp. 626–7). For this purpose capital employs an aggressive weapon—competition. By way of competition undertakings are rendered idle; what remains of their property is bought up by other capitalists who incorporate it in their own undertakings; the previous owner comes down in the social scale and sooner or later he ends, with his family, in the proletariat. (*231*)

This capitalist expropriation by way of competition as a legal procedure, does not deprive the owner of the value of his property. The person who is expropriated, though he loses his property, receives its equivalent in the form of money, thus retaining the value of the object, the economic property, after he has become dispossessed of the material object. No objection can be taken to the legal transaction which is only the winding-up of the prior economic catastrophe in legal forms. If "expropriation of capitalist by capitalist" brings about concentration of undertakings (*Capital* i, p. 640) competition enforces the merger of one undertaking in another, in which the rate of payment for the former is determined by the residuary value. We shall see later that this is only one special instance and perhaps not even the most important case of Marx's "attraction of capitals".

Values in the hands of the owners have here been destroyed by competition even before the owner was able to transfer them or indeed wished to do so. The first stage is not legal expropriation but the depreciation of property which precedes legal expropriation. The property remnants, thus depreciated, always make cheap booty for the expropriator, even if he has to pay the full or even an extravagant price for them. This "annexation of capitals" (Marx's term)—illustrated by the legend of the fishes— big fish eats small fish—is, according to Marx, by no means the main form in which capitalist accumulation takes place. Yet every change in industrial technique is accompanied by a decrease in the value of capitals which are less highly organised, it is accompanied by a depreciation of undertakings whose technique has become obsolete. They may remain for a long time the legal property of their owners, until competition has overcome them; the legal relations between the *persona* and the *res* of the property right can be conserved, and legal expropriation need not even take place at all. Side by side with the ruins of old castles we see in the countryside more and more ruins of industry, abandoned furnaces left to decay, which no-one will buy. But just as legal property must be distinguished from economic property, the former referring to the object as an item of nature, and the latter regarding it as an incarnation of value, an object with a capitalist function; so must it be admitted that economic expropriation is possible as well as legal expropriation, just as economic property exists independently of legal property.

This is expropriation as understood by Marx, a reduction or abolition of the capital function, as takes place in the cases described above. If there is both legal expropriation and appropriation, as in the case of sale, it implies, of course, on the average, an exchange of equivalents. But this legal transaction has been preceded by a process of economic expropriation, namely, depreciation of values. It is the final realisation of this economic process, which only now becomes apparent and measurable. In the case of expropriation as in the case of property, capitalist development results in a split between the legal construction and its economic substratum.

Expropriation, as we have outlined it here, [1] is still incidental

---

[1] We must distinguish between expropriation and dispossession (forcible dispossession and occupation). Somebody who has actual or legal detention of an object can be put out of detention *de facto*. This means that he is dispossessed. This distinction can become important in the course of social development. A capitalist who acts as his own entrepreneur, though generally without function in his capacity as capitalist, can be indispensable in his function as entrepreneur. It would in this case be wrong to dispossess him, though it may become necessary to expropriate him. Conversely

to every crisis, but it was most widely spread in the initial stages of capitalism. It led then to the ruin of innumerable masses of rural farmers and urban artisans, devaluating their possessions and bringing them to auction. In its beginnings the proletariat was mainly recruited from these newly expropriated artisans and peasants who had suffered economic collapse and still nourished a burning hatred against the expropriators. Nowadays the proletarians of the second and third generation are the overwhelming majority, and they no longer spontaneously appreciate the meaning of the old cry for revenge, the demand to "expropriate the expropriators". The disastrous economic upheaval of the war, however, has again left us with an army of new proletarians for whom Marx's expropriation is again a fresh and personal experience. (*232*)   Every economic catastrophe increases their number, re-awakening the pain of their experience. [2] Nevertheless this expropriating function of capital, as outlined above, is now very largely a matter of past history.

4. MUTUAL DISPLACEMENT OF SURPLUS VALUE AND WAGES REVENUE

Whatever we may think of capitalist expropriation, the method of capitalist appropriation is of fundamental importance, and develops on a constantly expanding scale. The titles to surplus value increase progressively in aggregate value, though neither undertakings nor possessions are fully concentrated. It is quite possible that a considerable part of these titles (shares, debentures, mortgage bonds) is dispersed among the middle classes, providing an additional income for them. Yet there is an opposite tendency which largely cancels out this dispersal of possession: the majority

the general occupation of factories by their workers is an absurdity to the lawyer. During the process of production the workers have detention of the place of work in any event; legal ownership, however, is due to the whole of society and not to them: moreover, they understand only one of the many functions connected with ownership and prove unable to assume other functions. Dispossession and occupation therefore lead only to a stoppage of the work in the undertaking and to economic confusion. If the functions of property have become sufficiently developed and differentiated, this way of re-expropriation is impossible (Russian and Italian experiences). Occupation and dispossession are therefore very doubtful social means which must not be confused with the legal expropriation of the property title.

[2] Karl Marx's life work, especially *Capital*, his principal work, belongs to a definite period of history, the middle of the last century, and must therefore be read with the eye of the historian. Yet this applies only with reservations. Wherever capital invades a society that is half feudal or based upon simple commodity production, Marx's words still have the old striking effect. So also in times when great catastrophes like the World War bring about sudden mass expropriations. This explains the propaganda power of Communism in the East of the Old World and its failure in the West.

of individuals, even members of the propertied classes, already to-day draw an increasing proportion of their income not from property, but from salaries. People of substance often prefer to take up employment, and it is often more painful for them to lose their position than to lose part of their property. Even now, more social prestige attaches to a position than to property. Man increasingly becomes a worker, and his interest in his possessions takes a place second to his interest in his work. The innumerable hybrid masks more and more tend to resemble each other, and the traits of the wage-earner superimpose themselves on those of the mere appropriator of value. Yet it is true that this change is to-day only in its inception, and probably was scarcely noticeable in the time of Karl Marx.

NOTES, CHAPTER II, SECTION III

(*215*) Whether this functional *"universitas rerum"* was ever as prominent in the social and economic history of this country as it was on the Continent may be doubted. The most essential point in Renner's analysis of the age of simple commodity production is the identity of physical ownership with the economic basis of the livelihood of the urban and rural population. It pre-supposes a system of universal peasant proprietorship. Even on the Continent it existed—before the French Revolution—only in certain countries. The prototypes Renner envisages are the independent craftsman and the yeoman farmer.

(*216*) The technical term is *"Haus- und Gutsübernahme"*. This transaction—of the greatest possible social significance in Austria as in Germany—is the transfer *inter vivos* of the farm by the retiring peasant to one of his children (often the eldest son). It is, from an economic point of view, a simple transaction—an anticipation of inheritance—, from a legal point of view a most complex phenomenon: a conveyance of land and transfer of movables, coupled with a novation of debts, and with the creation of rights to maintenance and alimony, often secured by rent-charges or mortgages. (See note 17, above.) The words *"Haus- und Gutsübernahme"* have been translated as "settlement inter vivos", words connoting the nearest equivalent of the institution in English law. While, however, the settlement of land upon the eldest son was originally a habit of the upper classes in this country, and while it usually leaves the settlor in possession as tenant for life (and also leaves to him the remainder in fee simple), the *Haus- und Gutsübernahme* is a peasant custom applied not upon the coming of age of the eldest son, but upon the retirement of the father from active participation in the management. The contrasts between the two institutions reflect those of two different social systems.

(*217*) The I.O.U.—which is only a piece of evidence of a debt, not its "embodiment"—belongs to the creditor as creditor. He is not the creditor because he is the owner of the I.O.U. He is the owner of the I.O.U. because he is the creditor. Hence the subservience of physical ownership to an incorporeal right can be demonstrated in a particularly striking fashion with the help of this example. It should be contrasted with those documents—alien to Roman law and entirely the creation of medieval and modern mercantile law—which "embody" an incorporeal right: documents of title (e.g. bills of lading, see above, note 171), bills of exchange and other negotiable instruments, share warrants (Sect. 70 of the Companies Act, 1929). Legitimate possession of these documents is the pre-condition of the exercise of the right: a debt evidenced by an I.O.U. can be assigned though the I.O.U. be lost, the rights arising from a bill of exchange can only be transferred by delivery of the document (with—or in the case of a bill payable to bearer without—endorsement). The incorporeal right has, in these cases, been crystallised into the physical ownership of the document which is its symbol.

(*218*) For a discussion of Renner's conception of legal ownership see the Introduction and notes 22 and 23 above. The "helplessness" of the Romanistic property concept is a striking fact. It is matched by that of the conception of "corporate entity" for which English law offers numerous examples.

(*219*) Renner presupposes the Continental system of company law and practice which gives to the "paper", the "certificate" a significance different from that which it has in English law. The English share certificate is merely "prima facie evidence of the title of the member to the shares" (Companies Act, 1929, sect. 68), although a company is, in many cases, estopped from denying this title (*Dixon v. Kennaway*, [1900] 1 Ch. 833) or (*Bloomenthal v. Ford*, [1897], AC 162) the fact that the shares are fully paid up if they are so described in the certificate. But, unlike the (not very frequent) share warrant (sect. 70 of the Act), the certificate is not a document "embodying" the share. The share is not transferred by a handing over of a certificate, but by a different procedure culminating in the registration of the transfer in the company's register of members (sects. 63, 65, 66 of the Act). On the Continent the issue of bearer shares by joint stock companies is the rule, not—

as in England—an exception. The paper is the embodiment of the membership right, and that right is transferred by physical delivery of the paper.

(*220*) There is, perhaps, no case of a discrepancy between legal and economic property which is as familiar to the English lawyer as this. The "One-Man-Company" has been recognised as legal since the decision of the House of Lords in *Salomon v. Salomon and Co. Ltd.*, [1897] AC 22. Even if the company is completely dominated by a single shareholder, it is not regarded as the latter's agent in its commercial dealings, and the shareholder is not, therefore, liable for the company's debts. Outside the actual field of application of this principle, however, both statute (especially revenue) and case law have been compelled to disregard the fiction of corporate entity, and to attach consequences to the economic rather than to the legal ownership (for a summary see 5 *Modern Law Review*, 54). The provisions about subsidiary companies and consolidated accounts in the Companies Act, 1947 constitute an attempt to define—or rather, in view of sect. 127 of the Act of 1929, to re-define—one aspect of economic ownership, and to attach important legal consequences to it. It is interesting to note that the principal test of economic ownership is to be "control", i.e. the power over the appointment of directors (Cohen Report No. 118), a development foreshadowed by the famous decision as to "enemy character" of corporations in *Daimler Co. v. Continental Tyre and Rubber Co. (Great Britain), Ltd.*, [1916] 2 AC 307. The power over the "complementary institution" (appointment of directors) becomes the test of control, i.e. of property in the economic sense. Berle and Means, l.c., p. 70, use the same test.

(*221*) The contradiction is less apparent from the English translation than from the German text. The words "economic ownership" (*ökonomisches Eigentum*) have a grating sound in the ears of a lawyer, but not only of a lawyer. The phenomenon analysed by Renner, the emasculation of legal ownership, is thus described (in connection with mortgages) by Prof. Aereboe, one of the leading German agricultural economists (*Agrarpolitika*, p. 471, quoted Hedemann, l.c., p. 96): "The modern credit system makes it possible to separate ownership (*Eigentum*) and property (*Vermögen*). If a farmer, who has hitherto been free from debts, encumbers his farm up to the chimney pots . . ., he mobilises his property (*Vermögen*). His ownership (*Eigentum*) in the farm is not, however, affected as long as he fulfils his obligations. . . . It is true that this is commonly known as mobilising landed possession. Strictly speaking, however, it ought to be called mobilising property (*Vermögen*) in immoveables while preserving the right of ownership (*Eigentum*)." This sharp antithesis of ownership and property by an economist illustrates Renner's terminological difficulty.

(*222*) The "contradictory development" which Renner tries to express in his deliberately contradictory terminology is, in this country, reflected in the ambiguity of the word "property" (see the Introduction) which will for ever continue to haunt writers on jurisprudence in the English language.

(*223*) In this general form the statement comes near to, but does not fully represent the actual English law. The measure of damages for the non-delivery of an article by a seller to a buyer is, generally speaking, neither the cost price, nor the capitalised yield, but the market price of the article (Sale of Goods Act, 1893, Sect. 51), although there are cases, especially where there is no "available market", in which a loss of special profits may be included in the damages (see *Benjamin on Sale*, 7th ed., p. 1004). There are, however, cases in which the non-delivery or late delivery of yield producing objects (land, ships) may entail liability for a refund of lost profits. Thus, in the law of tort, "mesne profits" are recoverable in an action for ejectment or for withholding possession, and where a vendor or lessor of land delays or refuses the performance of his obligation to give possession to the purchaser or lessee, he may have to refund profits lost (Cases in *Chitty on Contract*, p. 269, and *Mayne on Damages*, 11th ed., p. 228). Similar principles govern the calculation of damages for the wrongful detention of ships, breach of a charter-party by a charterer who fails to load, etc. The subject is one of great complexity, but it may be said that English law rejects the "cost" test as a standard of measurement for damages, without generally accepting the "yield of profits" test. It prefers the "market value" test which, in many instances, will be substantially identical with the "yield" criterion, and, in any event, illustrates Renner's thesis that the "cost" criterion is not part of modern law.

(*224*) A reader who is unfamiliar with the Marxist theory of accumulation, with the theories of production and re-production, of surplus labour and surplus value, and with the technical conceptions of expropriation and concentration, will find a succinct recent analysis in Schumpeter's *Capitalism, Socialism, and Democracy*, Part I. Chapter III is of particular importance in the present context.

(*225*) The distinction made by the *Usus Modernus Pandectarum* between *fructus naturales* and *fructus civiles* has nothing to do with the English distinction between *fructus naturales* and *fructus industriales*. According to Roman law (see I. 2, 1, 35; D. 50, 16, 77) *fructus (naturales)* were (in the words of Prof. Buckland, *Manual of Roman Private Law*, § 55) the "organic and, usually, periodic products" of a thing, the wool of the sheep, but also the lamb; crops and timber, but also the yield of a mine or quarry. *Fructus civiles*, a term used by the Pandectists, but not occurring in the sources were the yields of a thing accruing from a legal transaction, such as rent (D. 22, 1, 36—Ulpian) and—perhaps—interest (D. 22, 1, 34—Ulpian; per contra: D. 50, 16, 121—Pomponius). The Pandectists included interest and any other kind of "legal" yield among the *fructus civiles*. This distinction between *fructus naturales* and *civiles* was adopted by the Code Civil (Art. 547). There, however, we find a subdivision of "*fruits naturels de la terre*" into "*fruits naturels*" proper and "*fruits industriels*". This corresponds to the English distinction. Both *fructus naturales* and *fructus industriales* (in the English sense) are *fructus naturales* in the Roman sense, the first being the "natural profit of the earth" (grass, timber), the second being "those vegetables . . . produced by the labour of man, which ordinarily yield a present annual profit" (Benjamin, l.c., p. 196). The notion of *fructus civiles* is unknown to English law.

(*226*) For *Specificatio* see above, note 162.

(*227*) For *fructus civiles* see above, note 225.

(*228*) And, for this very reason, incapable of legal formulation. The economist's conception of "title", i.e. of an opportunity for obtaining some advantage, and the lawyer's conception of "title", i.e. a right to have or to claim a defined legally protected interest, are (and must be) irreconcileable.

(*229*) See further for this point below, Section V, No. 2, p. 230.

(*230*) The Marxist concept of expropriation, which (as is not always sufficiently appreciated) has nothing in common with the legal institution bearing the same name, is explained below. Its principal characteristic is that it is one of the functions of property itself.

(*231*) That the dispossessed bourgeois would, in any relevant sense, become a proletarian was, it is submitted, a wrong prognostication based on a mistaken diagnosis of middle class mentality. It will perhaps by future historians be regarded as one of the most fatal errors of the working class movement. The gigantic expropriation which occurred in Central Europe during and after the inflation of the currencies did not result in the victims becoming "proletarians", except in a purely economic sense. That middle class mentality and habits would survive a middle class basis of existence, that the dispossessed bourgeois would refuse to be a proletarian, and that, owing to their psychological need for a new ideological basis of a feeling of superiority, the expropriated would become the willing tools of the expropriators, was a lesson of the 20th century which 19th century thought did not anticipate. Nevertheless, a sociological as well as a jurisprudential analysis of Fascism might take the phenomenon of expropriation in the Marxist sense as its starting point. Much of Nazi legislation before and during the war (labour legislation, wholesale closure of small undertakings) was expropriation in this sense, expropriation for the benefit of large monopolistic groups which controlled the state.

(232) The "old" lower middle class—independent craftsmen, small traders, professional men—as well as the "new"—civil servants, salaried employees, etc.—were victims of the economic upheavals mentioned by Renner. But, contrary to expectations, they did not either of them develop a "proletarian" mentality. They were both recruiting grounds for Fascism. The "pain of the experience" which Renner mentions translated itself into a "false consciousness".

Section iv. Capitalist Property and the Law Relating to Associations

Capitalist property of the period of simple commodity production, the "patrimony", was thoroughly individualistic, as regards both its substratum and its concept. The world was based upon the individual and his property. Individual self-help and self-responsibility were the watch-words of a period which was at first suspicious of every form of association or coalition, in its urge to overthrow all those restrictions on the individual which dated from feudal times. The first French revolution prohibited *coalitions*, threatening them with punishment. (*233*) The civil law of this period of transition did not recognise any form of association apart from the civil *societas* of Roman law, and large trading companies were possible only by special privilege (the East India Company, etc.). (*234*) Only the codifications of the 19th century, (*235*) from Napoleon's *code de commerce* to the German commercial code brought about the full capitalist freedom of association and provided a large variety of legal forms for the purpose of associations. (*236*) The need to accumulate, inherent in the amassed surplus-values, was the motive power in this development.

I. ACCUMULATION AND ASSOCIATION

The surplus product which has been appropriated by industrial capital in the course of production is acquired by the capitalist and brought to market. The sale of the product realises the whole value. The value of the surplus product or surplus value is at first an undifferentiated part of it, and it can be made distinct only by calculation. It appears as the balance remaining after deduction of the money advanced for the purpose of production, and this balance is the property of the entrepreneur. As money which for the time being is inactive, it is not yet capital.

Appropriated surplus value changes into capital, into value which begets further value, and this conversion takes place in various forms. Capitals are accumulated in the same individual enterprise where that undertaking is expanded. "At the same time portions of the original capitals disengage themselves and function as new independent capitals. Besides other causes, the division of property, within capitalist families, plays a great part in this. With the accumulation of capital, therefore, the number of capitalists grows to a greater or less extent" (*Capital* i, p. 639). It is not contrary to the principle of accumulation but a consequence thereof, that accumulated capital is again split up into an increasing number of individual capitals. This, in Marxist terminology, is "repulsion of capitals".[1] It enlarges the total capital at the disposal of society and at the same time increases the number of capitalists.

Thus the accumulated surplus-values which demand employment are not always invested in existing undertakings as additional capital[2] since they arise by increments in the course of production. Yet they clamour to be invested, and this is possible only if the individual increments are combined into units of a higher order.

In this situation the particles of surplus value are not active, only potential capital (*Capital* iii, p. 712), property-objects belonging to many owners, dormant property fragments. They can only come to life and assume the function of capital, if they are made into a homogenous aggregate, one *res* to which the law can apply as to a single unit. Their economic centralisation requires one of two things: they must either be amalgamated into an aggregate object of ownership, held by a number of subjects, e.g. joint property or property held by a partnership according to civil law. (*237*) Or else, if obstacles or difficulties stand in the way of such legal transformation, the owners of the particles must be expropriated and their properties must be transferred to a single person, either physical or artificial. (*238*) The co-owners vest their properties in the association by act-in-the-law. This amalgamation of fragments of potential capital, their combination to a unitary, a virtual individual capital, is the attraction of capitals, as Marx has termed it. He distinguishes two forms of amalgamation: where it is brought about in a peaceful manner, by legal transaction, by way of association, it is centralisation. Conversely, forcible subjection and appropriation of competing enterprises by

---

[1] Repulsion and attraction are chemical terms (in German, *A.S.*) describing the behaviour of molecules of diverse elements towards one another. Capitals repel each other when, for instance, one family has inherited a large mill and a foundry and the sons divide their capital by giving the mill to one and the foundry to the other. Capitals attract each other when for instance two spinning works in one place are amalgamated, perhaps by marriage.

[2] Additional capital can also be brought in by way of association, for instance, in the form of the capital contributed by a limited partner or as debenture capital contributed to existing joint stock companies. (*239*)

way of economic competition is concentration, with which we have dealt above.

2. ASSOCIATION AND OWNERSHIP

Capitalist parliaments have developed a number of legal institutions to make this centralisation possible. All these institutions, however, are based upon ownership, and therefore they do not change the legal structure of property. Associations, (*240*) companies, co-operative societies, establishments (*241*) and corporations are the principal legal institutions complementary to property in its capitalist function: their fundamental legal principle is that of association for the purpose of joint performance as distinct from the exchange of performances (*do ut des, do ut facias*). The association, the union for the purpose of joint performance is in itself neither capitalist nor socialist, it is merely an empty legal frame,[1] a vessel without content. Only the purposes of the association and the means which it employs determine this content and show its functions. The association, moreover, is only one form of aggregate body. The workers of a factory are also associated individuals, they also form a body aggregate, but this is a passive collective, based on subjection and compulsion. (*243*) The association, on the other hand, is an active collective, differentiated from other active collectives by its foundation upon individual agreement, it is a collective based upon contract. (*244*) The association presupposes individuals who have self-determination, it is therefore founded upon property and a capitalist economic order.

The attraction and centralisation of capitals brought about by associations for the purpose of joint performance always keep intact all capitalist functions of property, even if ownership is legally surrendered. The owner retains the title to surplus-value, this title to surplus value which is now no longer burdened with physical substance. Legislation now gives a new substance to that legal title which in itself is non-corporeal, in the form of a document which the law regards as a thing, and therefore as a possible object of ownership: the negotiable security (share warrant, bond,

---

[1] It would be wrong, therefore, to regard the associations simply as forms for socialisation. But it is true that Marx himself often uses the term of socialisation (*Vergesellschaftung*) when he deals with mere forms of association of capital. Marx's *Vergesellschaftung* therefore must not be understood as socialisation pure and simple, though he always regards the association as a preliminary step towards socialisation. (*242*)

etc.). (*245*) This title established by the law corresponds in value
to the surrendered property-object.

Property in its economic capacity, as social object, as capital,
therefore remains in the hands of the associated individuals; but
in its technical capacity, as natural object, as use-value, it belongs
to the collective person, the association. If this association has
legal personality, if the law recognises it as a person, then the
legal picture of the situation is changed. The previous owner
ceases to be owner, and the association alone assumes ownership.
Individual ownership is abolished, as far as the law is concerned;
it is replaced by a mere debt of a certain kind which, (*246*) in the
case of debentures payable to bearer, is linked to the mere detention of a piece of paper without intrinsic value; such a debt is a
"frozen" right *in personam* which, though never property in a legal
sense, can circulate like property by virtue of its incorporation in
a bond. Thus the law transforms a personal right into a new
object in order that it may circulate like a commodity. (*247*)

Where the law thus provides a determinate structure to
economic matter, it consolidates its form but does not change its
substance. No new content is given to these economic relations
by those legal constructions which shape certain relations of wills
into legal types, [1] whether or not they formulate them in terms of
legal personality, in terms of simple I.O.U.s or debentures payable
to bearer or to order, or in terms of joint ownership. The original
owner remains the economic, i.e. capitalist, owner; he retains the
title to surplus value. He surrenders only the natural item, the
use-value of his property, an item in which he never was interested,
or if he ever was has long ceased to be so. (*248*)

However, associations do not necessarily serve capitalist purposes only. The formula of association for the purpose of joint
performance expresses a relation of wills which may derive its
content from all kinds of activities which need not be connected
with economy at all. (*250*) The union of two persons for the
performance of conjugal duties, as it is called, is neither capitalist
nor socialist nor is it in itself economic. A performance in the eyes
of the law is either a *dare* or a *facere*, a giving or doing. The

---

[1] The law can always achieve its aim by an association based on contract, and this
is the form which all associations first assume. Only when joint stock companies, co-
operative societies, etc., have actually been established, when certain articles of
agreement have become typical, only then does the law convert the type into a norm
and create laws relating to joint stock companies and co-operative societies as blanks
to simplify business for the contracting parties. (*249*) Limitations of the freedom of
contract or the content of the contract do not affect the functions of property.

association therefore can be a *unio dandi* or a *unio faciendi* or both. The *unio faciendi* is an association for the purpose of joint performance, but this joint performance need not be labour; it can be any kind of activity or function which the law recognises as performance. Only in so far as a union is an association for the purpose of labour, does it operate towards immediate socialisation, and is even to-day a step in the direction of a socialist order of society.[1] On a capitalist basis, however, associations are always also *unio dandi*, as they presuppose investment of capital, however small in amount, and therefore they are as a rule capitalist. In most cases they are also *unio faciendi*, associations for the purpose of joint activity, but this no longer applies to joint stock companies. (*251*) This activity may be labour in a sociological sense, but it can also be the mere function of managing an undertaking, as in the case of the trading company. All associations, with the exception, perhaps, of the absolutely unequivocal joint stock company, are hybrid forms in so far as they are based upon property and the functions of an undertaking (even if this is true only to a minute degree, as in the case of the labour associations). The association therefore always rests on a twofold foundation of *dare* and *facere*.

The decisive factor is, however, the purpose of the association. As a rule associations aim at the realisation of capital functions and are therefore purely capitalist. Even co-operative societies cannot eliminate the capital function which is necessarily bound up with ownership, but they can make it subservient to their members and harmless for them: they can, in particular, restrict merchant capital and usurer's capital. No association, however, can completely eliminate the capital function which is necessarily linked with property. Conversely, this form of association, if it is made profitable for the owners, provides an opportunity for them to push on the capitalist method of production to the climax of its development.

3. ASSOCIATION AND CREDIT

It is mainly by means of associations that a new power arises within the capitalist system of production, the credit system,

---

[1] This again is not the only impetus of the development: the compulsive association of the workers in the factory is on a par with the association for labour based on contract.

which, "by unseen threads . . . draws the disposable money, scattered in larger or smaller masses over the surface of society, into the hands of individual or associated capitalists" and thus becomes "the specific machine for the centralisation of capitals" (*Capital* i, p. 641).

The social function of property where it is held by the joint stock company, is in the first place to deprive the economic owner himself of his functions and to expose his superfluity; secondly to bring about the self-abolition of property even within a capitalist system of production, for even to the law the owner is either no longer owner or merely one among a multitude of owners without influence; and finally to transfer the capitalist function to paid managers, so that the contract of employment, the *locatio conductio operarum*, takes over the last remaining function of general service to the community as a whole, of those fulfilled by the institution of property. This previously insignificant legal institution has thus deprived property of all functions connected with social production and reproduction, making property itself an inoperative and thus an antisocial institution, [1] to which only one function is left, that of obstructing the future development of society.

"This is the abolition of the capitalist mode of production within capitalist production itself. . . . It is private production without the control of private property" (*Capital* iii, p. 519). It is this kind of property which yet operates as social property, this economic property of the share or debenture holder of which Jaurès rightly said that it "has become so estranged from the owner that he must consult the newspaper to get information about its position" (quoted from "*Theorie und Praxis*", p. 259). But this abolition of the capitalist method of production by no means implies the abolition of the methods of appropriation, as this is the core of property which no automatic development can destroy. In like manner, the cartels are an abolition of the capitalist method of production within the framework of the capitalist order of society, but again they do not abolish the appropriation of the social surplus product by individuals who fulfil no social function. All functions which property fulfilled in the period of simple commodity production, and which it acquired during the evolution towards capitalist production, may be relinquished in the course of development, all but one: the function

---

[1] Here we shall not enlarge on the connections between the credit system and the system of associations. Cf. on that subject: *Wirtschaft als Gesamtprozess*, p. 205 ff.

to be title to surplus value, to accumulate the surplus value appropriated.

NOTES, CHAPTER II, SECTION IV

(*233*) For the Loi Le Chapelier see above, note 104.

(*234*) This is broadly true of the legal history of the joint stock company in this country. Until 1844, i.e. until the registration of companies with corporate personality was made possible by the statutes 7 and 8 Vict. c. 110, joint stock enterprise had to take the form either of a partnership (which corresponded to the Roman *societas*) or of a corporation created by special statute or by royal charter. That this state of affairs was permitted to endure and capable of enduring in a country in which corporate trading and, at a later stage, manufacture played so vital a rôle may, at first sight, seem surprising. The legal difficulties inherent in the carrying on of what was in fact corporate business in the form of a partnership were almost overwhelming. (See for a vivid description Formoy, *Historical Foundations of Modern Company Law*, pp. 32 *sq.*) That they were tolerated and had to be tolerated was largely due to the shock which public opinion had received by the South Sea Bubble of 1720 and to the Bubble Act of that year which had been its consequence. Had it not been for the law of trusts—which enabled the "partners" to appoint the directors trustees under the "deed of settlement" (which was, in fact, the constitution of the joint stock undertaking)—the position would have been so impossible that incorporation by registration might have been provided for before 1844. The situation in England was aggravated by the fact that the "*commenda*", the *société en commandite*, or "limited partnership" did not exist. (An attempt to introduce it in Ireland by an Act of the Irish Parliament of 1782—21 and 22 Geo. III, c. 46—proved a failure.) This form of enterprise, so important on the Continent and introduced in many States in the United States in the first half of the 19th century, did not become part of English law until 1907 (Limited Partnerships Act, 1907). By that time, however, the development had turned full circle. During the 18th and the first half of the 19th centuries the law of partnership had been pressed into the service of joint stock enterprise, a norm designed to enable a small number of associated entrepreneurs to carry on a business in common had acquired the uncongenial function of regulating the mutual relationships of hundreds or even thousands of owners of joint stock. At the beginning of the 20th century, company law which since 1844, and especially since the conferment of the privilege of limited liability in 1855 (Limited Liability Act, 1855), had been the legal form of joint stock undertakings, had come to annex the functions of the law of partnership. The private company had become so popular by 1907 that the law of limited partnerships has almost remained a dead letter. For details of the history of English company law,—a history full of interest from the point of view of the functional transformation of norms,—see the book by Formoy, quoted above. The first comprehensive statute was the Companies Act, 1862, which marks the inception of modern company law. It will be noticed that it was almost contemporaneous with the General Commercial Code for the German Confederation.

(*235*) See note 191, above.

(*236*) This "large variety" included: the "civil" society and the "commercial" society (both corresponding to the English partnership), the limited partnership (see note 234), the ordinary incorporated company, and the incorporated company the managing shareholders of which are personally liable (see Companies Act, 1929, sect. 147). The incorporated company (*société anonyme, Aktien-Gesellschaft*) corresponds to the English public company. Later legislation in many Continental countries added a form of company similar to the English private company, known as *société à responsabilité limitée* or *Gesellschaft mit beschränkter Haftung*.

(*237*) The German word "*Miteigentum*" means, in strict legal terminology, ownership "in common". Each co-owner has a share in the property. The value of the property is, as it were, divided between the co-owners, though the physical substance is undivided and the right to possession can only be exercised jointly. On the death of a co-owner his share in the property passes to his personal representatives. "Joint ownership" in the legal sense is something different. The value of the property is not divided. All the co-owners together own the whole property, they hold it, as it were, "with one hand" (the German word for joint ownership is *Gesamt-Hand*), and, since there is no "share" which, upon a co-owner's death can devolve upon his personal representatives, his right accrues to the other co-owners, and, upon the death of the last surviving co-owner, the property passes to his personal representatives. This form of co-ownership exists among co-trustees, and, since the Law of Property Act, 1925 (sect. 1, subs. 6, sect. 34 to 36), it has been the only form of legal co-ownership of land, so that ownership in common is only possible in equity. The division of the value substance into "shares" exists only as a matter concerning the internal relationship between the co-owners, as regards the outside world the property is undivided, a legislative technical device which has greatly facilitated conveyancing. It means that the legal joint owners hold the property as trustees for themselves or others in their capacity as equitable tenants in common. While this form of co-ownership of land has been made compulsory by the Act of 1925, it was, long before the Act, extremely usual, and has in this country provided that type of "economic centralisation" which Renner calls "joint property". Thus, many "unincorporated associations", such as "members' clubs", trade unions, etc., are established in this form: the property is—legally—vested in trustees as joint owners, and the members' rights are merely contractual or equitable (in the case of registered trade unions and friendly societies this is required by law, see Trade Union Act, 1871, sect. 8; Friendly Societies Act, 1896, sect. 49, 50). Translated into terms of English law, what Renner says is that there is an alternative between the trust system and the partnership system. For the term "civil" as distinguished from "commercial" society (partnership) which has no parallel in this country, see above, note 167.

(*238*) The word "expropriation" is, of course, used in its technical Marxist meaning. Berle and Means, l.c., p. 3, call the same phenomenon a "surrender of wealth" which amounts much to the same thing.

(*239*) The limited partnership is a convenient and comparatively inexpensive method of attracting capital in circumstances which, in this country, would call for the formation of a private company.

(*240*) The word which is translated as "association" ("*Verein*") signifies an incorporated or unincorporated body, as a rule formed for non-economic purposes. It has no counterpart in English law, its place being taken by a variety of legal institutions, e.g. unincorporated associations which use the mechanism of the trust for the management of their property, companies limited by guarantee, "proprietary clubs", charitable trusts, etc.

(*241*) The legal institutions mentioned here may—directly or indirectly—promote the attraction of capital, but it is not in every case their objective to make the "morsels" of contributed capital profitable to their owners. The *Verein*—see previous note—usually attracts subscriptions for non-profit making purposes, *Körperschaft* (corporation) is a *nomen generale* comprising a large variety of species from the incorporated *Verein* to the joint stock company, and also non-voluntary bodies, e.g. the State itself and municipal corporations. *Anstalt* is not a voluntary body at all, but a segregated and incorporated piece of public administration or enterprise (see above, note 125). Indirectly, e.g. through the mechanism of central or local taxation, all these bodies attract capital, but only in some instances with a view to the distribution of profits.

(242) Two lines of development should be distinguished: the increasing use of the corporate ("association") *form* for purposes of nationalisation and for the management of public enterprise: the "public corporation" for which the laws both of this country and, particularly, the Soviet Union provide examples, and—much more significant—the separation of economic enjoyment, management, and control, the splitting of the atom of the property concept within capitalism itself (see Berle and Means, l.c. p. 7, pp. 119 *sq.*) through the growth of the joint stock company. It is this latter phenomenon which, within the framework of capitalist society, prepares the ground for socialisation.

(243) See above, notes 39, 113.

(244) It is not based on "contract" in any sense in the case of *Anstalten* or of public law corporations. But even in the case of "voluntary" bodies we must be careful in the use of the word "contract", more careful perhaps to-day than was necessary when Renner wrote his book. If we use the word "contract" in a purely formal—technical legal—sense, then every voluntary corporation can be said to be based on "contract", but if we use it thus, then we are constrained to say that the "association" of the workers in a factory is also based on "contract". This is obviously not what Renner has in mind. He thinks of "contract" not as a legal form, but as a relation of co-ordination. In that sense, however, the "voluntary" association is to-day in the most important instances hardly more "contractual" than the association of the workers in the factory. The subjection of the shareholder to a power of "control" in which he does not participate has been described by Berle and Means, l.c., *passim*. The conditions under which trade unions are joined by individuals—even in the absence of a "closed shop"—and, more significant in the present context, the shifting of control inside the unions from the circumference to the centre, make it difficult to lay much emphasis on the "contractual" element there. The fact is that, not only in the employment relationship, the "contractual" feature of the organisation of capitalism is dwindling, the line between "voluntary" and "compulsive" action becoming more and more fluid, and the neat antithesis postulated by Renner is losing its validity.

(245) See above, note 219, for the legal aspect of this type of corporate organisation. At one time there may have been "correspondence in value" between the property objects surrendered by the shareholder and the title which he receives. But this is no more than the starting point of a development which has

frequently led—and was bound to lead—to what Renner himself describes as an "expropriation" of values. The share and the debenture (here envisaged as the negotiable bearer debenture which is in universal use on the Continent) may still be a title to "surplus value", but they are no longer of necessity a title to the control of the surplus value.

(246) It is a "debt" only in the case of debentures, not in that of shares which—from a legal point of view—are membership rights and which produce "debts" only on certain contingencies (declaration of dividends, etc.). In substance, the difference is not as important as the legal construction would seem to suggest. Commercially there is much less to choose between, say, a cumulative preference share of a prosperous company and a debenture of the same company, than would appear from a law student's textbook learning.

(247) It goes without saying that the difference in outward form between the English type of registered share and the Continental type of negotiable share document does not affect the substance of Renner's argument at all. Registered shares (and debentures) do not, in the legal sense, "circulate" like commodities, in the economic sense they do.

(248) This sentence—indeed the whole of this chapter—brings home to the reader that, since Renner wrote it, the economic structure of corporate enterprise has changed almost beyond recognition. Nothing could be further from the truth to-day than that the "legal" structure of corporate enterprise does not change the substance of the economic relationship. Nothing, moreover, could justify the statement—made by Renner at the end of the next paragraph—that the joint stock company is "absolutely unequivocal". On the contrary, the joint stock company has become an empty frame, a colourless and neutral institution, like property and contract themselves. Like them it serves an infinite variety of economic purposes. It may be nothing but the outward form in which one entrepreneur or a small group of entrepreneurs continue to carry on their undertaking. This is usually the case with the private, and sometimes the case with the public company. If it is the case, and even if some of the shareholders are "friends" whose capital has been invested in the undertaking or the relations of one of the original entrepreneurs who has died, then Renner's statement that the economic relation has remained unaffected can still be upheld. It can also be upheld where a—parent—company chooses to manage part of its undertaking in the form of a subsidiary company. Where, however, the joint stock device fulfils its original appointed purpose of attracting large numbers of shifting morsels of capital, the business corporation is liable

eventually to become part of the "order of power" in society, and, as regards the social function of property itself, a disintegrating agent. It divorces beneficial enjoyment from control, and, some-times, control power from management. The analysis of this process in Berle and Means' *Modern Corporation and Private Property*, although written with the special American conditions in view, reads like a voluminous gloss to Renner's text. In this country the difficulties encountered in the process of framing uniform rules for all joint stock companies, or even for all private companies (see, e.g., Report on Company Law Amendment Cmd. 6659, No. 53) illustrates this development. Joint stock enterprise has become the dominating feature of capitalism. It has not left the economic property relation unaffected, it has revolutionised it. What happened to "property" and to "contract" during the transition from the age of simple commodity production to that of industrial capitalism has now happened to the company as a legal institution: it has ceased to be the mirror of an economic relation and become a "maid of all work". Society has, in the most important cases, taken this "brick" out of the order of property and built it into the order of power.

(*249*) Nothing could illustrate this better than the history of joint stock enterprise in England under the régime of the Bubble Act of 1720. It was the Act of 1844 (7 and 8 Vict. c. 110) which converted the "type" into a "norm". See above, note 234.

(*250*) The best example in this country is the company limited by guarantee. (For its definition see Companies Act, 1929, Sect. 1 (2) (b)). This is a joint stock company the members of which do not undertake to contribute any capital while the company is a going concern. They merely "undertake to contribute (a stated amount) to the assets of the company in the event of its being wound up". This form is therefore incapable of serving profit making enterprise, but well fitted to be used for associations pursuing "ideal" purposes which look to outside subscribers for their working "capital".

(*251*) Even a joint stock company may be an *unio faciendi*, e.g. where shares are allotted for "services". For technical legal reasons (due to the operation of the doctrine of consideration) shares cannot be allotted for past services, except as bonus shares, but, since shares may be allotted for a consideration other than cash, a member of the company who "contributes" his skill or experience may be—and sometimes is—promised to receive shares as part of his remuneration for future services. English law is probably too liberal and not sufficiently cautious with regard to transactions of this kind (for details, Kahn-Freund, 7 *Modern Law Review* 54).

Section v. Property and the Law of Family Relationships

The "own and patrimony" of days gone by ensured the basis of existence for the family from generation to generation.[1] The family was only one aspect of this "own", in theory set apart from it, but in fact inseparably bound up with it. The house connoted man as well as matter, the family was nothing but that aspect of the house which was concerned with reproduction of the species and with consumption.

All the most important events in the life of the individual, birth, marriage, death, were linked up with the "own", which wove around it a network of sacred traditions.

Above all it was the unity of "own and patrimony" which served the family as a fund for life. Procreation gives life to the individual but it does not maintain it. The character of the family is determined by the manner in which consumption is regulated and in which the social fund which serves this purpose is raised and used, just as the character of the individual is in many aspects determined by the family. With the differentiation and specialisation of the "own" of simple commodity production, with the disintegration of the microcosm, the family has been dissolved into the merely sexual relation of matrimony and a number of platonic relations of kinship. Neither husband and wife, nor brother and sister live in a community of labour, except the very wealthy who may perhaps live in a community of idleness. Every human being that can stand on his own feet, now seeks his revenue in some other way outside his house, or outside the substitute for his house, his "lodgings".

I. FAMILY AND INCOME

Nowadays the purpose of all economic activities as it appears to the individual is to secure that individual revenue which makes

---

[1] On the importance of the family as the legal institution for preserving the species see F. Engels: *The Origin of the Family, Private Property and the State* (transl. by A. West and D. Torr, London, 1943, pp. 1–2): "According to the materialistic conception, the determining factor in history is, in the final instance, the production and reproduction of the immediate essentials of life. This, again, is of a twofold character. On the one side the production of the means of existence, of articles of food and clothing, dwellings, and of the tools necessary for that production; on the other side, the production of human beings themselves, the propagation of the species. The social organisation, under which the people of a particular historical epoch and a particular country live is determined by both kinds of production; by the stage of development of labour on the one hand and of the family on the other."

individual consumption possible. Thus it is the satisfaction of individual wants which regulates all individual and social economic activity. In the period of simple commodity production, such a point of view was absolutely unintelligible. This is, however, the subjective reflection of the real state of affairs on the modern mind, a "frog's eye view" of the world as seen from the standpoint of the individual. Mankind is not, however, merely an aggregation of individuals, a whole arrived at by mechanical addition of the parts. The human individual does not exist apart from the species or prior to it, he is conditioned by the species more strictly than any other organic being, and in a different manner. Man as a member of society acts quite differently from the mere abstraction "individual". This is merely an abstract concept, it does not exist but in his own imagination.[1] Physiologically, the individual is determined by an infinite sequence of past generations. He is a mere link between changing generations, in body and soul a product of heredity. His mind is nothing but a meeting point of manifold tendencies of social thought, emotion and volition. Society dictates the forms of his thought in language, and the content of this thought is given on the one hand by traditional ideologies and on the other hand by social facts as they exist at the moment. Society trains his will power from childhood onward and prescribes his values. The psychology of the individual is a product of his environment. Physiology and psychology become more and more aware of the fact that "the concept of the individual is untenable".[2] In the field of economics, Marx has shown that the apparently independent self-determination and self-evaluation of individuals, a necessary product of the existing legal and economic order, is in reality their general social dependence; in the capitalist epoch this means complete subjection of man to matter, which, so long as society does not regulate directly the relations between human beings, must remain an unconscious expression of man's social nature.[3]

It is impossible to understand consumption if we regard it as an affair of the individual, and we are even less able to explain the

---

[1] We mean, of course, the purely self-contained individual which to our consciousness appears as a necessity and to philosophy as the only real and empirical datum.

[2] *Mach: Analyse der Sinnesempfindungen*, though in a different context.

[3] "Only thenceforward would man make his own history, fully conscious of his own actions; only thenceforward would the social causes, set in motion by himself, produce mainly and in an ever-increasing measure the intended results. It is the leap of mankind out of the reign of necessity into that of freedom" (F. Engels: *The Development of Socialism from Utopia to Science*, p. 28).

whole of economics in terms of individual consumption only, as has been attempted by the theory of marginal utility. That the capitalist accumulates for a period extending beyond his life-time in order to provide for his family, but accumulates none the less if he has no family, is no more comprehensible from this point of view than that the capitalist producer produces use-values which he himself cannot employ.

Consumption as a concept of economic theory[1] is preservation and reproduction of the species, it is production of human beings, of labour-power. The mere act of procreation, of paramount physiological interest, is in this connection the most simple factor. Societies which, like savages and barbarians, mainly live by occupation (252)—where labour therefore still remains in the background—regard the function of procreation and natural selection as their supreme social interest. Hence their constitution according to *gentes*, the admirable regulation of procreation by means of law, which is nothing other than the law of natural selection, declared as a rule of social conduct as soon as man became conscious of it. It is a natural law which has become a legal norm. (253) Our institution of matrimony is a mean and paltry remnant of this constitution, which has been pushed into the background, disintegrated and partially deprived of its functions by the social regulation of labour. The fact that the family is even to-day still partly household, an establishment for the purpose of joint consumption, is an indication of the indissoluble connection of propagation and consumption established by the preservation of the species.

In the period of simple commodity production the "own and patrimony" serves production, consumption and procreation alike; production and reproduction of man and of his means of subsistence are contained within one microcosm. In this respect, property, too, proves to be a universal and homogeneous institution. Even to-day social consumption and thus reproduction of the species is regulated by property, but in another and widely different manner, above all outside the home and the family. The family in most cases does not amount to more than the sexual union of marriage together with the union for consumption, the household, often not even union for the purpose of propagation. It is not the home but the tide of the labour market which determines

---

[1]Consumption as an individual act is a concept of physiology and, as such, a concept to be presupposed by economics.

the number of children, their standards and means of living, the place where they live and die. Marriage is for the owning classes often primarily not the union of two bodies and souls but the amalgamation of two estates, the attraction of capitals: it becomes the main function of marriage to serve accumulation, not propagation.

Therefore we must leave the institution of matrimony and return to property in its now differentiated form together with its complementary institutions, in order to find out which fund provides for the maintenance of the individual, the reproduction of the species; in short, for the population.

We know that capital supplies the capitalist with annual profits, that the soil supplies the landlord with rent, and that labour-power under normal conditions supplies the worker with wages. After deduction of what is set apart for accumulation, these three component parts of the value that is annually produced and their corresponding parts of the annual social product may be consumed by their respective owners, without exhausting the source of their reproduction. They are the annual income of three classes, the revenue of the capitalist, the landowning and the working class. (Cf. *Capital* iii, p. 956). Thus we see that an originally unitary regulation of consumption and propagation is replaced by a multiplicity of regulations brought about by property.

2. THE CAPITALIST'S HOUSEHOLD

The capitalist himself is aware of this. "So far, therefore, as his actions are a mere function of capital—endowed as capital is, in his person, with consciousness and a will—his own private consumption is a robbery perpetrated on accumulation" [1] (*Capital* i, p. 603). But with the development of wealth, "the capitalist ceases to be the mere incarnation of capital. He has a fellow-feeling for his own Adam" (ibid. p. 604). Whereas in the earlier stage of capitalism the urge to become rich is predominant, and it is regarded as a sin not to accumulate, accumulation is now regarded as the old-fashioned foible of "abstinence", and spending and luxury become the purpose of existence, they even become a means to improve one's credit. (*254*) "Although, there-

---

[1] ". . . in book-keeping by double entry, the private expenditure of the capitalist is placed on the debtor side of his account" (*Capital* i, p. 603). The capitalist appears in his own eyes as the administrator of alien possessions.

fore, the prodigality of the capitalist never possesses the bonâ-fide character of the open-handed feudal lord's prodigality, but, on the contrary, has always lurking behind it the most sordid avarice and the most anxious calculation, yet his expenditure grows with his accumulation, without the one necessarily restricting the other. But along with this growth, there is at the same time developed in his breast, a Faustian conflict between the passion for accumulation, and the desire for enjoyment" (ibid. p. 605).

It is not necessary to dwell here on the breeding of the capitalist class; the luxury of their fancy women, a luxury which has the effect of enticing away from their real purpose the most beautiful women, those most worthy to bear children; the luxury of domestic service which removes an ever-increasing percentage of social labour-power from productive labour, a waste of a whole generation, a robbery committed against human society itself. Capitalist ownership in this form operates directly towards a negative selection, towards a waste of goods and labour-power, damaging the reproduction of the human race; and at the stage of consumption its effects are as antisocial as they are at the stage of production.

3. THE WORKER'S HOUSEHOLD. SOCIAL INSURANCE

At first, the working class has only one means of subsistence and reproduction at its disposal: the contract of employment by which it is chained to the owner. Since the working class consists of non-owners,[1] property must from their point of view appear as a complementary and not as an operative institution. The workers obtain a part of the total social product by means of contract. Yet this portion is not given to them as a right for permanent use, like the right of ownership. It must be secured by private legal transaction with the opposite class that must constantly be renewed.

But the life of a human being, even if he is only a proletarian, is not an act-in-the-law to be entered into from time to time, it is physiologically a continuous process, long lasting and somewhat delicate in nature. Even if a glut of labour on the market has deprived the last marginal quantity of labour of its value, the

---

[1] Obviously, everybody is in some way an owner in the eyes of the law. But from the point of view of economics he is an owner only if the quality and quantity of his property permits the fulfilment of the social functions outlined above, so that it can operate as a title to surplus value and assume the function of capital.

labourer must still live and therefore consume, he must absorb victuals. A part of the means of subsistence, provisions for instance, are daily consumed and must be replaced, others like clothes and furniture, last longer. Apart from daily rations, weekly, monthly and yearly rations are required for the mere maintenance of the labour-power. But this labour-power must also be reproduced. Even if the law endows the individual with full capacity of disposal of his labour-power at the age of 12 or 14, giving him majority in regard to work (to be distinguished from majority in regard to full enjoyment of the rights of ownership) at this early age, there remains a period of minority of 12 to 14 years during which every individual requires consumption goods which he cannot provide for himself by legal transactions. The same often applies to consumption during protracted periods of disablement. Moreover, each couple once requires a special life portion for the establishment of a household, which we may call their matrimonial portion—illness, accident, etc., may be left out of consideration for the time being. All these portions are made up from consumption goods which no longer have the functions of capital. They are provided for the majority of the contemporary population by one legal institution which yields piece wages, daily, weekly, or in the best case, monthly wages. With this equipment, the individual is now confronted with the task of allotting an average weekly or monthly amount to a life of uncertain duration, to an indefinite number of children, and to incalculable incidents.

As we have seen the manner in which property, that is capital, regulates the labour fund, is unreasonable, even absurd. As long as there has been human life, there has been no social order so insensate in the administration of its fund for consumption. Its administration by property during the period of simple commodity production, though automatic, was not so irrational. Cattle breeding yields to the owner a daily or yearly produce, agriculture a yearly produce, and surplus is adjusted against want at the fairs. A wood lasts for a generation and provides household furniture for the new generation. In the microcosm of the "own and patrimony" the rations for consumption are automatically distributed. The wage-labourer, however, has to allot the small amount of his wage to various purposes in a manner which would do credit to the most expert insurance actuary.

Yet the capitalist class is interested in an undisturbed reproduction of its labourers. As the distribution of the labour fund by means of the contract of employment is an insult to reason, it has compelled the working class to a partial collectivisation of this fund. This is achieved by deductions from the variable capital in form of taxes on consumption goods and the like, and also by a certain socialisation of the rearing of the proletariat by means of foundling's homes, schools, hospitals, and so on. Moreover, by means of the Poor Law, it keeps in being a general reserve in Poor Law institutions maintained from taxation. All these public institutions supplement the contract of employment, indeed, they were caused or conditioned as complementary institutions by the expansion of this contract of employment.

The working class itself, by means of Friendly Societies of all kinds has gradually provided for a reasonable allotment of the labour fund, it has attempted a collectivisation which would make it a communal property of the whole class. Thus the idea of collective payment suggested itself to the capitalist class, (255) whereby the capitalist class as a whole would supply at least part of the wages for the working class as a whole. This collective payment, which assumes the form of social insurance, is of course not a socialist but an individualist institution and an expensive detour. If the whole of the labour fund were to be allotted in this way, and all long term instalments for consumption taken into consideration, there would need to be insurance premiums to cover the cost of illness, accident, old age, disablement, burial, pregnancy, motherhood, education, training, equipment and so on. But how much would then remain by way of weekly wages paid out to the workers? And would there be any further purpose in clinging to the form of insurance? (256)

During the forty-five years after the death of Karl Marx most of the civilised states have adopted a scheme of social insurance, and this legal institution is of the greatest sociological importance. The foregoing exposition which I wrote twenty-five years ago throws some light upon its intrinsic nature. It represents a partial socialisation of the wage relationship; it requires however a more detailed analysis of its functions than it is possible to give here.

4. ADDITIONAL CONTRIBUTIONS TO THE WAGES FUND

This inadequacy of the contract of employment gives rise to a large number of phenomena which have been erroneously interpreted. As certain portions for consumption are needed over periods of different length, the workers must provide funds of reserve out of their earnings. According to the economic position of the country and to their own intelligence they do this either by hoarding cash, or commodities (e.g. jewellery which is pawned periodically), by purchasing small portions of real estate (which they can also use and thus partly consume), by investing money in mortgages or in savings accounts, annuities, shares or lottery tickets. Thus they assume the legal character mask of owners, creditors and the rest. Yet the economic significance of this type of property is only that it provides a reserve fund for the subject, a fund of reserve for the purpose of consumption, not for the accumulation of capital, and it therefore in no way fulfils the function of capital for the owner. Capitalist production, as we have seen, produces a whole hierarchy of highly qualified workers who draw correspondingly high wages and save funds for the education or dowry of their children. These funds have the same character as the workman's savings. Thus variable capital is consolidated in all kinds of property fragments, varying in extent from small to medium and entirely devoted to the purpose of consumption. The existence of such funds and their growth do not disprove the concentration of capital.

These funds of reserve derived from the variable capital are in themselves not necessary, as insurance statisticians will be ready to admit. If the working class of a country is taken as a whole, there will be in every month a certain average of births, deaths and marriages so that the rate of consumption, calculated for the class as a whole, is not subject to periodic fluctuations, or subject to them only to a small extent. If the labour fund were to be distributed by collective regulation (on an actuarial basis), every incentive would disappear to build up reserve portions out of wages, salaries, etc. The administration of the labour fund would be simple; it would provide equally for the whole of the working class. We could imagine such a state of affairs within a capitalist framework of society, but it would be difficult to realise it fully. Wages paid out individually would have to be collected again in the form of premiums or taxes on provisions, so as to become a collective amount. Variable capital that is split up into many small parts, must be re-invested, incorporated in property and by way of credit handed back to capital for further use. All these funds are mere deposits for the owners to whom the small rate of interest is scarcely of any serious importance. They fulfil, however, the functions of capital for the depositaries, the banks, savings banks, etc., in which they are accumulated and centralised and thus may well fulfil the specific capitalist function of property.

It is only a seeming and ephemeral metamorphosis of the variable capital to capital pure and simple which we have described above. It is countered by a parallel metamorphosis, the constant conversion of simple, pre-capitalist property direct to variable capital, which I will call *an additional contribution to the labour fund*, since for the capitalist it saves part of the variable capital which he would otherwise have to pay to his workers. [1]

Capitalist production, wherever it has established its sway over small owners (e.g. proprietors of small houses, of allotments, or of simple means of production), can depress the wage below the cost of reproduction of the labour-power which it would otherwise have to bear. (*257*) A dwelling house is nothing but a means of consumption, and an allotment providing potatoes and vegetables is from an economic point of view not different from an ordinary consumption good. Property of this kind, property in the eyes of the law, does not fulfil the economic function of capitalist property, it is merely invested variable capital. The capitalist pays the worker here in the same manner as the state pays the civil servant, by giving him official quarters, the subtle distinction, though, is that the worker here provides these quarters for himself. It is obvious that it does not make any difference from an economic point of view whether the labourer has saved up for such a house or whether he has inherited it. The house always operates as a reserve fund of variable capital, in favour of the capitalist who therefore sometimes takes the trouble to provide the worker with house and allotment. (*258*)

The category of additional contributions to the labour fund covers a number of other phenomena, for instance, the mortgage of non-inheriting brothers and sisters. When the children of a deceased peasant settle the distribution of the estate, it is the rule that the brothers and sisters who receive compensation in money invest their portion in the form of a mortgage on the land of the heir proper, and if they do not become industrial workers, they become agricultural labourers for their mortgage-debtors. They

---

[1] A worker with some possessions is a better object for exploitation than one without any property. Thus property in most cases develops into a curse for the worker, whether it belongs to himself or to his employer.

consider this mortgage mainly as a safe-deposit, but in so far as
they draw interest, this appears as a direct part of their wages,
which are thus depressed. As soon as these labourers establish
their own households, they withdraw the mortgage (which is
replaced by another one, granted by a credit institution), and they
convert their capital into furniture or use it for the education and
endowment of their children, in short, for purposes of consumption. With the passing of generations, all this consolidated capital
becomes mobile and is eventually consumed.

Obviously the labour fund of society can have no other legal
form in a capitalist social system than that of property. Not only
wages, but also reserve funds of all sizes, from the dwarf deposit to
the annuity of the industrial executive for consumption in his old
age, from the factory worker's small potato patch to the country-
house of the factory director, from the accounts of the savings clubs
to the millions which make up the reserves of the insurance companies, are brought about by the hierarchy of labour-powers. For
the legal owners this kind of property is and remains only a fund
for the purposes of consumption which is temporarily deposited; it
exercises the function of capital only in the hands of the capitalist.[1]
This is of paramount importance for the appraisal of this property
from a social point of view. A society which established a complete
regulation of consumption would put a stop to this fictitious
accumulation, removing every resistance to the expropriation of
the property of these small owners (seeing to it that they were not
expropriated); that is, if it did not consider it more convenient
to allot a small house to every young couple. (259)

5.   THE FAMILY OF THE WORKER

The reproduction of the working class is ensured by other legal
institutions besides the contract of service: by the Poor Law, by
charitable donations, by foundations; (260) and furthermore, by
the first universal collectivist establishment within the framework
of a capitalist order of society, the board schools, i.e. compulsory
education as a legal institution, that palladium of the working
class. It would be a special task to discuss the social functions of
these institutions, the part which they play in the economic order
of society. Otherwise the regulation of the reproduction of social

---

[1] It is labour-power which is accumulated here in an indirect way; funds of reserve
may serve the increase of the population but not the direct increase of capital.

labour-power is as half-hearted and chaotic as that of social distribution.

What does the family of the worker look like, after all these changes? It is an algebraic sum of individuals united under the number of a tenement flat, not subject to parental control, for the father does not see his family from morning till night. Every grown-up member, not excluding father and mother, is subject to the control of a different employer, juvenile apprentices are subject to the control of a master, the children are subject to the supervision of the teacher, and the babies whine alone in a locked-up room. Parental power, formerly comprising all means of control, is split up and transferred to quite disparate holders of power. There is no "own" which provides for the life of the community, the adults bring home their wages from different quarters of the town. If paternal power should find expression, then woe to the children; for in that case the father lives on the children's earnings. But if everyone draws his wages individually, then everybody who is old enough to work, is also old enough to marry. The child now leaves the family at the most tender age, and it would be a blessing for many to be orphaned from birth. But even amongst well situated workers the family is not an organic community. How could a human life possibly be built on a weekly wage? How could anyone set up house on a foundation not of stone, not of earth, not of sand, but founded on a contract of employment which can be dissolved at will and for which the prospects are always precarious? How could anyone possibly make a home on the basis of a quarterly rent? (*261*)

Notes, Chapter II, Section V

(*252*) "Occupation" in the sense of the Roman *occupatio*, i.e. the taking possession, and appropriation of, things (immovable and movable) which belong to nobody.

(*253*) It is doubtful how far this statement can be upheld in view of the highly artificial "legalistic" character of the agnatic family. Not only is there no trace of a matriarchal system in Roman and very little of it in Germanic law, but adoption—the existence of which is the very negation of Renner's thesis—was one of the most ancient institutions of the Romans, and of other peoples (Jolowicz, l.c., pp. 118 *sq.*, Hübner, l.c., pp. 514 *sq.*

Pollock and Maitland, l.c., Vol. II, pp. 240 *sq.*   See also Vinogradoff, l.c., Vol. I, pp. 232 *sq.*, and Pollock's Note K to *Maine's Ancient Law*).

(*254*) See the admirable analysis of these phenomena in Veblen's *Theory of the Leisure Class*, especially ch. iv ("Conspicuous Consumption").

(*255*) The history of social insurance in Europe begins, of course, with the voluntary and autonomous benefit systems of the British trade unions, described in Part II, ch. i of the Webbs' *Industrial Democracy*. Bismarck introduced his social insurance—accident, health, old age pensions insurance—legislation in the 1880's. This must be viewed against the background of the Anti-Socialist Law of 1878 as an attempt "to take the wind of the sails of Social Democracy". Before doing so he had caused the German Consulate General in London to make inquiries into, and report on, the practices of the British trade unions. They obtained a report from George Howell, who, until shortly before, had been secretary of the Trades Union Congress Parliamentary Committee (I owe this information to unpublished material kindly put at my disposal by Prof. Gustav Mayer). From Germany social insurance of the working classes as a statutory system was imported into England in 1912. Now, under the National Insurance Act, 1946, insurance in this country has lost its necessary connection with the employment relation. It is to-day more difficult than ever before to maintain that social insurance constitutes a collective payment made by the capitalist class to the working class, since participation in the insurance system is becoming universal.

(*256*) Under the National Insurance Act, 1946, and under the National Insurance (Industrial Injuries) Act, 1946, most of the benefits mentioned by Renner are covered by insurance. These statutes should, of course, be read with those providing for other social services, such as the Unemployment Assistance Act, 1934, the Family Allowances Act, 1945, the National Health Service Act, 1946, and the Education Act, 1944. The Exchequer contribution to the "insurance services" alone will ultimately amount to 50 per cent., to the social services in a wider sense (including Unemployment Assistance and Health Service) it is expected to amount to 64 per cent. (White Paper on Social Insurance, Cmd. 6550, No. 7). This fact—but not only this fact—renders it questionable whether the form of insurance is more than a form, and why it should still be maintained. Lord (then Sir William) Beveridge tried to answer this question in his Report on Social Insurance and Allied Services (Cmd. 6404, No. 20). His answer was that the contributory system was "what the people of Britain desire". The justification for the insurance form of certain social services rests on ideological grounds. The payment of contributions by the employer, whether or not they are from an economist's point of view part of the wages, reduce the wage level to a minute extent, but it certainly does not affect the essence of the employment relationship.

(*257*) See above, note 174.

(*258*) It is extremely doubtful whether this statement can claim any validity under the conditions now prevailing in this country, i.e. whether the provision of small houses and of allotments for the working class has in fact an adverse effect upon the wage level. Only if the existence of statutory and voluntary (building societies) machinery serving these purposes has led to a reduction or prevented an increase in the general wage level, can Renner's contention be upheld.

(*259*) Is it not true, on the other hand, that these "reserves", whatever else they may be, are also "reserves" of the worker, which strengthen his bargaining power and, in times of unemployment, diminish the effect of the "industrial reserve army" on the wage level?

(*260*) The word "foundation" is an attempt to translate the German word "*Stiftung*". A "*Stiftung*" (see, e.g: German Civil Code §§ 80 *sq.*, Swiss Civil Code Art. 80 *sq.*) is a corporate entity consisting of a fund dedicated to a purpose which is usually a "charitable" object within the meaning of English law. It has no legal equivalent in this country. Its function is fulfilled by the "charitable trust" which, without being a "person" in the eyes of the law, has, in many ways, a similar organisation. See Maitland's essay, *Trust and Corporation*, quoted in the Introduction.

(*261*) Though the illustrations which Renner uses in this chapter reflect the conditions in Austria fifty years ago, the substance of this chapter is of present day significance. It is suggested that, in this field, sociological research has still many fruitful tasks to perform. The economic transformation of the family and the effect upon the law of the dissolution of the family as a unit of production, of its weakening as a unit of consumption, and of the changing position of women in society, should be investigated. The law of maintenance between husband and wife, and parent and child, the property relations between husband and wife in the working class, etc., have not been in the forefront of the interest of legal scholars in this country. That a factual community of property exists between husband and wife with regard to consumers' goods (including furniture and even dwelling room and allotment) can hardly be denied. It exists behind a legal veil of artificial constructions, most of which are taken from the—entirely unsuitable—law of agency. The wife who buys "necessaries" for the household is still regarded as her husband's agent, the money he gives her for the management of the household is administered by her as his agent, etc. Renner's method may prove to be useful for an investigation into these discrepancies between a dynamic social development and a static law. The Family Allowances Act, 1946, which introduces an entirely new legal conception of the family may mark the starting point, not only of a new legal development, but, one hopes, also of a new endeavour in the sociology of law.

Section vi.   OWNERSHIP AND THE LAW OF SUCCESSION

ACCORDING to Unger, (*262*) it is a truth implied in the nature of law and firmly established in the general conviction, that death has no power over the legal organism, just as it has no power over the world of the spirit. [1] In more sober terms, this means that although the individual must die, the species remains immortal. The individual is only a most transitory incarnation of the life of the species, though a necessary agent in this life. The species sets so little store by the individual that it may deprive him of his individuality, in that he may be executed strictly in accordance with the forms of the law. "The individual may die but there remain his legal relations which are not absolutely personal. The temporal owner of possessions may pass away but his goods outlive their master. Other people take the place which has become vacant, they fill the vacancy which death has caused." The persons are "changeable and accidental", but society is "continuous and essential".

As society is existence pure and simple, and as it is only possible through its fortuitous representatives and through the control of nature, it is compelled to give all controlled items of nature into the detention of individuals. Accordingly it must substitute a new individual for every one that passes away, it must appoint a successor to his place. Every society has its order of succession and vocation. But in the course of history succession has not always been mediated by a law of inheritance.

There have been societies in which the law of inheritance was practically the only order of succession and in which it provided for the appointment of all public functionaries, from the rural constable to the Count and up to the head of the state. The Church was the first institution completely to remain outside the system of hereditary succession. At a time when succession by inheritance held universal sway in society, celibacy was the only way to achieve vocation to the Church. Canon Law supplies a comprehensive range of forms for succession and modes of nomination, from election to appointment, arranging at the same time for a wide division of power in various forms among the various appointing agents. In this matter future societies may find much to learn from Canon Law.

The law of inheritance is thus not the only order of succession in

[1] *Erbrecht*, Introduction.

the history of mankind, just as the institution of property is not the only one for the regulation of detention. Both institutions are peculiar only to definite historical periods, and it was in the period of simple commodity production that they were most completely developed.

In the eyes of the law inheritance does not constitute a right but gives a certain qualification to a person. (263) The heir is a person who is qualified with regard to a certain estate: he has the status of heir, just as the offspring has the status of son. Certain legal consequences are generally connected with the status of a person, and here the specific legal consequence is succession to the estate.

The estate is not only a conglomeration of property-objects.[1] It consists of a greater or smaller number of legal relations all of which have lost their *persona*; above all it consists of claims and debts, of rights against and duties to other individuals and to the state. As long as these relations are not "purely personal" (264) they are capable of assessment; in their entirety they form a person's assets and liabilities. The estate is therefore not a natural or individualist concept, it is a social relationship which is distinguished on the one hand by the unity of the individual to whom the estate belongs, and on the other hand by the multiplicity of other legal subjects related to this individual by links forged by the law. This form and the individuality of the subject do not of themselves give this aggregate of assets and liabilities its intrinsic nature; if this were the case, the death of the owner would lead to its extinction. The relationship is purely social. It is not for the sake of the deceased but for the sake of society and of the continuity of the economic system, or, in capitalist terms, for the sake of debtors and creditors, of the preservation of the legal order as a whole, that society appoints a new subject. This aggregate of assets and liabilities is the estate.

[1] Goods in the hand of a legal subject, the aggregate of his particles of property, are in the eyes of the law a unity only by virtue of their relation to the subject. If this legal individuation were real, intrinsic and material, then every estate would at the moment of the owner's death become a drifting mass of ruins like the wreckage of a ship struck by lightning. In most instances, this is not the case. The estate is, as a rule, an economic undertaking, a household as an establishment for consumption, an economic whole, and only in this capacity does it require a legal successor; otherwise his appointment is meaningless. The owner is the soul of the body of goods which exists as a social unit, but this material body is not the objectivation of the individual: when death removes this soul, society creates a new soul by appointing a new successor. This is true at least for the sociological purpose; such is the social function of a law of inheritance. The capitalist whose property has lost its function, may however, leave as his estate a safe full of various shares and bonds without any economic unity; and here the law of inheritance, like property, has lost its function.

The heir is the individual whom the law has qualified to succeed to the estate. If society consciously establishes this legal qualification, it must be defined in a manner most favourable to the production and reproduction of society, it must be an economic qualification of the person who is to be the heir. If the law of inheritance is to fulfil its function without friction, the legal qualification of succession coincides with the economic qualification.[1] There is no doubt that this was so in the period of simple commodity production. The heir intestate is the next-of-kin, as a rule he has grown up in the "own", his father has taught him how to employ and use every part of his property, he has learned nothing but the work with his "own", the goods of which he has partly himself helped to produce. The law of intestate succession provides the best heir for the estate; at the same time it gives the fellow-worker part of the results of his labour. The confidant of the deceased also knows all his legal relations; thus the continuity of the economic order is assured in the best possible manner. This beautiful harmony between law and function may easily lead to the belief that this regulation is an immutable, eternal and sacrosanct institution, or a natural right; it is expressed in the term "own and patrimony".

Practically all functions of a social order were fulfilled by this "own and patrimony". It created a robust regulation of power and labour, based upon blood ties, where the hardships of compulsory labour were softened by the love of kinship, and the proceeds of the work were eventually assigned to the children who had played a subordinate part in the labour process. The "own and patrimony" fulfilled all functions of distribution and consumption, providing an efficient incentive for accumulation, and regulating reproduction of the species strictly in accordance with the opportunities for maintenance. In short, a complete harmony between legal form and social function was characteristic for this institution.

If there was no heir intestate, however, the law left it to the testator, who obviously knew his own business best, to appoint a qualified successor. (265) Whereas by intestate succession the law made direct provision for the qualification of the heir, here it sanctioned private division of inheritance, acknowledging this as its own. If there was a number of heirs intestate, as usually

---

[1] Like Marx, we use the term "economic" in a wider sense, implying also reproduction of the species and maintenance of the population.

happened only if the "own and patrimony" could support more than one successor, the law provided the opportunity for the testator to use his own judgment in dividing up the economic undertaking into a number of partial undertakings, *peculia*, as it were, which were established as separate units and given to separate successors, while the original concern was left either to one heir or to a number of co-heirs for their collective use. Legacies came to supplement the appointment of an heir. (*266*)

As the estate ceases to be a natural unit and becomes intrinsically value, that is capital; and as the individual assets come to be regarded as mere amounts of money; succession, which was formerly economic, now becomes mathematical, a mere succession into value. (*267*)   Every case of inheritance now becomes a calamity for the undertaking.   The son of the house, whom capitalist development by its completely new regulation of labour has led away from the house at an early age, now as a rule no longer continues to run the concern.   The estate is liquidated, the price divided, or one of the children who still clings to old-fashioned beliefs, and keeps to the old methods of work, is saddled with the undertaking and in consequence is burdened with I.O.U.s and mortgages in favour of the departing brothers and sisters.   Wherever the estate has assumed the character of a merely capitalist property without any functions, inheritance presents no difficulties, since the owner has no other functions than to amass and consume the revenues, and he can do so whatever the degree of partition.   If the law of inheritance is antisocial in the lower strata, because it interferes with the continuity of the undertaking, it is antisocial in the higher strata because property itself has here become antisocial.   Here the tail follows the dog, for it is evident that, once property has become antisocial, the inheritance of property must be antisocial as well.   Marx therefore scarcely wastes a word on the law of inheritance. (*268*)

In the case of small and medium holdings, the law of inheritance seldom if ever now serves the function of succession.   Where this function is preserved by a law of entail, all descendants but one are immediately thrown into the proletariat, for the population no longer increases according to the provisions of the "own and patrimony", but according to the increase of variable capital.(*269*) If the law permits free partition, mathematically calculated portions of inheritance gradually become additional contributions to the labour fund; they are frittered away on equipment, training, consumption, and the like, if not in the first, then in the second and third generations. For it is a very ordinary occurrence that the heirs to a holding of medium size buy up small holdings whose owners have been expropriated by capitalist development, maintain them for a time by sacrifices of energy and capital and possibly even leave them to their heirs. But these hereditary portions are mainly only a contribution to the income which the final heir will consume.

As the law of inheritance operates in this peculiar way, it fills in all intermediate stages in the scale of possessions and often causes the gradual decline of families into the proletariat; though in the course of this process, individual members who use their hereditary portion for the purpose of study may frequently attain to high, even the highest ranks in the hierarchy of labour or pass into the liberal or bureaucratic professions. Thus property, by means of its complementary institutions, preserves itself in all categories of size. But its functions in all these categories are diverse and changeable.

The law of inheritance nearly always regulates succession in a manner that is contrary to reason or is absolutely ineffective. In most cases the enterprise is sold to third parties [1] either by the testator himself during his life-time or by his heirs after his demise; or it is leased out, as is often arranged by courts of guardianship on behalf of infants. Thus economic succession which ought to conserve the enterprise, in practice nearly always results in its transfer by act-in-the-law *inter vivos*, whereby it is split up and squandered. This legal institution which has preserved its original function in exceptional cases only but otherwise has become completely antisocial, may lead to inheritance by lateral relatives who are out of touch with one another or the deceased, who sometimes live in different continents, for whom the inheritance is, from an economic point of view, like the winning of a lottery. It may encourage the appointment of heirs in recognition for dubious services, or it may reward the efforts of grasping legacy hunters, amateur or professional.

Let us enquire into the reasons for this inconsistent functioning of the law of inheritance. The estate as a natural object, from the point of view of technology, is a partial unit of the whole social organism, technically speaking a concern. At the stage of simple

---

[1] See p. 125, note 1, about the sale, the legal and economic qualifications of the aggregate of assets and liabilities.

commodity production it serves production, consumption and education, and at the capitalist stage it serves at least one of these functions. Capitalist economy, however, conceives of the estate merely as value, as an aggregate of values which can be assessed in figures and expressed in terms of money. Succession into the enterprise becomes distinct from succession into value, just as in general creative labour has become differentiated from inactive possession. Actual succession becomes distinct from legal succession, the person who buys up the concern and succeeds into the estate is not the heir, and the heir who succeeds into the value does not succeed into the concern. Whoever succeeds into an undertaking must be capable of independent economic management, (270) he must be qualified for specialised activities and labour. Whoever succeeds into value need only have a title to profit or rent, so that the division of inheritance becomes a mere matter of arithmetic. It is compatible with any number of heirs, hereditary portions of any amount, but in order to pay out these portions, the value of the estate must be realised. As a rule, therefore, the estate is sold or encumbered with debts or, in the most favourable case, converted into a company, Inheritance in practice nearly always works out in a way that is contrary to the *raison d'être* of the legal institution. It leads to disarrangement or disintegration of the undertaking instead of ensuring undisturbed continuity. It impedes development or even has retrogressive consequences, and this tendency is strengthened by the accompanying and constantly repeated splitting up of the social fund of accumulation.

In the period of simple commodity production the law of inheritance had the further function of ensuring the social accumulation, by providing everybody with an equal incentive to accumulate in order to provide for their families. The life of the species was securely based on the traditional family fortunes. Even to-day the law of inheritance is a spur to accumulation for all families. What little owners of small or medium property can accumulate to-day, must after the passing of two generations always fall into the fund of consumption, where in the most favourable case it becomes an additional contribution to the labour fund. For the working class, this legal institution (law of inheritance) is completely illusory. In the working class the goods of consumption owned by the deceased are usually during his lifetime given to those around him, if they have not been exhausted by the cost of his disablement and illness.

Thus substitutive institutions have taken over the material function of the law of inheritance, the transfer of undertaking and labour to a new subject.

To-day accordingly it is no longer inheritance which regulates the vocation to labour nor even to capitalist activity, the function of the entrepreneur. This function has been taken over by the purchase of an undertaking as a whole, or by various other institutions which are based on the contract of employment and develop it further. The members of the working class are appointed for short-term periods and then are cast off again, whereas appointments in the higher strata of labour are more or less stable.[1] (*271*)   In consequence of the general insecurity appointments for life are practically negligible. Appointment by election or ballot, by commission or delegation, by proposal and confirmation, sometimes occur. These legal types are to-day only occasional and there is no great scope for them, but they may be capable of a development which cannot even be imagined to-day. The contract of employment with its thousandfold variations, this most universal institution of our time which fulfils the greatest number of functions, has therefore replaced all institutions of succession fashioned by history, it has replaced the *old-established order of vocation*.

Notes, Chapter II, Section VI

(*262*) Josef Unger, 1828–1913, the famous Austrian jurist, Professor at the Universities of Prague and Vienna, and later President of the Austrian *Reichsgericht*, the highest Court in matters of public law. His principal work: *System of Austrian Private Law*. He was in many ways the founder of systematic and scientific legal research in Austria. For a short biography and an appreciation of Unger's contribution to legal scholarship see Sinzheimer, *Jüdische Klassiker der deutschen Rechtswissenschaft*, Amsterdam, 1938 (pp. 105–115).

(*263*) This pre-supposes the Roman and Continental legal conception of "heirship" which is alien to Anglo-American law. The

---

[1] Just as the labour-relationship develops into "position", so the *locatio conductio*, still the legal construction of to-day, develops more and more clearly the character of appointment. Public law, especially old Germanic and Canon Law, provide many patterns for this relationship which, in special cases, e.g. with regard to university professors, has already received normative regulation. For this relationship a new analysis and a new legal construction will be required.

"heir" succeeds, upon the death of the deceased, to the whole or a defined portion of the estate, whether he does so upon an intestacy or under a will or other disposition *mortis causa*. The appointment of an executor is optional, and the executor's powers are not usually as far reaching as those of an English executor. As a rule the heir (or heirs) combines (or combine) the functions of an English executor with the rights of an English residuary legatee. A "legatee" (unless he be a "*légataire universel*" according to French law, i.e. in fact an heir) has a mere claim against the heir or heirs for the payment of a sum of money, the delivery of an object bequeathed, or the conveyance of land devised to him. "Heirship" is therefore a kind of status, not only where, as in the case of the Roman *heredes domestici*, the French *héritiers légitimes* and *héritiers naturels* and the German *Erben*, the heirs succeed by operation of law without an act of acquisition, but also where some sort of *aditio hereditatis* is necessary. It is a status because it does not simply give a right to a given sum of money or object, or even to a fund, but involves a mixture of rights, powers (of administration) and liabilities. The heir is generally liable for the debts of the estate, though there are ways and means by which he can limit his liability to his share in the property devolving upon him.

(*264*) "Estate" is the translation of the German word "*Vermögen*". For the meaning of this word see the Introduction. "Purely personal" rights are those which do not survive the person entitled or the person liable. In Roman law the *actiones vindictam spirantes* (e.g. the *actio injuriarum*) did not survive the creditor, and no *actio poenalis* (i.e. action for penal damages), such as the *actio furti*, survived the debtor. Modern Continental systems have varied these principles. Thus, according to German law, the claim for "pain and suffering" arising from civil delict (Civil Code § 847) and the claim of a woman for breach of promise to marry in so far as it is a special claim on the ground of seduction (ibid. § 1300), are "purely personal" and do not pass to the heir. In this country the transmission of tortious liability both on the active and on the passive side was seriously curtailed and, to a large extent, negatived by the principle "*actio personalis moritur cum persona*" (itself in this form "manufactured" by Coke—see Plucknett, l.c., p. 333). But this principle was abolished by the Law Reform (Miscellaneous Provisions) Act, 1934. It was replaced by a rule not dissimilar to that of Roman law: tortious claims survive both the creditor and the debtor, except in the case of certain "purely personal" rights, e.g. rights to exemplary damages, rights arising from breach of promise, etc.

(*265*) We should not, however, overlook the serious limitations on the testator's freedom to dispose. For the *Usus Modernus*

Pandectarum their basis was Justinian's 18th and 115th *Novellae* which gave to the next-of-kin in the direct line of ascent and descent a right (even against a will) to a (varying) portion of their shares, defeasible only on certain grounds such as an attempt to kill the testator. In a number of cases Roman law also gave indefeasible rights to lateral relations. This was greatly modified by a large variety of customs, notably the *"droit d'aînesse"* which a Jacobin called a *"coutûme ridicule"* (Hedemann, l.c., p. 50). Modern Continental laws have, in one form or another, adopted a system by which the rights of certain near relations are indefeasible (see above, note 203).

(*266*) For the meaning of "legacy" as opposed to "heirship" see above, note 263. The legal map of Europe during the age of simple commodity production showed a bewildering tangle of systems of intestacy, partly established by enacted laws and partly by custom. Even the Prussian Code of 1794 did not claim to override local customs with regard to the succession of children, and vestiges of local laws remained in force side by side with the German Civil Code (Art. 64 of the Introductory Law), while the Code Civil aimed at a complete unification of French law. The Code Civil abolished the *droit d'aînesse*, and, through the institution of the *réserve légale*, made its continuance by testamentary custom difficult. But in Austria decrees were passed in 1790 and 1791, and as late as 1850, with the object of preventing the splitting up of farms upon the death of the peasant. The inquiries instituted by the Nazi Government in connection with the Hereditary Farm Law into hereditary customs with regard to agricultural property in Germany and Austria revealed that, in many parts of the country, the custom of leaving the farm undivided to the eldest or—in some parts—the youngest son, had survived many centuries of *Usus Modernus* and the introduction of the civil codes. It has ex post proved the correctness of Renner's statement.

(*267*) The provisions of the Settled Land Act, 1925, mentioned in the Introduction, have, in this country, re-inforced the tendency towards a substitution of a succession to values for a succession to a particular real estate.

(*268*) This is a reminder that it is not the institution of inheritance by succession which determines the social function of property, but that the nature of property determines the social function of inheritance. The development since 1900 has made this abundantly clear. The "mobilisation" of small industrial and trading enterprises through the institutions of company law has, to a considerable extent, nullified the effect of the law of succession upon the continuity of undertakings. It is, however, nowadays

9

impossible to discuss the social function of the law of inheritance without taking into account the effect of the death duties.

(*269*) This is what usually happened in those areas in which (see note 266) the law of primogeniture or some such system was in fact continued by testamentary custom. The Nazis tried to go further: through the Hereditary Farm Law they made the dis-inheritance of the younger (or elder) children compulsory and coupled it with a doctrinaire revival of the agnatic *gens* which went so far that—partly in view of the war casualties and partly in view of the resistance amongst the peasants themselves—they had to mitigate it by a Decree of 1943. In the case of this Nazi legislation, however, the relegation of the disinherited children into the proletariat was not an inevitable by-product of this system of succession, but a deliberate move towards the creation of a landless rural proletariat available for the enforcement of a settlement policy in conquered territories in the East.

(*270*) See the Introduction. The most important contemporary example is the succession to the management and—largely—the control of companies by the appointment of salaried directors. In the field of agricultural property the provisions of Part II of the Agriculture Act, 1947, provide another important new order of vocation.

(*271*) The line between the "lower" and the "higher" orders of wage and salary earners is blurred, the more statute law and, particularly, collective bargaining gives security of tenure to the manual workers. The "guaranteed week" is the beginning of an approximation between "wage" and "salary" earners. See further above, note 152.

CHAPTER III

SOCIOLOGICAL ANALYSIS OF FUNCTIONAL CHANGE

WE have come to the end of our journey through contemporary civil law. We have encountered everywhere a continual process of change, and we have attempted to take note of every land-mark and to describe the changes affecting it. In the confusing sequence of details the reader will have seen for himself here and there the inherent connections, and he will have recognised that our research is concerned with sociological problems which demand systematic exposition. The main theme of this enquiry is the relation between law and economics in the evolution of history, observed and examined here from the aspect of legal institutions; regarded with the eye of the jurist who, with a vision extending beyond his native field of legal rules, recognises that everywhere the law is as much bound up with economics as economics is bound up with the law. The legal expert who has accompanied us in our observations will have made the surprising discovery that law and economics, though appearing to be indissolubly bound together, if considered as static at any given moment, yet undergo unequal development in the course of history. Contradictions and contrasts emerge, and their mutual relations are not seldom reversed. Thorough examination of the vast field presented by civil law for inductive investigation soon leads to the discovery of common characteristics within this dialectical development. It thus becomes possible to read its laws from these facts. The following summing-up will serve to bring our observations into a systematic order.

Section i. Norm and Substratum

The legal institution of property, as shown in the second chapter, has undergone an extensive development in a relatively short period. It has suffered a drastic transformation which has not, however, been accompanied by noticeable modifications of its legal structure. This fact proves our first thesis, that *fundamental changes in society are possible without accompanying alterations of the legal system.*

I. CHANGE OF THE SUBSTRATUM: ECONOMIC EVOLUTION

A second thesis is also proved, that *it is not the law that causes economic development.* All the examples given above demonstrate that the existence of society as it is, depends on and presupposes a determined, historically conditioned, legal order. The latter, however, has never caused social change. A legal order adapted to a definite historical substratum, simple commodity production, derived its significance from the substratum; its purpose was to hold it together and to stabilise it. But this legal order does not prevent changes in the substratum. The essential character of the social process as preservation and reproduction of the species undergoes continual change while the form of the law is constant. The form of the law is not the *causa causans* which brings about the change. The social function undergoes change unaccompanied by a juridical change of the legal institution.

This seems to imply a third thesis, that *economic change does not change the law*, as it has been our leading assumption that the juridical character of the institutions is constant. Thus our investigation seems to prove that the legal superstructure is absolutely independent of its economic substructure, its substratum; and that changes in the legal system must proceed from other than economic sources. Yet this would be a premature conclusion. A supplementary investigation of the change of norms might show that the economic substratum would eventually transform the law also, though strictly in accordance with forms of creation specific to norms. So our third thesis is valid with a reservation, that *economic change does not immediately and automatically bring about changes in the law.* (272)

How does this change of functions come about? We have seen that it proceeds steadily, continuously, imperceptibly, like the growth of grass, according to the law of all organic development. As the process of growth cannot be understood by a glance at the plant, but only by study of the whole successive development from germ to fruit and again to the new germ; so the change of functions can be recognised only at an advanced stage and then only by way of historical comparison: it can be recognised only when it has matured. Hence our fourth thesis, that *development by leaps and bounds is unknown in the social substratum, which knows evolution only, not revolution.* [1] We may imagine, though, that the legal super-structure necessarily obeys different laws, we may assume that revolutions are familiar in the realm of the law and that reper-cussions therefrom may affect the substratum. This, however, will take us beyond the scope of our enquiry.

Now we have proved that the law does not create the develop-ment of capitalist economics although it may be a condition of it. [2] For example, it confers upon the owner the power to act, but it does not prescribe definite forms of action. It makes possible the transformation of property into capital, but it does not cause it.

One could argue that this is the case with property only, as the law itself refrains here from exercising any influence upon the owner, the institution being of a negative character. (*273*) One might suppose that the law would be the determining factor of the development whenever it were to enforce a definite action. This, however, would not be correct. One should not make the tacit assumption that a new law could command to-day what was not yesterday commanded by an abrogated order. Such an assump-tion would imply a change of norms, and we would first have to answer the question of the origin of the new norm. Where, how-ever, as in the case of the father's duty to maintain his children, the obligation to definite action has existed since time immemorial, there is no further consequence beyond the fact that the father supports his offspring as he did a thousand years ago. Any valid law can be changed but does not itself change society, it does not bring about social evolution; for it is the very purpose of the law

---

[1] K. Marx, *The Poverty of Philosophy*, transl. by H. Quelch, London, 1900, p. 160: "It is only in an order of things in which there will be no longer classes or class antagonism that *social evolutions* will cease to be *political revolutions*." This dictum of Marx clearly expresses his appreciation of the difference between revolutionary changes in the legal and social field.

[2] It is true that the evidence upon which this proposition is based is limited, and its validity restricted to a single period—that of transition from simple to capitalist commodity production. Yet, in so far as the categories of these periods are nothing but specific manifestations of universal categories, they also have general validity.

to conserve. Therefore our question can be only: how can it be conceived *a priori* that the law binds and yet does not bind, that development *praeter* or *contra legem* can take place?

2. EXTERNAL LIMITS OF THE EFFICACY OF THE NORM

All law is the imperative voice of society—as an entity conscious of itself—addressing the individual. It is expressed by the formula: total will—individual will. There is no doubt that valid law has the power to bind; it is the purpose of the total will to bind individual will. [1] But obligation of the individual is by no means an obligation of society itself. The arm of the law extends even further, to bind also the economic actions of the individual. The individual's economic actions are always legally relevant facts, they are either acts-in-the-law or exercise of rights, yet their legal character is but one aspect of their economic significance. Moreover, the total will does not exist outside the individuals, though its embodiment in writing as a code gives it an appearance of independence, since society's consciousness of itself as an entity cannot exist but within the consciousness of individuals. It is individuals who are the exponents of the total will, they are the bearers of power, and it is to them that the will of the individual is subject. The formula: total will—individual will can only be conceived as: will of the power—will of the subject, that is to say it can exist only as a relation between two individual wills.

We deduce from these premises:

A.   The legal order can address its commands to human beings only, not to nature. It cannot order the horse belonging to A to be subject to A. This shows that the current common conception of ownership is erroneous. The law does not give the owner the real power of disposal over a thing: it is beyond its capacity to do so. It commands only all other individuals to refrain from seizing the object. In the same way, in general, the control of the law over nature is indirect: the law, by its very nature, can only endow the individual with power and authority to rule over nature. Between the individual who rules and nature that is ruled, however, there is an individual and technical relationship over which the law has no power.

---

[1] We do not examine here by what power the law so binds, nor do we raise the question of the force (*Geltungskraft*) of laws, i.e. the limits of the *immanent* power of law. Purely a problem of legal analysis, this is different from our problem—the external limits of the efficacy of the law.

The relation between the individual and the natural object, the technical power of man, the productive capacity of the individual, all these develop under the eye of the law but not by means of the law. (*274*)

B. The law can address its commands only to individuals. Where it aims at the control of groups, the law cannot do more than address itself to the individual. Leaving out of consideration the merely subjective resistance of the subject's will, the law must resolve all collective relations among men into rights and duties of the individuals. (*275*) Wherever men enter into a definite but extra-legal relationship, as for instance in the form of co-operation for manufacture or of a body of factory workers, in actuality they merely constitute groups whose collective actions (e.g. a strike) are beyond the reach of the law. (*276*) Even a casual gathering of individuals, such as a crowd, develops potentialities for social action outside the direct control of the law. Co-operation has, *inter alia*, the effect of developing the relation between individual and natural object into collective productive capacity. Just as the law has no control over the term of the first degree, individual productive capacity; so it has none over the collective productive capacity, which is of the nth degree. It can provide aggregate bodies with legal forms, such as association,[1] and confer specific powers on them, but lacking a complete control over the element, it can have but a partial control over the whole.

As a consequence of mere contemporaneity and propinquity—leaving all law out of consideration—definite yet mutable connections are formed, by this mere juxtaposition, between all members of a society. (*277*) All changes in temporal, local and technical conditions affect the whole of society without always becoming present to the mind of the individuals. Even less do they become so to society as a whole, which ought to respond to new facts with new laws.

C. Side by side with this inter-connection there is the inter-connection of the natural objects, which exists independently of any human intervention. The world of objects is a cosmos like the world of men. An important consequence follows: if the law confirms the relations between the individuals A and B, this relation of A to B seemingly becomes a purely private relationship which is of no interest to other members of society. If the law links the

---

[1] The law may treat the association as a person (legal person), but only by binding the individuals can it aim at this effect and achieve it to a greater or lesser extent.

natural object N to the individual A, the relation between A and N
seems private. Yet from the very beginning these relations have
been social, and when a society undergoes a change below the
plane of the law, the relations between A and B acquire another
content or meaning; and a change in the technological significance
of N within the whole of the social structure may give qualities to
N in the hands of A which are quite different from those which the
legislator had in mind when he originally established the relation
between A and N.

Thus we see that the lever which the law uses upon social facts
is too short to control them. Legal ties are mere threads compared
with the herculean power of natural life. Yet this Hercules
stretches his limbs so gradually and imperceptibly, that the threads
do not suddenly snap in all places.

D.   Moreover, the law can express its commands only through
the instrumentality of human beings. The individual who has
power and would exercise legal control in the name of society must
have actual power as an individual as well, power which must be
either physical force or moral authority. The law can only define
the power he is to wield. The conditions under which he exercises
this power, however, are facts of real life, not of law. Whether
the law is armed with bow and arrow or with machine-guns,
whether the squire himself is the local authority or whether
authority is exercised by a chief constable and his subordinates
who are appointed by means of a contract of service, is a question
of the social conditions prevailing at that particular historical
period: there are strict limitations to the choice of the law in this
respect. If the law has installed a holder of power and provided
him with instruments to exercise this power, the question arises
whether, to what extent and for what length of time the person
and instruments can adequately serve their purpose.

 We have been able to give only a brief outline of these fundamentals of the law; yet these considerations show clearly that it is
the isolated individual will which constitutes the essential means
at the disposal of the law and which is its point of application.
Yet the law aims at the control of the organic texture of nature, of
the inter-connections among men and between man and matter.
The whole of this intricate structure forms the substratum, the
foundation of the law. And since this substratum is subject to
change, the same applies to the law. But the imperceptible process
of change does not immediately react upon the norms. At first it

is scarcely noticeable to the individual, much less to the community, and so the norm remains constant. The legal institution remains the same, as regards its normative content, but it no longer retains its former social functions.

3. THE CHANGE OF FUNCTIONS AND THE ABSOLUTE LACK OF FUNCTIONS

The evolution of the "own and patrimony" to capitalist property reveals these matters more clearly than any other development. In support of our thesis we will consider one example: a certain amount of coins is the property of an individual who has hidden them in his stocking against a rainy day. The law ordains that no-one may take them away from him. In economic terms, this money constitutes a hoard. Later a neighbour's house is burnt down, and it is not the law which is responsible for this fire. The neighbour needs money, and the man who has hoarded his coins lends them to him at a high rate of interest. The function of being his own safeguard against dire want gives place to the function of exploiting the need of another person. The existence of men and goods at the same time and in close proximity, and changes in their modes of existence and possession taking place outside the sphere of the law, have not abolished the norm, nor have they abolished the legal institution, but they have wrought a difference in the effects of either.

This change of functions due to a change of the economic and natural foundations of society can result in a complete abolition of the functions. This is the explanation for desuetude, the practical abeyance of a legal institution, though the law itself has not abolished it. If a legal institution thus loses its function, it may disappear from society without any ceremony. The members of society need not even notice this disappearance, far less need it be proclaimed officially. If the economic development were to bring it about that nobody made a last will any more, everybody leaving his possessions to the next-of-kin, then in the course of a few generations the legal institution of testament would have disappeared from our memory, and its abolition would have been due to the quiet force of facts. (*278*) But not all legal institutions are constitutionally capable of falling into desuetude.

Desuetude requires first that no subject succeeds any longer into the legal institution, and secondly that no object of relevance to the law forms its substratum. But as long as the norms of property are valid, every object must necessarily belong to a natural or artificial person, and every derelict object must fall to the occupier (*res nullius cedit occupanti*). As bourgeois society knows no other mode of detention and as, whatever the form of human society, every object must be held by somebody, property cannot fall into desuetude. The fact that a legal institution falls into desuetude, however, is always evidence of the impotence of the law to control its substratum permanently.

4. INEFFECTIVE FUNCTIONING. "IDOLATRY OF THE DECREE"

The power of the law over economics is therefore already restricted by the narrow technique of the law; it is only in theory that the law is omnipotent. It is true that the imperatives of the law can interfere in a creative way; but although it has not been our intention to examine this intervention of the norm, the evidence we have gathered has already led us to recognise that the inter-connections among men, between man and matter and among material objects exist as a datum independently of the law in every epoch of history. Like the sculptor's block of marble, this substratum of legal creation must exist first; yet, quite unlike the block of marble, it controls the norm rather than is subject to control by the norm. Above all the art of legislation lies in the correct appraisal of the mutual effects which norm and substratum have upon each other.

Here we mention only one of the many historical examples. At the height of the Middle Ages, when the economic system was affected neither by traffic nor by money, the public official was called to office by the king in the forms of vasselage, he was endowed with the flag and had to swear the oath of fealty. He was enfeoffed with his office (*officium*) and with landed property (*beneficium*) so that his dignity should not lack substance. Breach of fealty led to forfeiture of both—and so, originally, to death. The newly appointed dignitary was ceremoniously invested with office and land. Under the then prevailing economic conditions it was impossible to reward public functionaries in any other way than by assigning a natural ground rent to them. The order of vocation is indeed predetermined by the economic order, by the substratum itself. This, however, soon becomes more powerful than the norm. The lifelong connection of person and soil, owing to the precarious nature of the instruments of control at this period, is so strong that the fee first becomes hereditary as a matter of fact (*via facti*) and office and possessions become hereditary at the same time. With the return of an economic system based upon trade and money, in the second half of the Middle Ages, the instruments of power have changed. The rising bourgeois state appoints public functionaries on a salary basis and the office of the feudal lord—his *officium*—becomes effete, though the control of the land, the *beneficium*, still remains. The bourgeois revolution abolishes the office even in form (abolition of the nobility) and declares property in land to be free. (*279*) We see from this process which has taken place in one millennium, that the original norm had its purpose, its intended function, but in the course of time the intention is no longer achieved, the institution becomes ineffective, it assumes misdirected functions; so that at first the original intentions are distorted and possibly reversed and in the end every function disappears. The trend of development due to economic laws which are inherent in the substratum is more powerful than the power of the law.

We recognise that the art of legislation, the legal art, has an immense importance for society. Neither economic nor legal analysis can adequately supply the tools for legislation, but only the investigation of the problem which we have raised in this enquiry: the problem of the complicated interrelations between law and economics, this wonderful interweaving of legal institutions and economic structure. The traditional analogy of substructure and superstructure, or Stammler's distinction of form and matter, scarcely indicate this interconnection; at best they do not describe its real substance, or they partly misrepresent it.

As soon as human society has become conscious of its social character, which means that it has developed its common will and thus realises that it has attained potential mastery of itself and its surroundings,—as soon as it has performed the "jump from the realm of necessity to the realm of freedom" (to use Engels' phrase), this consciousness is enhanced to a profound faith which believes legislation capable of performing miracles. This is particularly true for the emotional disposition of the masses after every successful revolution, when this conviction becomes very strong and overwhelming. The law is thought of as omnipotent. Archimedes' Δός μοι ποῦ στῶ, the axiom of the physicist, is here repeated on the part of the lawyer: "Give me the lever of legislation and I shall move the world". This idolatry of legislation, "decretinism" as it has been called, is by no means confined to the Bolshevist revolution, but there it was especially pronounced and has led to disastrous consequences. (*280*)

Let us suppose that a victorious revolution of the dispossessed classes has abolished the bourgeois law of property, especially with regard to the land: on the day after, the same individuals would again have the actual detention of the goods, and at first there would have been no change in the material position. The law therefore would have to work out new regulations of detention in some way. If it was decided to abolish the private and absolute nature of the right of ownership and convert all detention into a kind of onerous fee, which would mean that all private property was converted by one stroke into communal property; such a measure, in my opinion, though it would be far from meaningless, could not abolish the capitalist nature of the economic system. Our whole journey through civil law has given direct proof that property, even in this new legal form, would retain all its functions, and that it would have, in combination with its complementary institutions, the same social effects as private property pure and simple. So the new law would have failed and the faith in legislation would be shattered as an illusion. The agrarian constitution of contemporary Russia is an irrefutable proof of this argument. (*281*)

NOTES, CHAPTER III, SECTION I

(*272*) This paragraph should be read as a comment to the statement that law may be a condition of capitalist development, but does not create it. Not only negative norms—duties not to interfere—but even positive norms—duties to do something, e.g. a legal formulation of the rule *pacta sunt servanda*—cannot and do not make any material contribution to the evolution of capitalism. If it is thus understood the statement is almost a commonplace. It is easy to prove its truth from English legal history. During the period of the Industrial Revolution—Dicey called its central stage the "period of legislative quiescence"—the law did not enforce many "positive duties". Where it did—the Poor Law is the outstanding example—it was designed to create conditions favourable to capitalism. The "considerable changes" (Dicey, l.c., p. 95) of the period—e.g. the enactment and repeal of the Combination Acts—were negative in character, positive changes— e.g. the first Factories Acts—were tentative and not very significant. The subsequent period saw indeed the most far-reaching legislative reforms, but, broadly speaking, the legislation which was informed by the spirit of Benthamism was mainly intended to remove what Dicey called (l.c. p. 111) "the intolerable incongruity between a rapidly changing social condition and the practical unchangeableness of the law". This is true of much of the criminal law and procedural reforms of the period, and legislation (such as railway and public utility laws) which did enforce positive duties, was intended to curb monopoly where new technical developments might have interfered with competitive enterprise whose undisturbed existence was the principal aim of legislation. The truth of Renner's remark follows from the very essence of a laissez faire economy. If, however, his statement was understood as a general remark on the place of law in society in general, it could hardly be upheld. Fundamental principles like *pacta sunt servanda* or a parent's duty to maintain his children cannot, of course, be created by law unless they express social convictions and economic needs. But, especially in what Laski calls "the positive state," the law and the positive obligations which it enforces do transform society. Who can deny that social legislation—insurance law and factory law, minimum wage law and (in America) the legal duty to collective bargaining—have changed society? Who, remembering the vast economic effect of taxation and the social effect of conscription, can give to Renner's statement an application beyond the isolated case of capitalism in its formative stages? True enough, legal duties remain ineffective unless society is prepared to accept them. But there is a long way between endorsing this truism and denying that the crystallisation of social convictions and needs in positive law can have a transforming effect on society. That this transforming effect has its limits, is clear from the contemporary experience of Anti-Monopoly legislation in the United States and in Germany. If economic tendencies reach a certain magnitude of strength, the law is indeed impotent.

(*273*) See for an explanation of the conflict between these two views of property the remarks made in the Introduction.

(*274*) Here, again, the experience of the "positive state" prompts a query. Does legislation against soil erosion, does a legislative scheme harnessing water power (like the T.V.A.), does the enforcement of standards of estate management and good husbandry, nothing to develop the productive power of the individual?

(*275*) It is hardly necessary to point out that the "theory of the real nature of corporate personality" is the principal target of this attack. Its principal protagonist was Gierke.

(*276*) The development of the English law of criminal and civil conspiracy illustrates this statement. It was the intention of the Courts to bring the criminal law, and, during a later period, the civil law of damages to bear upon collective action. They were, however, unable to formulate the "collective" element otherwise than by the mechanical test whether one person or several persons had been concerned in the act. A comparison of the cases *Allen v. Flood*, [1898] AC 1, and *Quinn v. Leathem*, [1901] AC 495, shows that conduct which does not give rise to a claim for damages if only one individual is sued (though he may in fact have acted for a "collective" entity) may constitute a "conspiracy" if it can be shown that at least two individuals were involved. There is no doubt that this crude test is still part of the law. It was recognised as such by the House of Lords as recently as 1942 in *Crofter Harris Tweed Co. v. Veitch*, [1942] AC 604, but it was severely criticised on the ground that it disregards the overpowering influence one individual or corporation may have in a society such as ours. It is probably due to the diminishing importance of legal interference with collective action that this test was able to survive at all. Whatever its historical origin, it is based upon a tacit assumption that all individuals are equal in power, and that, therefore, two are necessarily more dangerous than one. (See for further discussion and literature Friedmann, *Legal Theory*, ch. 26; Salmond's *Law of Torts*, 10th ed., pp. 604 *sq.*).

(*277*) The English law of negligence is based upon the conception of a "duty of care", a duty owed to persons who, in the words of Lord Atkin in *Donoghue v. Stevenson*, [1932] AC 562, at p. 580, "are so closely and directly affected by my act that I ought reasonably to have them in contemplation as being so affected when I am directing my mind to the acts or omissions which are called in question". It is not the law which determines the range of "proximity" in this sense, it is the development of social organisation and of technique which continuously enlarges (or restricts) the number of persons who are, in this sense, my "neighbours". The law does not create the "definite yet mutable connections (which) are formed between all members of society" (Renner), the "infinite variety of relations with their fellows" into which, as Lord Macmillan said in the same case (at p. 619), human beings are thrown or in which they place themselves in the daily contacts of social and business life. All this takes place "under the eyes of the law", not by virtue of the law. But, and this is where the development of the English law of negligence during the last fifteen years has taught an interesting lesson, "the conception of legal responsibility may develop in adaptation to altering social conditions and standards. The criterion of judgment must adjust and adapt itself to the changing circumstances of life" (Lord Macmillan, ibid.). The test of "reasonableness"—which is intrinsically meaningless—has proved to be a blank which is filled by the changing facts of social life to which the law reacts. It has, in certain limits, made the "lever of the law" adjustable to the varying state of social conditions.

(*278*) It is only in this extreme case that Renner departs from his positivist assumption. In the case of a mere change of function he insists that "the legal institution remains the same", only where it ceases to operate altogether can its existence be affected by its social effectiveness. One of the principal characteristics of English law is the continuance of former legal realities as mere symbols. This symbolic continuity is apt to veil the social fact of desuetude. The history of the Royal assent to Acts of Parliament is the most prominent example. Sometimes an attempt to revive as a reality what has long ceased to have a more than symbolical existence leads to the formal abolition of a legal institution (as was the case with the "Appeal of Felony" after the decision in *Ashford v. Thornton* (1818), 1 B. and Ald. 423). In other instances we can surmise that institutions which are still extremely prominent in the textbooks are condemned to be emasculated by desuetude: this may, for example, be true of the common carrier's "absolute liability" which seems to be suffering the fate of being eliminated *via facti* (by contractual practice and statutory rules: see Kahn-Freund, *Law of Carriage by Inland Transport*, p. 13). Others, like, e.g., the limited partnership or the company with unlimited liability of its directors, need not die because they are stillborn. A genuine case of *desuetudo* appears to be that of the Unlawful Societies Act, 1799, and of the Seditious Meetings Act, 1817 (the legislation under which the Tolpuddle Labourers were convicted in *R. v. Loveless* (1834), 6 C. and P. 596). These Acts have never been repealed, and are still "law", but ceased to operate *via facti* (see Slesser, *Law relating to Trade Unions*, p. 17).

(*279*) Although Renner uses as his example a development which was peculiar to the Continent, we can find parallel instances of "ineffective functioning" in this country. The law of copyhold, for example, had completely lost its original function when the Law of Property Act, 1922, set out to abolish it. By that time it had merely become a cumbersome method of conveyancing. The law governing the crime and the tort of "maintenance" (originally designed to prevent the overpowering influence of local potentates from being brought to bear upon juries) has completely "missed" its function. Doctrines like those of consideration in the law of contract or of *ultra vires* in company law—at one time necessary corollaries of innovations in the law, such as the universal recognition of the rule *pacta sunt servanda* or the introduction of the joint stock company—have become mere instruments of legal vexation (see per Lord Dunedin in *Dunlop Pneumatic Tyre Co., Ltd. v. Selfridge and Co.*, [1915] AC 847, at p. 855, and the observations of the Cohen Committee on Company Law Reform No. 12). The "contract under seal", once a necessary legal institution at a time of widespread illiteracy, has lost whatever *raison d'être* it possessed in the past. (See the Memorandum by the present Lord Chief Justice attached to the Sixth Interim Report of the Law Revision Committee, Cmd. 5449.) But the chief contemporary example is the limited liability company, which at an earlier stage of capitalist development was a necessary institution promoting a sharing of risks, and has now, to a considerable extent, "missed" this function. During an era of expanding capitalism it served the attraction of capital for objects beyond the financial power of individual entrepreneurs or small groups of investors. What it does to-day, has partly been described in the treatise by Berle and Means, quoted above. In addition it has become an accounting device, an instrument of tax avoidance and a supplement to the law of succession by inheritance.

(*280*) Is this "idolatry of legislation" peculiar to victorious revolutions? Has it, perhaps, a parallel in the views of those economists and lawyers who—on both sides of the Atlantic— seriously believe that the inherent tendency of capitalism towards monopoly can be checked by anti-trust and similar laws? Was it not an act of wisdom on the part of the English Courts that, by reducing the law of conspiracy to a minimum, they disclaimed any belief in the power of the law of forcing a competitive economy upon an unwilling community? It would appear that the "idolatry of legislation" castigated by Renner was a characteristic of Russian legal thought only during the first stages of the Revolution. It was abandoned with the advent of N.E.P., and the "Commodity Exchange School" described by Schlesinger, l.c., pp. 152 *sq.*, and represented, *inter alia*, by Pashukani's *General Theory of Law and Marxism* (1925), which would seem to represent the very opposite of "decretinism".

(*281*) This was written in 1928, and still reflects the impact of Soviet legislation upon agriculture during War Communism and N.E.P., as expressed in the Land Code of 1922 (see Schlesinger, l.c., p. 99). One year after Renner had published the second edition of his work, the Central Committee of the Communist Party passed its resolution of December, 1929, which inaugurated the policy of large scale agricultural collectivisation (Schlesinger, l.c., p. 178).

Section ii. The Change of Functions and Its Various Forms

We have dealt with the general theoretical possibilities and causes of the change of functions. Now we shall attempt to investigate the forms in which these changes manifest themselves.

1. PURELY QUANTITATIVE CHANGES

The norm is addressed to individuals, endowing them with rights or power or imposing on them duties or commissions. Every legal institution calls for persons to act as its agents. The number and character of these agents determines the subjective scope of the institution. [1] Property as a legal institution assumes a different character according to whether the whole population, a majority or only a minority are actual owners. (282) A legal institution can continue to exist as a norm but may disappear in practical life if no individual any longer acts as its agent; and where the institution is confined to a minority, it can become illusory for the majority. Viewed from this angle, such changes are in themselves of a purely quantitative character, and, in theory, they do not constitute a change of function. It is, however, palpable enough that in consequence of this extension or restriction of the number of agents, the effects of the institutions may assume different qualities. Once again, we have reached the point where the category of quantity turns into the category of quality.

Apart from the subjective relations, every legal institution has an objective content. Property in particular has as its object a corporeal thing, an item of nature, a quantity of matter. The right of ownership assumes a different social character according to the quantity of objects which it comprises. This increase or decrease of quantity, too, affects its social function, at least in practice, though not in theory.

Changes in these two aspects, mere changes of quantity, are the first to become apparent, and superficial observation penetrates no deeper. Thus certain social democrats regard the concentration of property-objects in the hand of only a few *personae* as the only

---

[1] Thus property in the form of the *allodium* was conserved under the feuda system as a mere exception. As the cities developed, this soon became the rule in such particular and exceptional urban areas, though the relations of possession in the country proper remained unaffected.

guarantee of social development; and they most anxiously examine the property-statistics, although such quantitative relations do not by any means constitute the essence of a change of prime importance in the function of property. Thus many social reformers regard the introduction of maximum and minimum holdings as a palliative. But this kind of mechanical conception does not go deeper than the surface of the phenomenon.

There is no doubt that in capitalist economics an unceasing change of property-subject and object takes place, expropriation and appropriation without cease. This alone already constitutes a functional change. The "own and patrimony" was firmly held by the *persona* and his successor, it belonged to the family, and this stabilisation of economy was its *raison d'être*. Nowadays *personae* and *res* continually change hands and positions. Doubtless this reversal is brought about in such a manner that the property-objects tend to become concentrated in the hands of a few. But this tendency to concentration is counteracted in many cases by the splitting up of property owing to hereditary succession, as we saw when we dealt with the attraction and repulsion of capitals. In consequence of the unavoidable division into fund of production and labour fund, at least a portion of the goods must always return into the hands of all, and from a legal point of view, nobody is entirely without property. Such quantitative consideration can in the end have only one result: the conservation to eternity of property as it is to-day—a pyramid of property which tapers off at its highest point.

2. SOCIAL INTERCONNECTIONS

This indirect change of functions which is brought about by extension and restriction of property with regard to its subjects and objects, recedes into the background when compared with the direct change of function which up to now has been completely neglected in socialist literature.[1] This change consists mainly of the following: property is *de jure* nothing but the power of disposal of a person A over an object N, the mere relation between individual and natural object, which, according to the law, affects no other object and no other person. The object is private property,

---

[1] This is sometimes true in spite of Karl Marx's researches which have strikingly demonstrated this very fact. There are many who go about, swearing by Marx or cursing him, without having grasped the essential point of his social criticism.

the individual a private person, and the law is private law. This was in accordance with the facts in the period of simple commodity production, when the institution too operated in a private, non-social and non-public manner; because the substratum of the right, the actual distribution of goods and labour-power, made this possible and indeed was the cause of it. Since the substratum has changed, the relation between individual and natural object receives quite a different content: the connexity between all members of society and all natural objects makes it into a relation among men which is disguised as a relation among things. (*283*) A person's clearly determined control of a thing becomes his control over other persons; masked as a relation between objects, it becomes control of society itself.

The function of a right *in rem* is not revealed by *persona* or *res* alone, nor by the legal power of the *persona* over the *res*, which is merely freedom of action granted by the law. Its function is revealed in the active use of the right, in the manner of exercise; which in most cases lies outside the sphere of the law. This exercise in the period of simple commodity production appears to be a private and isolated act; but in fact it is always a part-process of the whole social life process, performed by a cell of the social organism on an atom of the whole social material. The exercise of the right of ownership, however, takes place within the microcosm of that period, as we have portrayed it in a previous chapter. As soon as this microcosm is dissolved and its ruins are made part of the social concern, the method of exercise is socially determined and of social significance. If the individual peasant left his land fallow, he wronged no-one and only shortened his own subsistence. (*284*) But the mine-owner who closes down his mine cuts down fuel for everybody, deprives his workers of their livelihood and perhaps enlarges his income by increasing the price of coal. The exercise of the right, however, is not only of social relevance, it is itself determined by society. The isolated peasant decides at his pleasure how to use his land, but the capitalist producer is motivated by the position of the market, by society. Legally free, he is economically bound, and his bonds are formed by the relation between his own and all other property-objects. Since the exercise of a right is not determined by the law but by facts outside the legal sphere, the law loses control of the matter.

3. THE DIVORCE OF TECHNICAL FROM LEGAL USE

As the property-object of the period of simple commodity production was universal, the exercise of the right of ownership at
this period necessitated the owner's universal power of disposal.
The economic development, however, dissolved the microcosm
into its component elements. Each individual part now requires a
specific manner of disposal, and this is determined by the technical properties of the *res* and the technical qualifications of the
persona who disposes: he now must be an expert. If the *res* is an
instrument of production only, mental or manual labour can
make use of it, and if it is a means of consumption, its use is
restricted to the consumer. But the owner has neither universal
capacity for labour, nor is he specialised in being merely a consumer. As he ceases to be the master of the individual object in a
technical sense, he must give up detention in order to put the
object at the service of society. He cannot retain technical
ownership, and he does not want to surrender legal ownership. As
he can no longer make technical use of his right of disposal, he is
quick-witted enough to cultivate the legal aspect of his right. He
alienates the object, gives it into the detention of other persons by
act-in-the-law and makes it profitable by means of mere legal
transactions.

How is this possible? The legal system must make provision for
giving the things into the detention of those who have the technical
means of controlling them, otherwise society would cease to exist.
But there was a solution to this problem before it became pressing.
The gaps in the institution of hereditary property were filled in
by many old legal institutions; for no legal system solves its task
completely and every system needs stop-gaps. Sale and purchase,
loan, deposit, rent existed previously, yet their range was very
small, with regard to the *persona* as well as to the *res*; they were
merely subsidiary institutions. Now the time of their evolution
had come. As detention by the owner was an absolute impediment
for the owner as well as for society, the question arises whether the
legislator should have abolished the property-norm. But the
legislator was scarcely aware of this impediment, since the owner
himself had previously found a remedy and made subsidiary
institutions into correlatives of property.

The sale of one's patrimony was formerly illegal or at least condemned by society. The idea that property existed only to be ex-

ploited by legal transactions, only in order to be sold, was inconceivable to anybody. But now the *res* has become a commodity that cannot be used in any other way than by sale or purchase; or it has become a machine and cannot be used in any other way than by putting others to work on it by means of contract, by giving its detention to these others and entrusting them with the necessary technical exercise of the property-right; or it becomes land which is suitable and proper to lease out and so to give into the detention of a man who understands all about fertilisers. The right of ownership is exercised by act-in-the-law. Every item of property with special technical and economic functions now can have social existence only in connection with its complementary institution. It is this complementary institution to which the technical and economic function is attached, and ownership is reduced to a function that is merely private, to the unfortunate function of freezing the legal detention of the property-object in the hands of those who cannot detain it in fact and yet have the right of detention. From the point of view of society, property thus acquires the most striking function, but in order to develop further according to economic laws, it must be redeemed piecemeal by the very society that conferred it, against a tribute payable to the owner.

Ownership at the period of simple commodity production was essentially and with few exceptions exercised without any intervention of other legal institutions and required no other act-in-the-law. The soil was cultivated and its fruits were consumed. In so far as property served a system of production by artisans, the work was done directly for the customer or for a local market, generally in the form of a contract of work and labour (*locatio conductio operis*), or of sale and purchase. But sale and purchase here relate to the finished article alone, there was no incessant flow of sale and purchase involving anything and everything. The sale was merely the final act of the labour process, and the exercise of ownership was as a rule the technical disposal over the object. Now, however, the exercise of this right by act-in-the-law becomes the specific function of the owner, technical disposal becomes the specific function of the non-owner, and the owner acquires the social function of distributing the goods among labour and consumers. Let us reflect for a moment: what has happened? Did not the legislator endow the workers and consumers with ownership of the instruments of labour and the consumption goods in order to ensure to them for all time their steady detention from generation to generation? Was it therefore not the legislator who distributed the goods among labourers and consumers? Now the relation is reversed. The owner is neither worker nor consumer, but since the legislator has meanwhile retired, the owner takes over from him the function of distribution.

4. DISSOCIATION INTO PARTIAL FUNCTIONS

But quite apart from this: only now does property acquire its specific manner of functioning—each individual item of property begins to operate in conjunction with its own complementary institution. In the period of simple commodity production this obtained in part by virtue of a primitive law of obligations, the institutions of the market. Property becomes productive capital when it is combined with the contract of employment, interest-bearing capital when combined with the loan, modern landed estate when combined with the lease and so on. Thus typical combinations of legal institutions are created, higher amalgamations of legal elements, each of which calls for a special theoretical analysis (e.g. the law relating to real estate, to urban house property, to mines, to commerce, and so on). (285) Given that property fulfils its special functions invariably in connection with certain complementary institutions, it becomes evident that its function can no longer be deduced from the right of ownership alone. However carefully one may resolve the content of the property rights (the general power of disposal) into individual competences, one will not discover the noxious effects of property, as they develop only when property is combined with the contract of employment, the contract of loan, and the rest. Between the legal institutions there is a social interconnection just as there is between man and matter. The mere power of disposal over machinery does not tell us anything, however thoroughly we may investigate the title to ownership. Therefore theory cannot find fault with the rights themselves in isolation.   If social critics object to the absolute character of the power of disposal, as this permits also of possible abuse, waste or destruction of the good, the owner may rightly answer: "A man who wastes or destroys property ought to be in a lunatic asylum. Madness or mental deficiency of individual owners does not affect the institution of ownership. As to the absolute and unlimited power of disposal, my disposal is neither absolute nor wilful. I do not dispose except in a definite manner; I can do nothing else with the machines than either keep them going or leave them idle. Would you rather that they should be idle?" If the contract of employment is examined in isolation, it reveals nothing but the disarming fact of complete agreement on both sides, here again revealing no cause for misgivings. Only upon the combination of both institutions rests the foundation of their economic function. The exercise of one type of right, in itself a natural action, an extra-legal activity—indeed during a certain period it was nothing more than this—is here mediated by an act-in-the-law. The owner disposes of his property-object, the machine, by means of the contract of employment; the workers fulfil their contract by operating the machine, which is another person's property. One economic action is represented by two complementary legal institutions. (286) Thus every social function of property finds its legal expression in a special combination with another legal institution which developed in the course of history but whose quantitative extent has been enlarged, as explained above. The dissolution of property is at the same time an unforeseen evolution of the contract of sale and purchase, the contract of employment, and the loan, which formerly were only stop-gaps of the legal system.

5. THE FUNCTION AS A WHOLE

But neither the legal substance, nor the normative content, of the individual legal institution, nor the combined effect of its complementary institutions, reveals completely its social function; which can only be understood if the institution is seen within the whole of its economic context. For the sake of brevity we may call the whole process of a society's production and reproduction in its technical aspect: its working order. This working order of society prescribes for every individual a certain manner in which he should exercise his rights, but it does not do so by way of norms, but by way of general maxims for his actions. The law gives freedom of action, opportunity and power, but it is the social working order which determines the real activities and gives a concrete content to the blanks which the law has provided. It gives to every person an unchanging character mask and to every object a definite economic form. The whole of society is, as it were, implicated in every individual and material relationship, for it determines the social rôle of the individual and the economic purpose of the object. Thus society is the invisible and immaterial soul which reveals itself in man, matter and institutions; yet, like the centre of gravity of a ring, it always lies without.

An individual's possessions appear to him to be his own economic concern. Here a part-concern of the whole social concern is isolated and appears to be a whole; it is individualised by the law and becomes a legal unit. Every part-concern is property. This legal unit, this aggregate of possessions, however, in its capacity as a working concern remains part and parcel of the whole social working order. The law has the general function of establishing working concerns in terms of possessions; but the whole social working order co-ordinates these partial concerns, in certain circumstances dissolving them and shaping them anew. The working technique of the concern is in constant rebellion against the mode of possession, which is a permanent obstacle to the development of the concern. Human capacity for production does not always develop by means of property and often develops in opposition to it, and in spite of it; and the complementary institutions help to remove this obstacle—property—by redeeming it.

In every private concern, person, object and property together play their specific rôle and fulfil their appropriate function. A man is a factory-owner, a number of people are labourers; the whole of the property-object becomes industrial capital only when they are organised; and it is only in this conjunction that property has the capital function, the function of appropriating the product of alien labour for the owner. The same applies to a warehouse or a bank. It is for this reason that appraisal of property is so difficult. The same person, the same object and the same right can in another private concern change their function, even if there has not been much change in the working technique. They can themselves become objects of exploitation and appropriation instead of being means of exploitation and appropriation; as often happens, e.g. in the case of the capitalist tenant. If it is easy to understand the quantitative extension and contraction of property with its derivative modes of function, it is difficult to grasp and analyse the qualitative function of property in bourgeois society. The reason for this difficulty is that the qualitative function is based neither upon the individual, nor upon the material object, nor indeed upon the legal institution or the aggregate of legal institutions, but can only be understood if all those elements are considered within the context of the individual private concern, which again must be correlated to the whole of the social working order. It is its significance for the whole life of the human race which determines the social function of the legal institution.

NOTES, CHAPTER III, SECTION II

(*282*) Similarly, an institution originally designed for a minority may expand and be used by the majority. The institutions of a married woman's separate property (under the Act of 1882) and of settled land (under the Act of 1925) are examples in this country.

(*283*) In English factory legislation the employer appears in the mask of the "occupier". Safety regulations, and even limitations as to employment of women and juveniles, are imposed upon him in his capacity of a person controlling a thing.

(*284*) How the function of agricultural property depends on the economic character of that property, emerges from Renner's example to an extent not even demonstrated by himself. The tacit assumption of his statement is that the peasant uses his property for subsistence farming. Where he supplies a market on which the very existence of an urban population depends, Renner's assertion loses its validity. A community which, owing to the need for a restriction of agricultural imports, must rely on the farmer's output, will be driven to enforcing—if necessary, by the threat of legal dispossession (see Section 17 of the Agriculture Act, 1947)—compliance with standards of "good husbandry". The changed structure of the national economy has transformed the social function, and eventually the legal structure of the farmer's ownership right.

(*285*) Blackstone's Commentaries on the Laws of England (1765) consisted of four books. The first was devoted to constitutional law and to family law, the second to the law of property (mainly land law), the third to private wrongs (mainly torts and civil procedure) and the fourth to criminal law and procedure. Mercantile law hardly existed as a separate discipline, the law of contract was in an undeveloped state and occupied a short chapter in the second volume. To-day we have separate and important disciplines called "industrial law", "law of banking", "law of transport", "patent law", "insurance law", and so forth. In the curriculum leading to the Bachelor of Laws Examination in the University of London land law has recently ceased to be a compulsory subject. It has become one discipline among many. The laws of the "complementary institutions" have become its equals and, in some ways, its superiors. No one could have suggested to deprive the law of contract of its compulsory character. To-day a man may be a competent lawyer in many fields without knowing more than the barest elements of land law. But no one could practise law without a thorough grounding in the law of contract.

(286) Renner does not mention the law of patents and designs which, together with the institutions of ownership and of the contract of employment, constitutes the legal framework of industry. In many cases the owner of industrial plant exercises his right through the combined effect of these three institutions: property, employment, patent law.

Section iii. The Function becomes Divorced from the Legal Institution

WHAT we owe to Marx in the field of the law is a most precise analysis of the mode of function covering every article of property at every stage of the social working order. We have tried to bring the principal modes of function into a system that is easily grasped; and we have repeatedly emphasised the fact that every concrete case may be of a hybrid character and that numerous rudiments of functions have been conserved up to the present.

I. PROPERTY BECOMES DIVORCED FROM THE OWNER

One feature is common to all kinds of property, whether mole-hill or mountain,—they all control and exploit men, though in a small working concern this part is not always evident and in many cases it is insignificant. Strange as it may seem, as a rule it is not the person who has the technical and economic disposal, the technical detention of the object, but the person who has only the legal control of property and exercises this control by means of the contract of employment, the contract of loan or the contract of lease, who can realise his property in an economic manner to his own advantage. Economic ownership in an advanced capitalist economy is in fact identical with absence of disposal in a technical sense. The original relationship has been turned into its converse.

Yet the property-object is so much bound up with the capital function that the legal subject does not always benefit by it. The moneylender is for instance the legal owner of the sum loaned before the loan transaction by which he perforce loses detention of his own object; for he transfers the detention to somebody else by act-in-the-law, just as the landlord does when he leases his land. But when money is the object of the legal transaction, the very nature of this object implies that loss of detention is necessarily alienation in the eyes of the law, so that the property is legally transferred to the other person. Here the economic owner who uses the capital function to his own advantage has ceased to be owner in a legal sense, yet he retains the function of ownership. This function has become independent, it has been divorced from ownership as a legal institution. This is a frequent phenomenon. For example, it is obvious that when the mortgagee appropriates the ground rent, or the shareholder the profit of enterprise in the form of dividend, both have nothing to show but scraps of paper covered with print or writing—deeds or shares. Shareholder and mortgagee, without having the right of ownership, utilise a part of the functions of property for their own purposes. The legal institution of property here no longer comprises its whole material content. The contract of obligation, itself an institution complementary to ownership (formally), absorbs property by taking over its principal functions, thus opening revealing the true character of property as a mere title to surplus value. This example shows us that economic ownership is clearly distinguishable from its original form, that of legal property.

2. THE CAPITAL FUNCTION IS NOW DETACHED FROM THE *RES*

Yet these are neither the only nor the most striking instances of a situation where one person utilises the capital of an object though this object temporarily belongs to another. Nowadays the capital function is bound up with every property-object, even where the casual observer would least suspect it. Even the wage in the hand of the worker and the worker's goods of consumption which he has bought for this wage, remain capital: they are variable capital. The wage forms a part of the employer's working capital. From an economic point of view, it has only been advanced to the workers, and by this transfer its value is not lost to the employer, the wage remains part of his capital. This money is capital only for the entrepreneur; it is a mere exchange-value for the worker who has to convert it into consumption goods. Two functions are now fulfilled by the same object. This phenomenon provides a typical example of the cluster of objects and relationships from which the capital function must in each case be disentangled.

Legally the worker's loaf of bread is the worker's property. From the point of view of the law, this subject-object relationship is self-contained, simple and unequivocal. From an economic point of view it is different. Here the loaf of bread represents the wage, a sum of money which was yesterday at the disposal of the capitalist class; as reproduced labour-power it will again revert to this class. The loaf of bread represents money which to-day belongs to the worker; but, when the price is paid, the money is restituted to the capitalist class in exchange for the bread; and this very amount of money may even return to the individual employer who has paid it, as part of the price for the commodities which he has produced, and may thus demonstrate its function as a particle of capital which has been advanced. (*287*) One and the same particle of capitalist property, the economic property of the capitalist, rolls from hand to hand, rolls away from the owner, falls to another legal owner and yet remains his capital. This is typical for a situation where objects and relations form an intricate pattern in which the capital function is but one strand that must be disentangled from the others in every instance.

The capitalist will have it that the workers live on "his" money, though as far as the law is concerned, this money has already become the workers' property. He says that the commodity is "his" commodity even when it has become the property of the next vendor. He says that he must bring in "his" money if he wants to recoup himself for the cost of production by the sale of his commodity, even if "his" money has already become the property of innumerable *personae*. This is not merely a futile remark of the capitalist, for all these amounts appear as entries on the credit side of his account, and it is their sum which represents his capital. From an economic point of view he is right. All these objects belong to him, it is their relation to his person which gives them unity. They are set in motion by a uniform law, the will of the capitalist, and thus they become capital. And they do not cease to be his capital even if they are temporarily transferred into the ownership of X, Y or Z.

If we regard the object merely from X's point of view, its quality of being capital disappears altogether. There remain only the technological relation between the individual and the natural object, and the volitional relation of the *persona* to the *res*. Therefore the capital function clings to the property-object regardless of the temporary legal subject. The function of the capitalist, his economic character mask, no longer coincides with the legal character mask of the owner. A usurer who has given away all his goods and received I.O.U.s instead has no property in the eyes of the law. (*288*) If his debtors are wage-labourers and not capitalists, the capitalist owner has vanished altogether so far as the law is concerned. Yet capital and capitalist relations obviously continue to exist.

It is therefore essential to distinguish between economic pro-

perty and legal property, out of which the former has developed. [1]
Legal property is a corporeal object, it may also be an aggregation
of various parts, and it is accordingly an item of nature. (289)
Economic property, however, is an aggregate of values, and therefore it is *a priori* socially conditioned. The term "economic property" gives a correct indication of its origin and historical
development, but it is misleading in so far as it can easily be confused with legal ownership. The usage of the law has developed
an adequate category for economic property and calls the
economic property of a person his "aggregate possessions"
(*Vermögen*, which in German means also "power" or "capacity"
A.S.). An ingenious invention of language, for the very word
connotes the social power of a person (cf. below, Section V).

3. THE OBJECT ACQUIRES MANY FUNCTIONS. THE SUBJECT IS
DEPRIVED OF ALL FUNCTIONS

Many phenomena which may deceive the casual observer, are
due to this distinction between legal and economic property,
almost unknown to simple commodity production. Let us first
consider the differentiation of functions which we have already
had occasion to mention.

In the period of simple commodity production the property-
object as a unit of many component parts, as patrimonial property, is of universal service to the subject. All the economic
functions are undifferentiated and merge into one another, they
form a coherent whole. The unitary character of legal property
corresponds to an equally unitary character of economic property.
To-day, on the other hand, a piece of land is an asset and a source
of rent for the owner, but for the tenant and his labourer it is not
an asset but a title to profit and an instrument of labour. Thus
the functions of an object are split up in accordance with the
various persons who by virtue of the various complementary
institutions of property become concerned with it. To-day we
have again many modes in which one and the same object can be
held, we have again a whole system of *geweres* (seizins). (290)

Moreover, this differentiation explains the phenomenon of a
relative lack of function on the part of the subject. All occupied
items of nature, and in consequence all property-objects, fulfil a
social function which they can never lose. (It is for this reason,

---

[1] These two kinds of property, however, should not be fused into one another.

also, that many people are convinced that the abolition of property is absolutely impossible.)

As soon as property has developed separate functions, it has, with regard to every individual who comes in contact with it, one function only. The loaf of bread is for the worker only a means of consumption, it has no function from any other aspect. Yet the object itself must have at least one function in all relations of which it is an element.

But the same does not apply to the person. The property-object which is represented by a share, has, of course, quite specific economic functions. Not so the owner, who, indeed, fulfils no social function whatever, or, in other words, his function has become antisocial in its essence. The functions of property change—not in as much as the institution itself is deprived of its functions—but because the subjects become quite useless, like a vestal or a begging friar. Such relative loss of function does not bring it about that the institution itself falls into abeyance, indeed, it cannot do so, since its object can never be without function and all objects are under the present system *de jure* bound to be in somebody's ownership. Therefore there can be no desuetude for the institution of property, it can only be abused.

Notes, Chapter III, Section III

(*287*) It is hardly necessary to mention that this process is not in any way affected by Truck Acts. Within the framework of this analysis the price paid by the worker for the consumer goods which he buys "returns" to the employer in the market in which he sells the products. The money paid by the worker for his loaf of bread circulates from the baker *via* the miller to the farmer who uses it to buy, may be, the industrial product of the factory in which the worker himself is occupied.

(*288*) He has no "property" in the sense in which the term is used in the Continental Codes (except with regard to the valueless substance of the I.O.U.s). As soon as the word "property" is used with the meaning which it usually bears in this country (or, e.g., in the Fifth and Fourteenth Amendments to the United States Constitution), the capital function is no longer so clearly detached from the property object, because the legal right, the "chose in action" which has been created by the "complementary institution" (the contract) then appears as a "property object".

(*289*) "Legal property is a corporeal object",—it is strictly speaking (in Renner's sense) a right in a corporeal object. The—often noticed—use of the word "property" both for the right and for the thing is not confined to the English language. It has even been applied in the Continental Codes, e.g., in § 823 of the German Civil Code which imposes a liability for damages upon anyone who injures the life, body, health, liberty, property or any other right of another. What is meant is injury to the property object. The German noun "*Vermögen*" (see the Introduction) is derived from the verb "*vermögen*" which means "having the power to do something". "*Vermögen*" meant originally "power", and, subsequently came to be used as indicating "assets", "estate". As so often happens, the history of a word reveals a social development which ideologies are anxious to conceal. The dual meaning of the French word "*fortune*" is, in a different way, equally revealing, as is the English word "estate".

(*290*) See above, note 65.

Section iv. The Unit of Business and the Unit of Property Cease to Coincide

The question can therefore be only whether this degeneration of property can or must proceed ever nearer toward a state where all owners retain one function only, that of drawing surplus value from the object; or to a stage where the overwhelming majority of owners are so far removed from the process of production that their futility and perniciousness are exposed; whether a development is unavoidable whereby these owners, now deprived of every function, become such an object of hatred for the real functionaries of society that in the end the legal order itself must remove them. The trends of economic development brings the owners close enough to this kind of pillory and many Marxists even to-day build their hopes on it.

Yet this development is neither in general sufficiently advanced, nor can it everywhere automatically progress up to this climax; and this fact is due to the very existence of capital.

1. THE SIZE OF THE WORKING CONCERN AS TECHNICAL OPTIMUM

Every working capital exists in the form of a private working concern. [1]

Under all circumstances, even in a communist society, there is a technical division of the social working order as a whole into various part-concerns which are scattered over all regions where people live, and distributed among these people. A social order where the localities for the various social activities are not spread out in space, and where there is no technical division of labour, cannot be imagined. This division and distribution of concerns is entirely a technical question which must be raised even in a communist society. The principles are simple. The locality of the enterprise is determined with an eye to the market, and the organisation of the concern by the nature of the goods which are to be used for production, distribution or consumption; moreover the organisation is affected by the degree of development of human skill, and the theoretical and practical development of working methods, which, all taken together, can be described as the "social productive power". The organisation and locality of the concern at the period of the patrimonial property completely

[1] Public concerns as a rule are subject to private law. (*291*)

coincided with the legal form of the "own and patrimony", they both required productive microcosms situated in close proximity. [1]

But our present economic system has set free the individual productive powers and by its specialisation it has increased them beyond previous imagination in manufacture and factory. Labour-power and goods have not only been split up into atoms but have also been started on a process of continual motion, and all elements have become fluid—*corpora non avent, nisi fluunt.* A new process of grouping has started with regard to the goods, and labour-power must follow willy-nilly. Newly created enterprises are not self-contained entities, they are specialised concerns, technological part-concerns of one large macrocosm of economic life which is held together by national markets and later by the world market.

The fate of every private concern is determined by its position within this working order of society, but its size is exclusively dependent on the means and methods employed for production. The technique of the period determines the size of the enterprise; in theory this is always so and in social life the technique is at least the ultimate factor. It is easy to understand that iron nowadays must be smelted in large establishments, whereas cows must be milked individually. It is intelligible that men must disperse themselves all over the globe in order to extract raw material, whereas commodities intended for sale are conveniently stored in warehouses. Man follows the immobile means of production, while mobile means of production follow man. Under all circumstances labour-power and instruments of labour must adapt themselves individually, and the better they do this, the more expedient it is. But consumption, too, must be adapted to the individual consumers, just as the doctor must adapt himself to the patient or the shoe to the foot.

[1] This state of affairs is impressively described in Marx's *The Eighteenth Brumaire* (transl. by D. de Leon), New York, 1898, p. 71: "Every single farmer family is almost self-sufficient; itself produces directly the greater part of what it consumes; and it earns its livelihood more by means of an interchange with nature than by intercourse with society. We have the allotted patch of land, the farmer and his family; alongside of that another allotted patch of land, another farmer and another family. A bunch of these makes up a village; a bunch of villages makes up a Department. Thus the large mass of the French nation is constituted by the simple addition of equal magnitudes—much as a bag with potatoes constitutes a potato-bag."

True as this description may be for the case of the French peasant of 1848, it would be wrong indeed and lead to politically disastrous consequences to assume that it is valid for the peasantry of to-day in France or in any other part of Europe. Everywhere the overwhelming majority of the peasants have become producers for the market. This alone would account for a totally different psychology of the rural population.

Every part-product of society, like bread or wine, undergoes a large number of processes which are more or less distinctly separated from each other. Cotton might be made into shirts in one place, but equally well might there be different localities for the various parts of this working process, spinning mills, weaving mills and so on. It is for the technical expert to decide what is most expedient. But the growing of vines, the harvesting of grapes, the pressing, cellaring and retailing of the wine cannot all be done in one building adjacent to the inn. Crop growing, cattle breeding and dairy farming in particular can only be successful if they are performed in concerns which must not exceed a certain maximum size. Cultivated crops and highly bred animals require special care and attention on the part of the individual. All this is a matter of course.

Yet it is equally evident that this division of enterprises, which under special circumstances may favour even the smallest enterprises, does not remove the need for the co-ordination of these part-concerns to the whole of the social working order. This individualisation of enterprises must indeed always be a partial one. The man who is most skilful in milking cows is not always the most perfect veterinary surgeon, book-keeper, or—on our basis— merchant. A tiny cattle farm may therefore be most expedient with regard to milking and feeding, but not with regard to breeding, the manufacture and delivery of meat and dairy produce or the keeping of accounts. Even from a purely technical aspect there can always be only a partial individualisation of concerns, which necessitates in each case an equally partial supplementary co-ordination of these concerns. The economic plan, which is of paramount importance, should be conceived as one technical comprehensive plan for each given type of social production.

The question now arises how to attain this optimum size of the concern so long as the institution of private property remains in force as a legal institution.

2. THE SIZE OF THE CONCERN AS A FORTUITOUS INCIDENT OF THE LAW

The independence of these part-concerns, of whatever size— always a partial and relative independence,—cannot nowadays be expressed otherwise than in the legal form of absolute individual property, since ownership is our sole and universal mode of detention, and part-property must necessarily become individual property. (*292*) But the interconnection of all concerns is revealed at the same time as a necessary dependence of the part-concern on the social order, which in its turn is expressed, as a rule, by the dependence of the owner upon mercantile and finance capital. (*293*) Our present regulation of possessions as private property often allows partial concerns which are technically expedient, to remain private property and often even compels them to remain so, but this is not in any way evidence in favour of private property. From the point of view of the law these concerns are completely independent, they are private possessions which result from the chance of the law, as a rule from inheritance. (*294*) From the economic point of view, however, they are part-concerns of the social body, subject to those relations of dependence which we have mentioned above. This conflict between law and substratum causes permanent friction within the concerns; this friction becomes manifest at first as losses to the owner and as a rule it ends in making him dependent on finance and mercantile capital. It is this conflict, above all, which impedes the full development of the productive power of society as a whole. Herein we have the justification of the remark that property has become an obstacle to social development.

Whenever the legal owners are dependent upon capital in this manner, property itself is not automatically abolished, but a separation between legal and economic property is effected, with the consequence that the legal owner becomes a mere detentor on behalf of the economic owner. When the owners form associations to protect themselves against the noxious effects of property, they are neither willing nor able to neutralise them for the whole of bourgeois society, all they achieve is to secure the title to surplus value for themselves. The capital function of property remains indestructible, even when all owners in one branch of production co-operate in a joint economic plan, and, as in the case of a cartel, submit to a collective regulation of all collective relations of their concerns. If we consider the associated group of owners as a unit, property still remains a snag, a stumbling block for this united group.

We see that any enterprise, whatever its size, is compatible with and may assume the capitalist function. Hence a statistical examination of concerns as to size can no more be cited in evidence for or against property, or for or against socialism, than a statistical examination of the quantitative distribution of possessions. What matters is not quantity but quality, the manner in which property fulfils its functions.

3. PROPERTY AS AN IMPEDIMENT TO CONCENTRATION AND NATIONALISATION

But not only owing to its quantitative structure but also by the very quality of its essence, capital prevents an automatic and complete concentration. If it were otherwise, private property would not be an obstacle to development. The industrialist's capital is always split up into separate portions, constant capital is invested in enterprises and circulating capital is continually in motion. In part, as money and mercantile capital, it circulates from hand to hand and thus forms automatically smaller and larger property-units in the hands of third persons; and in part, as variable capital, it flows into the workers' pockets, thus making the workers, too, owners in the eyes of the law. Therefore capital is automatically divided not only into concerns of production and distribution, but also into numerous smaller or larger private concerns of consumption, so that it becomes responsible for the anarchical administration not only of the social fund of production, but also, and predominantly so, of the social labour fund.

The dissolution of all property into a mere title to interest and rent, the disappearance of the capitalist from the process of production, cannot therefore be universal, so long as the present law of property is in force; just as during the feudal epoch the feudal lord did not become everywhere and completely a mere parasite. It is not a mere phrase that a traditional legal order obstructs development; it is a hard fact and fortunately one that inspires us to action. The law of property establishes the concern as a property-unit, attempting to fossilise it in the hands of the owner. A change in the methods of social production results in changed methods applied to the management of private concerns, and the method of management comes inevitably to be permanently in revolt against the distribution of possessions. In some cases necessary changes in the management of enterprises call for additional capital for the purpose of expansion or intensification, and this additional capital must be borrowed as it cannot be accumulated in a small concern; in other cases the small concern becomes dependent upon commerce, and in still others the individual concern must be liquidated and its ruins are annexed by capital. Every change in the management of enterprises threatens the independence of the owner, and in consequence the owner is either expropriated or at least forced into subjection to commercial and finance capital.

The capitalists themselves are urged on by these dangers towards a collective economy. But in their capacity of owners they oppose total socialisation of their capital and are satisfied to combine merely individual aspects of their concerns within the modern associations. It is evident, though, that by these methods they do no more than give conscious expression to tendencies which are already inherent in the nature of their capital units. Even previously these capital units constituted *in toto* the aggregate capital of the capitalist class, from which everybody derived average profits. Thus the capitalists begin to form themselves into a class, in the eyes of bourgeois society and of the law; just as the working class became an established legal institution in consequence of the collective administration of the labour fund in the forms of social insurance. These associations have the tendency to stabilise and organise[1] the capitalist system, to perpetuate the exploitation of society by capital. Thus they are symptoms of a perfected capitalism, not symptoms of its incipient disintegration. But it is the curse of the capitalist class that it cannot perpetuate itself without collectivising property, at least in form, without socialising its subject-matter; in so doing it brings its property to a condition where it is ripe for transfer into communal ownership. Yet the form is not the essence; and the associated capitalist class does not cease to be a class, a mere part of society; and property does not cease to exploit in the capitalist sense, namely, to exploit the under-privileged.

But even this socialisation, which is merely formal, can hardly become universal. In a society where detention is only possible in terms of private property, all enterprises which form distinct technical parts of the social working order as a whole, must always become objects of private property. Thus the owner remains in numerous cases either working capitalist or worker, he does not lose his functions altogether, he retains a protecting and misleading mask, to be at the same time functionary and non-functionary.

[1] Our era has made much progress in this field and is rightly called an era of organised capitalism. Cf. on this subject Renner: *Marxismus, Krieg und Internationale*, 2nd ed., p. 15 ff., and also the Economic Resolution of the International Socialist Congress at Brussels, 1928.

Yet would it be true to say that the antisocial functions of property are abolished by this equivocal phenomenon?

No, those socialists are mistaken who believe that the progressive process of concentration will at any time abolish property and capitalism.

NOTES, CHAPTER III, SECTION IV

(*291*) See above, note 100. If one thinks of the law of public utilities and of railway law in this country one is tempted to argue that, in some respects, certain types of private enterprise are governed by public law. This is largely a verbal controversy as is the whole of the age old dispute about the borderline between public and private law. What is, however, a matter of substance, is the question how far we can to-day accept the statement that "every working capital exists in the form of a private working concern". It is true that, in this country, the Crown has "private property" in the land occupied by a post office or an ordnance factory. Exceptions apart, rules governing land law and the law of tort apply to such land as to any other, but what does this mean beyond the simple truth that legal institutions are colourless, and that they can be used for public as well as for private enterprise? As it stands, Renner's statement implies more than that. It implies that all working capital is privately invested, which is no longer true to-day. This, as Renner says himself, does not affect the technical problem of the optimum size of the working concern. This remains the same whether the concerns are privately owned or—legally incorporated or unincorporated— segments of public administration. Renner's statement is, however, the basis of his subsequent analysis of the impact of private property upon the realisation of the optimum of technical size. That the technical size of an undertaking subject to public ownership can be planned irrespective of the vagaries of the law of property, is indeed a point of no small importance.

(*292*) No longer! Renner describes a state of affairs which the economic development of our time has left far behind. We must distinguish between the technical unit, the unit of productive organisation, the "concern" (in German: *Betrieb*) and the commercial unit, the "enterprise" (in German: *Unternehmen*). One commercial enterprise (like I.C.I. or Lever Bros.) may comprise many concerns. Two enterprises may share interests in one concern. The question of legal ownership has become comparatively insignificant. Whether a company controlling a multitude of concerns chooses to manage all of them as operating subsidiary companies and to confine its own function to that of a controlling holding company, or whether it acts itself as the operating entrepreneur is a question of accounting technique, no more. Since Renner wrote his book, the economic development has proved his own thesis of the emasculation of property (in the legal sense) to an extent which he himself obviously did not anticipate.

(*293*) The control of finance (banking capital) over industry is a tacit assumption made throughout Renner's work. Within the framework of corporate finance, the size of the "concerns" controlled by an undertaking is determined by "controls" which may or may not be wielded by banks. Here, again, the work by Berle and Means, above, may be consulted as a description of developments which occurred in our own time. In Central Europe it was, amongst other things, the inflation of the currencies, which wrested the control of industry from the banks. Nor is it true to-day that merchant capital controls industry. The opposite is often the case (see above, note 168).

(*294*) Owing to the impact of company law, the law of succession has largely ceased to have this effect. The justification of the remark that "property has become an obstacle to social development" does not, however, rest on these examples. In this country the nationalisation of the coal mines was justified, *inter alia*, on the ground that the multitude of separate mining companies prevented the necessary rationalisation of the industry. An analysis of the effect of private property upon economic progress would have to go far beyond Renner's brief remarks on its relation to the technical optimum size of undertakings. It would, above all, have to take into account the obstacles to expansion created by monopolies, and the destructive effect of private control in times of falling demand. These are matters to which the sociology of law can hardly make a contribution.

Section v.　Modern Possessions.　The Aggregate of
Assets and Liabilities

THE change of functions is most strikingly revealed, if now, at the end of the development of property, we compare norm and substratum, as we did before (chapter i. 2) with regard to patrimonial property.

Property is an individual right to an object, its exclusive subjection to the individual will of the owner. But is there any individual disposition of his property on the part of the bank customer of a bank, of the share-holder or of the member of an association? Is it not the market which rules the most independent factory owner as well as the isolated peasant who lives alone on his solitary farm? The right of ownership is absolute: this means that it requires all other subjects of the norm to refrain from interference with the object. But the house-owner exercises his absolute right by taking in strangers from the street and setting them up in his so-called "own"; the landlord, by surrendering his possession completely to a tenant with his army of labourers, for ten or even for 99 years. The urban or agricultural tenant is protected in his possession: he can, with the help of the authorities, send away the interfering owner who enters uninvited. The owners of a railway even invite all and sundry to roam over their property, the more the merrier. Property establishes complete power of the individual over the object; but an economic object, the substratum of the right, is not an aggregate of objects, not an independent microcosm, it is merely a particle of the whole of society's working order, admitting of one special manner of disposal only. Even the number of revolutions performed by a spinning wheel is prescribed by the requirements of industrial technique. The universal power of disposal given by the law is confronted, in economic reality, by a most limited scope for the exercise of this power. Property is universal with regard to subject and object, any individual may own any kind of object, and this was actually so in the period of simple commodity production, when every individual[1] of full age had disposal of a microcosm which was made up of objects of every description. Now one part of the population, the great majority, owns nothing but a week's provisions, another part nothing but houses, another part nothing but machines and the raw materials to feed them, and still others nothing but printed paper. Modern

[1] In the case of journeymen and apprentices somewhat later.

possessions no longer form a cosmos, large or small, they are neither microcosm nor macrocosm. They are an amorphous agglomeration of possessions for the purposes of consumption and production, and in part they are mere "paper-possessions". These latter comprise shares in various railway undertakings at home and abroad, and in various manufacturing enterprises, government bonds and so forth: a loose pile of shavings which derives its unity only from its purpose, the purpose of securing average profits. These possessions represented by documents are in no way connected with the individuality of the owner, they can be increased as convenient. The legal character mask of a monarch is compatible with the economic mask of a distiller of spirits, the legal mask of a state minister is compatible with the economic mask of a gambler on the stock exchange, the ecclesiastic mask of an Archbishop is compatible with the economic mask of an employer of sweated labour. Such unity as modern possessions have, is a mere consequence of the legal abstraction which does not require a unitary substratum; their unity is artificial, easily permitting of arithmetical division by 2, 3, or 4 in cases of inheritance. Modern possessions form no material whole, only a mathematical sum.

Norm and substratum have become so dissimilar, so incommensurable, that the working of property, the way in which it functions, is no longer explained and made intelligible by the property-norm; to-day we must look to the complementary institutions of property. The lives of most of the people, even of the capitalists, are regulated by the law relating to landlord and tenant, their food is controlled by the law of the market, and their clothing, expenditure and pleasures are controlled by the law of wages. Property remains only in the background as a general legal presupposition for the special law that comes into operation, an institution of which we are dimly aware as the necessary consequence of the regrettable fact that there must be someone who is in the last resort responsible for the disposal of any object. But primarily disposal rests with the labourer in the case of the machine, the tool or the plough, with the tenant in the case of the house, and in general with the non-owner. The subjective, absolute, and all-embracing power of disposal seems to the casual observer to be completely eliminated; yet it is perpetuated as the subjective, absolute, and all-embracing power of the capitalist class to dispose of the whole of society, of man and matter and their annual surplus product.

But this fact is hidden from a merely legal interpretation; it is not intended, not expressed nor reflected by the norm. Norm and substratum can scarcely be said to correspond, they are no longer similar, and the present function of the norm is the result of a process in the course of which the relations of production and the relations of the law entered on a disparate development. The conflict between a growing (and partly completed) social working order which is conscious of its own unity, and a law which is still in existence although adapted to a previous system of private enterprise based upon economic microcosms, results in property assuming the function of capital. As the conflict increases, the functions of modern property become more and more distinct and differentiated. An increasing number of complementary institutions is developed, and it becomes more and more obvious that property itself has withdrawn into a position where it is solely concerned with disposal over, and acquisition of, values.

Section vi. THE DEVELOPMENT OF THE LAW

I MAINTAIN that Karl Marx deliberately set out to observe and describe each and every phenomenon of the capitalist epoch, correlating these to a continuous development of human society on the basis of an inherited legal system, rigid, retarded and fossilised. Those who expect from his critique of political economy a guide for economic behaviour, or an analysis of subjective valuations, or something similar, are therefore bound to misunderstand him. Only if the great historical drama is approached as he approached it, only then is it revealed in a true light: a society of small commodity producers has overcome feudal restrictions by dint of hard struggle, and at last establishes a system wherein the producer freely disposes over his means of production. It is now declared that everyone shall own his means of production, that everyone shall be free to exchange the fruits of his labours for those of everyone else, it is ordained that everybody shall peacefully enjoy and keep his own as he has saved it from the ruins of the feudal system. The law leaves to every individual the use of his means of production, permitting him to work as he finds expedient. As the product of everybody's labours automatically becomes his property, the law may safely do so. The law also leaves it to every individual to provide for his descendants, and it may safely do so: for the father's property forms a fund of subsistence for the inheriting children. This plain and simple regulation of property merely attempts legally to stabilise[1] the existing living conditions of society.

I. CHANGE OF FUNCTIONS AND CHANGE OF NORMS

But now we find the peaceful enjoyment of one's own property developing into the draconic control of alien labour-power, and giving rise to a new regulation of labour, more severe and in its initial stages more cruel than any regulation of feudal times or of the time of the pharaos—we need only mention child labour. Thus peaceful enjoyment of one's own object becomes constant appropriation of the proceeds of the labour of others; it becomes title to surplus value, distributing the whole of the social product as profit,

---

[1] The bourgeois revolution was so much easier because there was no necessity to form new social groups or to redistribute possessions, apart from the liberation of the peasants. Fundamentally it proclaimed only two commandments: a material one, that everyone should keep what he had, and a personal one, that everyone should mind his own business.

interest and rent among an idle class, and limiting the working class to the mere necessities of existence and procreation. In the end it reverses all its original functions. The owner has now no longer even detention of his property; it is deposited at some bank, and whether he is labourer or working capitalist, the owner cannot dispose of his own. He may not even be acquainted with the locality of the concern in which he has invested his property. Yet one function of capital is indestructibly linked up with his person, the function of appropriating the products of alien labour; and month by month the bank messenger delivers to the owner the revenue of his economic property.

This vast process of change, with all its accompanying phenomena, is unfolded before the eyes of Karl Marx; he exposes it as the problem of our time, as the vital question of the whole of human society in our present era. His thoughts cover the whole of human society and at the same time they concentrate upon the inherent and most secret principles of its existence; in his thoughts he is in advance of the overwhelming majority of our generation.

He has made it clear to us that property in the capitalist epoch fulfils functions quite different from those which it fulfilled in the era of simple commodity production, and partly opposed to these. He has made it clear that property has become antisocial, intrinsically opposed to the real interests of society. Yet all property is conferred by the law, by a conscious exercise of the power of society. When society was in control it endowed the individual with the power of disposal over corporeal things; but now the corporeal object controls the individuals, labour-power, even society itself—it regulates the hierarchy of power and labour, the maintenance and procreation of society. Mankind has become tributary to its own creation.

The norm is the result of free action on the part of a society that has become conscious of its own existence. The society of simple commodity producers attempts to stabilise its own conditions of existence, the substratum of its existence, by means of the norm. But in spite of the norm, the substratum changes, yet this change of the substratum takes place within the forms of the law; the legal institutions automatically change their functions which turn into their very opposite, yet this change is scarcely noticed and is not understood. In view of all this the problem arises whether society is not bound to change the norm as soon as it has become conscious of the change in its functions.

2. COMPLEMENTARY INSTITUTIONS DISPLACE THE PRINCIPAL INSTITUTION

An urgent demand for a human society that acts in freedom and in full consciousness, that creates its norms in complete independence: this is socialism. The very word expresses this. The passing of man from the realm of necessity to the realm of freedom cannot be conceived otherwise than as a marshalling of the organised will of society against the paltry presumptuousness of the individual, so that the object that has become the master of man may again be subjected to the control of society. Common will can achieve this only by a direct, controlled and well-aimed regulation of the relations among men and between man and nature, so that every person and every object may have its functions openly established and may fulfil them in a straightforward manner.

Utopians indulged in dreams and speculations as to how this could be achieved, fanatics of law and philosophy felt themselves obliged to preach fantastic remedies. It was thought that completely new legal institutions would have to be fashioned and the old ones abolished by decree, in order to bring about something that man had never known before. The socialists of this period, the Messianic era of socialism, failed to recognise that it is above all the way of experience which can lead to the new, that even the state of the future is conditioned by the past and that it cannot be otherwise. This era has long since passed away, nowadays we rely on empirical fact, and rightly so. But the socialists, and also unfortunately their leading group, the Marxists, disdain to apply this experience in the realm of the law and the state. They fail to comprehend and to investigate scientifically, how far it is true that the new society is already pre-formed in the womb of the old, even in the field of the law. May it not be true that here also new life is already completely developed in the mother's womb, waiting only for the liberating act of birth?

Some vista of the future, some answers to the questions which we have raised, must have occurred to anyone who has accompanied us on our journey through economics, who has joined in our study with critical regard to the sufferings of mankind. Every society requires a regulation of power and labour. Why do we not set out to create it directly? Why do we not appoint skilled teachers to be masters of our apprentices, why does society accept blindly everyone who takes over an enterprise by the chance of birth or inheritance, although he may be totally unfit to instruct? Why does not society select the best-qualified agriculturist to succeed into a farm that has become vacant, instead of the rich city man who buys it as a hobby, or instead of the fortuitous heir who may be no good? If hereditary appointments are now abolished as insufferable in the case of the most unimportant public office, why is it that the fortuitous heir may still succeed into an important economic enterprise which is responsible for the good or bad fortune of a thousand workers, and, maybe, for the adequate supply of certain goods the whole of society? Anyone can see that society is in immediate need of a regulation of appointments. Our expositions have shown that the real successor who serves the economic functions of a concern is appointed by contract of employment, so that the heir need only play the part of possessor of a title to surplus value without performing any function. We have seen that even to-day property is supplemented by complementary institutions which take over its real functions. Should we not come to the conclusion that the process of change towards a new legal order has already begun, that the complementary institutions already pre-shaped in the framework of the old order will become the principal institutions so that the institution which has previously played the principal part can be abolished, without any disturbance of the economic process, in so far as it no longer serves a useful social purpose?

Feasible as this idea seems, it nevertheless comes up against the most rampant prejudices. It would mean that the contract of employment would become the principal institution of the social regulation of labour, but this institution was during the last century denounced as the source of all social suffering. We are asked to revolutionise our conceptions completely. But we have already met two decisive reasons for changing this opinion. We have seen that the contract of employment, like all legal forms, is in itself neither good nor evil, that the value of the legal form is solely determined by the social function fulfilled by the legal institution. We have seen that it is not the legal form of the contract of employment but its connection with the institution of property which makes the former an instrument of exploitation. Secondly, experience has shown us that the contract of employment even to-day has developed into the established "position" and has to a large extent become socialised and made secure by means of manifold social rights.

3. COMPLEMENTARY INSTITUTIONS OF PUBLIC LAW FORCE THE PRIVATE LAW INSTITUTIONS INTO THE BACKGROUND

A second and probably even more important phenomenon becomes apparent and must be considered by the intelligent observer.

Property is a matter of private law. The whole body of our legal doctrine is based upon this fact. We distinguish between private and public law as the two principal branches of our legal analysis, as we understand it. (295) The normative content of our existing laws fully justifies this division and we cannot avoid making this distinction. Our observations, however, have led us to recognise that every legal order must grant to everybody a private sphere into which the common will does not intrude. After the victory of a liberalist philosophy with its concepts of natural rights, to which the victory of the bourgeoisie over the feudal system corresponded in practice, a theory of constitutional law was evolved which set limits to the powers of the state, affecting even the public law. Public law may not transgress these limits; within them the individual is free and not subject to the control of the state. (296) Here he is no longer a citizen of the state but simply a human being who enjoys freedom of thought and religion, freedom of convictions which the state may not touch. We hold this freedom of the individual in high esteem. It is not a present of nature and it was gained as a precious good of civilisation only after severe social and political struggle; and no thinking socialist would dream of surrendering it. [1] As far as we can judge looking into the future, material goods will also belong to this sphere, not only family portraits and other articles of sentimental value, but also the bulk of goods intended for consumption, household utensils, perhaps even the home itself. There will always be a private *"suum"*, a sphere of one's "legal own", even with regard to rights *in rem*, no matter what social order men may give themselves.

But contemporary property, capital as the object of property, though *de jure* private, has in fact ceased altogether to be private. No longer does the owner make use of property in a technical way; the tenement house serves a number of strangers and the railway

---

[1] This has not prevented Bolshevism from again establishing the omnipotence of the state, from stringently curtailing human freedom in the spiritual sphere. I think this is a disastrous retrogression. It is not justifiable to surrender achievements of civilisation even if they are branded as introductions of the enemy, the hated bourgeoisie.

serves all and sundry. Property in its technical aspect has been completely estranged from the owner. The Roman civil lawyer believed that *dominus rei suae legem dicit.* As far as ownership of capital is concerned, this pronouncement is no longer true: it is society that disposes of capital and prescribes the laws for its use. It may be maintained at least that the object has ceased to be private and is becoming social. An army of a thousand miners, an army with its own generals, commissioned and non-commissioned officers, all of them employees, have complete technical control of the mine; they search its depths and bring its treasures to light, securing not only its continuity but also its very existence; and they stake their own lives for this purpose. Evidently it is a mere provocative fiction that this army should be regarded as a disconnected crowd of strangers, and the share-holders, who may not even know where their property is situated, as the real owners. Language, indeed, revolts against such abuse.

What is it that makes this abuse nevertheless apparently tolerable? Public law has for a long time recognised that where the whole of society is in principle concerned with an object, it can no longer be treated as a matter that is merely private. So it comes about that private law is supplemented by rules of public law relating to the object; (*297*) a process that was cautious and tentative in the beginning but soon became more decided and in the end was developed in full consciousness.

In the liberal epoch the state considered every interference with the economic system and therefore with private law as contrary to reason and natural law; (*298*) accordingly it refrained from it completely and merely exercised the restricted functions of protection and administration of justice. But since the middle of the last century the state is no longer content merely to hold the mace and the scales, it begins to take an active part in administration. New norms are made year by year in increasing numbers in the form of statutes, orders and instructions of the administrators of the state. Administrative law develops into a special branch of legal analysis, and economic administration soon becomes the most extensive part within this branch. Grievances arise out of the application of the law of property and the contract of employment to the factory, and therefore administrative law must step in. Regulations relating to the normal working day, factory inspection, and protection of women and children are institutions of public law which increasingly supplement these institutions of private law. Insurance against sickness, accident and old age follow suit, public labour exchanges replace the private labour market, and so on. In the end the relations of labour are as to nine parts regulated by public law, and the field of influence of private law is restricted to the remaining tenth.

When we were dealing with the functions of capital, we nearly always had occasion to refer to complementary institutions of public law and to emphasise that these are new creations; in the main they were introduced or at least perfected only after the death of Karl Marx.

Thus we are led to surmise that a two-fold development is taking place: first, that the complementary institutions of private law have deprived the owners of their technical disposal over their property; and secondly, that the common will has subjected property to its direct control, at least from the point of view of the law. Elements of a new order have been developed within the framework of an old society. So it may not be necessary to clamour for prophets whose predictions of the future will flow from esoteric qualities of the soul. It may well be that there is no need to proclaim premiums for those who would draft the new legal constitution of a reasonable social order: perhaps the truth is that we can simply deduce the law of the future from the data supplied by our experience of to-day and yesterday. (*299*)

Should this be so, and we have good reason to believe it, our only problem would be to burst the shell which still obstructs the new development; to set free the complementary and supplementary institutions and to use them straightforwardly in accordance with their present and real functions, freed from restriction; to elevate them, the previous handmaidens of property, into the principal institutions; and to liberate them from the fetters of traditional property, which has lost its functions and has itself become a restrictive force.

Our observations have shown, however, that this cannot be the automatic result of a change of functions, that new norms are required to achieve it. For there can be no doubt that only a norm can break another norm. The norm, however, is a conscious act of will performed by society.

4. LEGAL DOCTRINE AND THE TASKS OF SOCIETY

If society has become conscious of the changes in the functions of property and its contradictory effects, the question arises

whether it must not change the norm. If it has surrounded property with so many barriers that these have gained the specific and
paramount importance of a legal construction *sui generis*, should it
not set free this new construction from the obstructions caused by
its origin? Or has it surrendered so much of its autonomy that
it can no longer perform this last step or dare not do so? Does
society still enjoy freedom of will, the power to create new
norms? [1] Even if it disposes of the instruments of legislation, if its
legal title to free legislation is beyond dispute, the question still
remains: is society still able to control technically the forces of
development which have been set free? Society is sovereign as the
legislator, but is it equally sovereign in practice? Or can it achieve
in practical life only what it must? We have already become
acquainted with the external limits which restrict the efficacy of
the norm. If the law changes its functions, does this enforce a
change of norms as well? Why do the norms not change equally
automatically? If a change in functions is always also the cause of
a change in norms, why is it that this cause cannot equally take
effect in the quiet way of facts? How is the law determined by
economics?

We have seen that the economic substratum dislocates the
functions of the norm, that it reverses them; but the norm itself
remains indestructible. The capital function also remains indestructible, and all development serves only its perfection.
Therefore it may seem as if the crudest change of function does not
react on this nebulous creation, this immaterial formula, those
imperatives which apparently have no existence or only modestly
vegetate in the documents of the statutes. Does it mean that the
norms are indestructible, eternal, changeless, or at least determined
by no other power than their own?

Given that, like all else under the sun, norms have their causes,
wherein do these lie? Given that they enjoy a real existence, what
are its characteristics, what is the mode of their existence and how
do they change? Given that their origin lies in the conditions of
life of the human race, that they are nothing more than a means of
preserving human society, what part do they actually play in the

---

[1] The law relating to labour and the law relating to economics are, as branches of
legal analysis, to-day overshadowed by the law of obligations on the one hand and the
law of administration on the other: these latter belong to a sphere where public law
and private law merge into one another. The trend of development indicates, however,
that these two latter branches will eventually be the basis of a new regulation of labour
and of society. (*300*)

existence and development of our own generation?

These are open questions of jurisprudence. The time has come to engage in an attempt at their solution. (*301*)

THE END

NOTES, CHAPTER III, SECTION VI

(*295*) Renner does not say that this distinction is itself the outcome of the *laissez faire* economy which he describes. We are, however, now in a position to say that the development which Renner foreshadows in his concluding pages does not mean that "private" law institutions are superseded by "public" law. It deprives the distinction itself (whatever meaning be ascribed to it) of its validity. The sanctions of "private" law and those of "administrative law" have almost become interchangeable in the Soviet Union. In this country the enforcement of certain standards of conduct, in the field of minimum wage legislation, of public utility legislation, and elsewhere is fortified by a structure of remedies in which the "public" and "private" elements have become indistinguishable.

(*296*) See for an analysis of the political and social context in which we should see "freedom of the mind" in our own time: Laski, *Liberty in the Modern State*, ch. ii. This chapter contains a number of contributions to the functional analysis of legal institutions in various fields. In order to demonstrate the ambivalent nature of the "limits of the power of the state" mentioned by Renner one would have to write a history of the United States Supreme Court from Chief Justice Marshall to our own day.

(*297*) See notes 100 and 295 above. This process began in this country with the first railway and public utility laws.

(*298*) This sentiment still finds powerful expression in the rules governing the interpretation of statutes, especially in the principle that there is a strong presumption against any invasion of common law rights. See the article by Jennings, quoted above, note 148. Some English lawyers are still inclined instinctively to consider the common law with its guarantees of property and freedom of contract as a crystallised rule of reason, and statutory "interference" as an intrusion of the politics of the day into the realm of eternal verities. The judges appear to them, not, as they did to Montesquieu, as "*bouches de la loi*", but, as it were, as "*bouches de la raison*", as a "neutral power" above the arena of social conflict.

Cardozo (The Judicial Process) and Holmes (see the Article quoted above, note 148) have effectively destroyed this claim, but it is still being made, and it is the foundation of the differentiation between "lawyer's law" and other law which influences the mentality of many members of the legal profession and much of the training we give to the younger generation. Above all, this relic from the age of *laissez faire* supplies the Courts with those canons of statutory interpretation which, in this country, take the place occupied in America by the established institution of "judicial review". See also note 23 above, for the corresponding Continental phenomenon: the conception of absolute ownership as "eternal", and limitations as "fortuitous".

(*299*) Much of the legislation which Renner mentions has indeed this "liberating" character. To put public town planning into the place of "building schemes" established by "restrictive covenant" means in fact to give its proper expression to a public function whose exercise was hitherto shackled by the law of private property. To entrust the safeguarding of standards of good husbandry to the agents of the Ministry of Agriculture instead of private landowners means much the same. To replace workmen's compensation by industrial accident insurance means, in effect, to transfer the public function of paying compensation to the victims of industrial accidents and diseases from profit making insurance companies to a public fund. Nevertheless, not all legislation of the type mentioned by Renner is of this character. Legislation for the protection of women and juveniles in factories, for the protection of tenants of working class houses, price control legislation, and many other measures are not "developed in the womb of society". They are social innovations, creating not only new agents of realisation, but new functions. Above all revenue law, one of the most powerful agents of social change in our time and not as such mentioned by Renner, is perhaps destined to have a more profound and a more permanent effect upon the structure of society than any other body of enactments.

(*300*) See above, note 124. On "economic law" in the Soviet Union—where it has a different meaning—see Schlesinger, l.c., p. 206. The essence of these two disciplines is that they coordinate, in accordance with their function, principles and institutions which appeared separate in the 19th century system of legal thought. Thus the torts of "passing off" and of "conspiracy", some aspects of the law of contracts in restraint of trade, much of revenue law, of administrative law, and of company law, would, in this country, belong to "economic law" as the sum total of all rules which affect the organisation of business and the question of monopoly and competition.

(*301*) Renner ends his work with a challenge to the jurist. Where, he asks in effect, is the effort made by the legal profession (and its academic branch in particular) to explain not only what norms contain and how they are interpreted, but also how they are made? Where is the science of legislation? Not only as a science explaining a technique (though even that exists hardly more to-day than fifty years ago), but as an exploration of the political and economic forces that go into the making of laws and of the process by which they translate themselves into fixed norms? Where is that union of legal and economic thought which Holmes demanded fifty years ago?

INDEX